A

COURSE

OF

ENGLISH READING,

ADAPTED TO

EVERY TASTE AND CAPACITY:

WITH

Literary Anecdotes.

BY

THE REV. JAMES PYCROFT, B.A.
TRINITY COLLEGE, OXFORD;
PERPETUAL CURATE OF ST. MARY'S, BARNSTAPLE;

AUTHOR OF
"RECOLLECTIONS OF COLLEGE DAYS,"
"LATIN AND GREEK GRAMMAR PRACTICE,"
"THE CRICKET FIELD," ETC.

THIRD EDITION.

NEW YORK:
D. APPLETON AND CO., 346. & 348. BROADWAY.
1854.

PREFACE

TO

THE THIRD EDITION.

MISS JANE C. divided her in-door hours into three parts: the housekeeping and dinner-ordering cares of life claimed one part; hearing two younger sisters say their lessons a second part; and during the third and most delightful remainder she would lock her chamber door, and move on the marker of Russell's "Modern Europe" at the rate of never less than fifteen pages an hour, and sometimes more.

Being so vexatious as to ask wherein her satisfaction consisted, I was told—in the thought that she did her duty; that she kept her resolution; that she read as much as her friends; that continually fewer histories remained to be read; and that she hoped one day to excel in literature.

A 2

A few torturing questions elicited that neither the labour nor the resolution aforesaid had produced any sensible increase, or more than a vague but anxious expectation, of available information or mental improvement. A painful suspicion arose that there was some truth in the annoying remark of a certain idle companion, that she was "stupefying her brains for no good."

The exposure of an innocent delusion is mere cruelty, unless you replace the shadow by the substance; so a list of books and plan of operations was promised by the next post. Adam Smith attempted in a pamphlet what resulted in his "Wealth of Nations" after the labour of thirty years. My letter grew into a volume, now offered for the guidance of youth in each and every department of literature.

Two large editions have been circulated, and a demand for a third enables me to notice many recent publications, and to profit by the suggestions of "gentle readers" and severer critics. In reply to repeated inquiries how the Author could have forgotten such and such works of undoubted authority, he suggests, that no student would thank him for transcribing the Catalogue of the Bodleian, however much it might add to his reputation for extensive reading. Without aspiring to direct the future studies of Mr. Macaulay in History, of Dr. Buckland in Geology, or of a Duke of Wellington in Military Tactics, he is happy to say, that very learned men have expressed their regret that in their early studies they had not the benefit of such simple guidance as this volume affords.

J. P.

Barnstaple, Oct. 1. 1854.

SUMMARY OF COURSE OF ENGLISH READING.

Advice more particularly to those who study

Literary Opinions and Remarks by distinguished Men.

281; by Bacon of Memoria Technica, 286; by Niebuhr of verbal memory, 287; by Medhurst of the wonderful memory of the Chinese, 289; of the memory of Mathews the comedian, 290; by Lady W. Montague of Addison's daughter, 291; by Prior of Bolingbroke's talent for languages, also of Xavier the Jesuit, and the Bishop of New Zealand, 291; by Eusebius of Esdras, by Seneca of Hadrian, by Petrarch of Clement V., by Cicero and Quintilian, of Memory, 291; by Johnson of improving by travels, 193; by Professor Sedgwick of Paley's "Moral Philosophy," 196; by Mackintosh, Dr. Chalmers, and Dr. Arnold, of Butler's Sermons, 197; by Fox of Burke's "Letters on the French Revolution," 200; by Sir W. Scott, of Sir David Wilkie's paintings, 214; by the Rev. H. Melville of the Scriptures tending to mental discipline, 226; by Coleridge of *Melite*, not *Malta*, 227; by Dr. Meuse of the Indian tradition of a deluge, 228; by Serle of the Trinity known to the Otaheitans, 228; by Mackintosh of Job xxix., by Wordsworth of Jeremiah, by Mrs. Hemans of St. John, by Coleridge of St. Paul's Epistle to the Romans, 229; by George III. of Watson's "Apology for the Bible," 238; by Dr. Chalmers of the Fathers, 244; by the Duke of Wellington of Paley's Evidences, 245; by Abp. Leighton of the Schoolmen, 247; by Robert Hall of Burke and Howe, 250; by St. Augustine of Cicero, 251; by Charles II. of Isaac Barrow, 252; by Johnson of Law's "Serious Call," 254; Lord Jeffrey on the abundance of Poets: Thomas Moore on Chaucer; Burke on Spenser 257-8; by Bolingbroke of Dryden's prose; by Mackintosh of Dryden's "Cock and the Fox," 264; by Mackintosh of obscurity in poetry — of Gray — of Johnson's injustice to Gray and Prior, 265; by Byron of Johnson's poems, 365; by Fox and Mackintosh of Crabbe, by Pitt of Scott, by Scott of Coleridge, by Mackintosh of Coleridge, 367; by Burns of Alison "On Taste," 268.

A COURSE

OF

ENGLISH READING.

PART I.

IN WHICH THE PATH OF LEARNING IS EXPLAINED TO BE NICELY SLOPED AND GRADUATED, AND SO PLENTEOUSLY STREWN WITH OBJECTS OF INTEREST AND CURIOSITY AS TO BE ENTERTAINING AND INVITING TO ALL.

"Est quiddam prodire tenus si non datur ultrà."
"If you can't do as much as you would, at least do as much as you can."

ALL the world would allow that a traveller would pass more easily from any one point to any other point, by having a distinct picture of the road before he started. All the world would approve of a traveller's stopping once or twice in his journey, and asking himself, "To what place am I going?" and "Is this the best way to reach it?" But how many myriads in this world aforesaid do set out on the long and intricate road of life without a map, and, while they can only keep moving, never stop to ask whether they are in their latitude or out of it. So blindly do men run after all the imaginary prizes of life, and just as blindly do they pursue any one of them. Consider intellectual pursuits. Many young persons have said to me, "I should so like to possess general information, and to be well-informed, like our very amusing friend. Is it not strange that, amidst all the toils of a most engrossing profession, he can find time to acquire so much knowledge on every subject?"

"Not at all strange; a few minutes a day, well employed, are quite sufficient."

"Really I do not find it so. What I read rarely interests me; so I forget nearly as fast as I read, and grow more and more confused."

"Too little interest, and too much confusion! Really you have enough to complain of. Do you know that this may constitute all the difference between your acquirements and those of your learned friend?"

"But he is so clever."

"Can he do as much in one hour as you in six?"

"No! certainly not—I see your argument. You are going to remind me, I have more than six times the number of hours to study."

"Is there no one subject on which you feel

yourself his equal? Think of gardening, drawing, scriptural reading," &c.

"True, but I am so fond of these subjects; for ——"

"For,—you would say, your attention never flags, and your memory never fails."

"Just so. But I am not so fond of certain other subjects, though I much desire to know them also."

"But do you not remember a time when you were not so *fond* even of these favourite subjects?"

"Certainly; you would infer therefore ——"

"I would infer, what I positively have experienced both in myself and others, that *a fondness and interest for study may be acquired, and under good guidance it is hardly ever too late to begin.*"

"And the advice you intend to give me is founded on ——"

"Is founded on certain simple and self-evident means of creating an interest in all we read, and thus insuring Attention, and consequently Memory. Suppose you wished to nourish a man's body, you would say, 'Feed him.' 'But he does not digest.' 'Probably he has no appetite?' 'Yes; he will eat some few things.' 'Then choose these few; attend to his appetite, and it will enable you to judge when and what he can digest.' So with the mind; attend to the Curiosity, which is the appetite of the mind: for, whatever the mind receives with avidity tends to its maturity and strength."

In this way I have reasoned with many of my friends; and I have had the satisfaction of seeing my advice attended with more success than I ever could have anticipated. My prescriptions are not like the panacea of the day, the same for all patients in all stages; but such as, being based on the same principles of mental health, are nicely modified to suit every age and constitution. If my rules seem obvious, and what all well-educated persons may be presumed to know, I answer, Do we not often hear readers say, "I like a book which begins at the beginning of a subject—which presumes not that I have knowledge, but that I am really ignorant?" Have the best informed never searched for information, though with affected indifference—they would not, on any account, be seen to do so—even in a child's story-book, or penny catechism? Hesiod, as quoted by Aristotle, divides the world into three classes:

The first have sense of their own.
The second use the sense of their neighbours.
The third do neither one nor the other.

Now all the advice I have to offer is addressed to

the second class, with a slight hope and a sincere desire to make converts of the third. As to arrangement, I will not promise to be very exact. As a traveller in the boundless fields of literature, I shall take the privilege of describing fair flowers and curiosities as they occur, and to quote the very words of many fellow-travellers. A man who will stand forth like a witness in a court of justice, and say not what he thinks, but what he knows and has seen, and what impression these occurrences produced upon his mind, may find his humble testimony decide knotty questions and promote high purposes, far beyond all conjecture. Thus, by truth copied from the plain tablets of memory, will I endeavour so to lay down the law that each may solve his own perplexity, and to hold up a mirror in which every man may see himself.

The first case which occurs to me,—the case of nearly all who have the ambition, but not the method, to be literary characters—is the following:—A young lady of great intelligence asked, "What would you recommend me to read?"

"That depends on what you have been reading lately—the new matter must assimilate with the old, or it will not digest."

"I have read nearly all Hume and Smollett,

and I want to know more of the History of England, and the continental nations too — shall I read Russell's Modern Europe?"

"Excuse me for saying you have rather a large ground-plan, for your Historical Edifice. Do you hope to build up in the same proportion? Remember the Tower of Babel and the confusion of tongues. A dozen and a half of thick volumes! Can you remember all this?"

"Oh no. The worst of it is I cannot remember even common facts, succession of kings, wars, and peace, and the like, which even children learn from their little books. I was so long over Hume, that I forgot the first part before I had read the last."

"And if you had only read the child's history through twice, you would possess more real knowledge at the present moment!"

This was allowed: my pupil also admitted that Hume dwelt too long on some topics in which she felt no interest, and too little on others; that with all long histories it was difficult to grasp the outline of events so comprehensively as to enjoy the advantage of comparing one period with another; and, that the more these disadvantages diminish our interest the more severely they tax our perseverance. An admission which called to mind the expression of another literary pilgrim, who exclaimed from the very slough of despond, "What am I to try next—I have waded through two volumes of Russell, and am heartily tired by a third?"

I now took a sheet of paper and drew what was intended for a historical tree. The trunk bore in straggling capitals the words Hume and Smollett, and, in smaller letters, the names of the sovereigns; each of whom was allowed a space commensurate with his reign. "Here," I said, "you have one continuous history; as it were, the stem and prop, or the connected chain of your knowledge:—a less substantial supporter than Hume would do as well at present, because you appear to have forgotten (which is about the same thing as never having read) Hume's History. I wish you to have a comprehensive knowledge of this whole chain; so take the History of England by the Society for Promoting Christian Knowledge, one small duodecimo of 140 pages, price 1*s.* 3*d.* This you may learn accurately in four or five days, and keep it in mind afterwards by writing out the answers of the questions given at the end. In this way your chain of history will be connected, and you may learn to run over in your mind all the events from Queen Boadicea to Queen Victoria; at least, I have known children of ten years of age do as much."

"Then what shall I do with Hume?"

"Hume's history will strengthen particular links in this fine chain I am supposing: it will make[illegible]aginary trunk the thicker, and better able[illegible]upport the weight of its branches. You will[illegible]ss that, by the branches and offshoots, I mea[illegible]phies and other works read in connection[illegible]he desire for which will be excited by this chain of reading, or appear to grow out of this Tree of History."

"A little more explanation if you please; and, remember your promise, not only to inform but to entertain. Hitherto, my studies have been literally 'bubble, bubble, toil and trouble.'"

"Tell me, first, what *desire* or curiosity has *grown out of* your chain of reading?"

"I have a curiosity to know more of Ridley, Cranmer, and their contemporaries."

"First cast your eye over the three or four pages of Mary's reign in the little history; you will then have a vivid recollection of their times; and then read a separate account of these champions of Christendom in some other books."

"But for this purpose must I wade through four or five volumes of the Reformation?"

"There is no necessity; continue to read about the martyrs only as long as your curiosity lasts. You may find a short account of them in a Cyclopædia or Biographical Dictionary; or you may turn to a full and graphic account in Southey's Book of the Church. See, I keep my promise; when 'toil and trouble' begins or interest ends, I allow you to stop and read something else."

My friend was laudably solicitous as to whether this was sound advice: she thought "that where there was no pain, there would be no cure;" so besides urging my own experience, I sought and found a high authority for my opinion in good old Samuel Johnson:—"*What* we read with inclination makes a much stronger impression. If we read without inclination, half the mind is employed in fixing the attention, so there is but one half to be employed on what we read;"* and this the Doctor said when sixty-seven years had rolled over his sober head.

Again Doctor Johnson observed, "Idleness is a disease which must be combated; but I would not advise a rigid adherence to a particular plan of study."—Now, my plan requires no rigid adherence, but allows full latitude, as the Doctor goes on to require; "I, myself, have never persisted in any plan for two days together. A man ought to read just as inclination leads him, for what he reads as a task will do him little good."—Vol. ii. p. 213.

* Boswell, vol. vi. p. 163.

My advice coincides with that of Johnson: I would afford all the assistance of method, without cramping the strong spring of inclination.

This advice was followed. A few evenings after, I found my pupil had read with the sharp edge of curiosity, and, of course, had digested, lives of Ridley and Cranmer, and had become curious still further about Henry VIII., Edward VI., and Mary. "What!" I said; "how came these characters to interest you more to-day than when you read of them in Hume?" "Because," was the natural reply, "the association was different. I care more about those who fought or befriended the pope, than about men who lost heads or won crowns; to say nothing of long chapters about primogeniture, a topic on which the accuracy of our friend used to surprise me once, though now I understand that he was assisted by its association with his law studies." My principle was now understood: that *every person has his peculiar curiosity, by attending to the dictates of which we ensure attention, memory, interest, and consequently general improvement—also that the sphere of our curiosity may be gradually enlarged.*

Let me relate another passage from my preceptorial diary:—"A most wonderfully retentive memory has that Captain Evans we met yesterday: he talks on every subject; strange that Mr. Wood, when here on his circuit, did not think more of him." "I should wonder more if he did; the captain talks for effect: he has more vanity than love of literature: Mr. Wood truly remarked that such a man was the very pest of a party; that he went away like a steam-engine on his own line, but clogged the moment he ran off it; pursued no game but what he himself had started; could fight but badly on his own ground, and was no match for the poorest antagonist on any other." Strangely enough, there was another person in the same company, of known depth and research, who heard this "captain bold" without taking the trouble to correct his facts, or question his conclusions; and who also observed the next day, he "only wished men would not worry their friends in the evening with what they had read without understanding the very same morning." How true is the observation that men who have not studied some one subject as a profession, or with as much assiduity and thought as a profession requires, having no standard of accuracy, can rarely speak creditably on any single topic! Lies, whether expressed or implied (and what is Affectation but "lies in a state of solution"), ever prove a discouragement to truth and to the humble endeavours of simple honesty: so, a youth honourably desirous of improvement was almost persuaded by this foolish exhibition of a shallow pretender, that the knowledge worthy of a man of good education is beyond ordinary ability to attain.

Let a vain, chattering character read the latest article in the "United Service Magazine," talk of the contents at the reading-room door with some of those portly gentlemen who are to be seen in every town like China jars, or male Caryatides, daily fixtures for fear any stranger should want a clue to the fashionable library; and, with the sum total of remarks and illustrations so collected, let him talk loud and long at his next party, and he will often be regarded as a man of general information. The ignorant do not discover the cheat, and the wise despise too much to expose it; or, should they venture to qualify the general praise, they are called jealous, and pass unregarded.

"Well," said my young friend, "certainly I should have felt more comfortable had I been better acquainted with the subject he was discussing. The last war — Napoleon — Nelson — and the Duke, are matters about which I have a very confused and shallow stock of information. How should I proceed?—'Gurwood's Despatches,' Alison, volumes of Southey on the Peninsula, and others on the Revolution, will take me so long, I shall starve for want of knowledge before I gain it at this slow rate."

My pupil soon understood that these were not the books for a beginner; he was warned with the mention of Robinson Crusoe's boat, too big to launch, and his first plan of a goat-pen, two miles round, which would have given him as little command of his flock as if he had no pen at all.

Long historical works, and most others, consist of two parts: — First, facts. Secondly, observations on facts. As to the facts, he did not want to know thoroughly all the minutiæ in the books above mentioned. A perfect knowledge of a very small portion would satisfy him for the present; a small collection would serve as standards round which other ideas might rally, — as fixed points, for association, in aid of memory; — as links, however coarse, to make the chain complete, till time was allowed to substitute links stronger and more minute. He had also the confidence to allow that, by comparison of facts, he might discern effects and causes, and have a home supply of observations; for, the larger stock of ideas we import the less we grow, and the more minds fall out of cultivation. I encouraged him with the prospect of becoming, in course of time, almost exclusively his own grower and consumer as to observations: and when books are to be read for culling facts alone, and when most observations are passed by as already known, he saw that cumbrous volumes would in effect be considerably reduced in size, and asked, "Is this the reason I see you with a book on your favourite subject, turning over the leaves without seeming to read five lines out of a page?" "Yes, frequently five lines are enough to show what the author is going to observe. By passing judiciously from one kindred author to another, we may learn to read books, as lawyers read briefs; for they rather recognise than read the well-known clauses." Let not readers be encouraged by these observations to fall into a careless and desultory habit. I allow them to miss what they already *know:* I do not say what they have already *read.* Accurate reading and reflection are their own reward, by saving time and trouble in the end. Sheridan once remarked, "Instead of always reading, I prefer to think: on every subject there are only a few leading ideas, and these we may originate for ourselves." While others talk of so many hours of daily study, and so many books read, those who really improve think only of questions solved and clear knowledge attained. "So, my friend," I continued, "to gain confidence in speaking of Napoleon and his contemporaries, take first of all a book of facts; do as I did some years since, in idle time, by the sea-side: — I took Miller's History of Great Britain from George II. to George IV. (published 1834, by Jones, Finsbury Square), one double-columned volume of 400 pages; giving something like an epitome of the newspapers, from 1760 to 1820, and bearing on each page, in two or three places, lines in capitals, drawing attention to the respective topics, as in pages 332. and 333.: ADVANCE OF THE BRITISH INTO SPAIN UNDER SIR JOHN MOORE; again, SIR J. MOORE'S RETREAT; again, BATTLE OF CORUNNA, AND DEATH OF MOORE."

I commenced at p. 207., which gave the history of the end of the year 1789: I wrote on the top of every page, "A.D. 17—, or A.D. 18—," and in this manner my book became a ready book of reference for any newspaper allusion to the days of our fathers. A few days' reading carried me through the 200 pages which gave the history from the beginning of the Revolution to the death of George III. Still I intended to read the same portion twice or thrice more. I was in haste to complete my chain, as I call it, in a fair, substantial way first, and strengthen it afterwards. I did not read from end to end; but when tired, I used to dip into interesting parts, such as victories and state trials; so, this history suited me in all humours, whether as a novel or work of memory. It would puzzle any one to guess what parts made most impression on my memory: they were not "the moving incidents by flood and field," but facts which I might probably have overlooked, had they not happened to form the subject of conversation, and thus became matters of special interest. There is a maxim among lawyers, that private reading makes little impression till legal practice shows its use, and fixes attention to important points. Daily intercourse with men and books serves the general reader as practice serves the lawyer; by fixing attention, it insures memory. Nor is this the only point of comparison. Do you think any lawyer's knowledge can comprehend all the ponderous volumes in Lincoln's Inn library, and all these, to the uninitiated, seem equally deserving of study? Certainly not. Then how do they know which to choose as most likely to bear upon all the cases that occur? Practice shows the general demand, and this they prepare to supply. So the general reader, like the lawyer, must study to be strongest on those points which conscious inferiority or the greater proficiency of his friends may happen to suggest. The same book may be read again and again with continually increasing interest and profit; because, the interval between each reading may call attention to a new order of facts, and elicit a new series of conclusions."

"And how did you proceed when you had read this part of history once?"

"I had a friend who was fond of discussing the same subject; one who had long lived by the sea, conversed with naval officers, listened with me to many an hour's yarn from an old Trafalgar man, while cruising in the Rose yacht off Tenby and Caldy, and had often surprised me with the apparent extent of his knowledge. His conversation increased my interest, and made my reading more profitable. I then read Southey's Life of Nelson, and the Life of Napoleon, 2 vols., in the Family Library. These books are quite easy reading, except allusions to the history of the times, a knowledge of which is always indispensable in reading for real improvement. One word of caution. I have suggested sometimes 'to read and skip;' but to skip only what we know, without indulging an idle habit. The historical allusions in the Life of Nelson I readily explained, by looking over the occurrences of the same year in my history. Thus, while the history explained the biography, the biography drew attention to the history. Certainly, all readers may occasionally be at a loss for an allusion: still, if they do their best to explain it, this is immaterial; but those literary

Epicures who touch nothing but dainties, and pick all books for the amusing, will never enjoy a sound intellectual constitution. If once you contract a habit of reading solely and exclusively what pleases at the moment, and if once you blunt that natural sense of satisfaction which a sound mind experiences in accurate information, from that moment you barter the literary resources of a life for the excitement of an hour. Neither need this custom of elucidating historical allusions interrupt the interest of the narrative. I often place on a fly-leaf a mark of interrogation, and against this I set the numbers of the pages containing difficulties, till I have finished reading, and then make all the references at once. Even if you should not succeed in your search at the time, this practice will fix the difficulties in your memory so firmly that you will be on the alert for future elucidations.

But what was the result of the line of reading I have mentioned? The result was, that my friend was quite surprised at the accuracy of my knowledge even in his own favourite parts of modern history: and, this was an idle man who had nothing to do but to read every periodical that came out—a man who had read numerous volumes on the topics on which I had read but three! My knowledge, I knew, was shallow, but his no longer seemed deep. This gave me confidence. I have since found that there are very, very few readers so familiar with any topic, that ordinary ability, with methodical application, may not greatly surpass them after only a few days of diligent study.

To continue my method with history: Miller's History has since served me as a book of reference, and stands on the same shelf with my Biographical and other Dictionaries. It shows, at one view, a picture of those by-gone days and departed heroes, of whom we hear old gentlemen talk, when they are wicked enough to perpetrate a little conversational monopoly, and swell with a very innocent kind of self-importance, as they tell of the cold perspiration that came over their patriotic brows the morning they heard of the mutiny at the Nore, the threatened Invasion, and the Bank stopping payment;—and how they laughed and triumphed in the truth of, if not their own, at least some near relative's prognostication, that Nelson would find the foe and beat him too;—how melancholy they felt as that Hero's funeral passed, and how they sympathised with the honest tars who followed in the mournful throng. To all such conversation it is improving to listen: but since all you will learn from it is inaccurate and unconnected, instead of being satisfied with half a story, go at once to book, to ascertain time, place, and characters, and thus "give to airy nothing a local habitation and a name." On this principle, in reading Ireland's Seven Years of France, from 1815-22, I cast my eye over the pages of Miller, on which I had marked the corresponding seven years: I did the same before reading every Biography relating to the same period. But, I shall be reminded that I promised to make my course amusing; and most amusing was the method I am relating; for, in course of time, I selected from old Reviews and Magazines only such articles as were amusing: but by that time the sphere of my amusement had become greatly enlarged; my mind was stored with facts on which I thirsted for more minute information; and since all these were read with an appetite, all were easily digested. In order to register my reading, and preserve order in my studies, I marked on the margin of the History what books or essays gave exact information on different subjects; vide Southey, p. —, or Gentleman's Magazine, No. —; or read Mackintosh's Observations on the French Revolution, p. —; Burke's Opinion, see Life, p. —. So my History became an index or Common-Place Book.

"Reading furnishes the mind only with materials of knowledge," says Locke: "it is thinking that makes what we read ours. We are of the ruminating kind, and it is in vain to cram ourselves; unless we chew over again, we shall derive no strength or nourishment:" without a certain digesting and assimilating process—it is but so much loose matter floating in the brain. It is a great mistake, Locke argues, to honour men of great Reading as men of great Knowledge, and to suppose that, by mere perusal, the author's knowledge is transferred into the reader's understanding. The stream of literature may flow through the mind without any deposit. All depends on the food's agreeing with the constitution of the mind, of which the appetite of curiosity is the only test.

The time at which reading is most improving, is when, as you glance over the table of contents, you feel impatient to begin the chapter, as containing exactly the facts you want to know—the very observations you wish to compare with your own. And this eager curiosity and zest for reading will find its sphere continually open and enlarge, till at last every book will have its interest. Even now, there rises before me a vision of one, an accomplished scholar and hard-worked man of active life, standing amidst a nursery of children, so riveted to a story book picked off the floor, that the young fry, spite of all their pulling at his skirts, and clinging to his knees, despaired in their impatience at moving him, till one cried out, "Ah, I knew if we did not keep our picture books away from him, he would not let us ride on his foot till he had read them all through."

None but those so eminently blessed with mental endowments, can conceive all the pleasures which spring from the well-formed and fertile mind. Such a mind seems ready fitted with little cells for all sweets, and to have a distinct pigeon-hole for every kind of communication: each of its acquisitions has a tendency, not to dissolve and darken, but to crystallise in brilliancy and beauty; however extended its chain, each link ends in a hook for joining more.

These are the minds which in society impart almost as much pleasure as they enjoy: they find companions even in those whom their friends apologise for asking them to meet. Dr. Johnson said he would rather sit next an intelligent man of the world than a scholar; for the man who has learned life from nature's own volume, is provided with a supply as varied and as rich, as is the store from which he draws! he can repay with genuine unclipped coin, in bold relief, fresh from Nature's mint: however small his after-dinner contribution to the common fund of entertainment, it still is sterling, pure, and unadulterated. Gray said of Boswell's Corsica, that it proved any man with talent or without could write a useful book, if he would only faithfully, and without affectation, detail what he had seen and heard in a sphere which the rest of the world had never seen, and was curious to know. In this point of view the man of well-formed mind regards companions; he is fully prepared to be entertained by the humblest relator of "things that he doth know:" he consequently is qualified to be always pleasing; for be it observed, men please in society not in proportion as they inform, but in proportion as they elicit; and who are so able to elicit as those who are not vainglorious to pour forth, but habitually intent on the great end of all society and of all conversation—to hear, to observe, and be improved?

Seek improvement, not only by books, but by conversation which will teach the use of books. Books furnish the arms, conversation teaches the use of them. Steele warns us against "coming charged into company, and unloading whether a fit opportunity offers or not;" still, he says, "you may prepare for conversation, by reading up each prevailing subject, just as our armies are besieging a town abroad, or a new measure is debating at home. A man buried in his study, and 'besprent with learned dust,' will lose in utterance while he gains in knowledge. He cannot adapt his topics to the taste, or his arguments to the conviction, of his company; nothing but practice can give "the power," says Johnson, "of changing a position and presenting it in different points of view, connecting it with truths already granted, fortifying it with intelligible arguments, and illustrating it by apt similitudes. He who has collected knowledge in solitude, must learn its application by mixing with mankind."

As to conversation, too many forget that it implies listening as well as talking; and none are so agreeable as those who, while they inform, elicit. Madame De Stael once pronounced a lady to whom she had been speaking, a most interesting person, who proved to be dumb! If you think only of those who hear you, you will please your company; if bent on display, you will please none but yourself. A talent for conversation is worth cultivating: it requires experience to discern at a glance the taste, the humour, and the intelligence you are addressing, and the topics most attractive, and the manner most winning with each. Without this nice discernment, some will inflict a lengthy dissertation where a passing remark, a sally of wit, or a smile of qualified acquiescence would obviate a question on which all argument were vain. Some, of course, can be more entertaining than others; still almost all persons may add something to the pleasures of society if contented to talk of what they understand, without pretence or affectation. Speak from the natural suggestions of the moment, and from the genuine impulse of a hearty and ingenuous disposition, and you will hardly fail to please. Never be afraid of men of real learning: the "world" is the book they enter society to read, and they are the last persons to complain of your knowledge being little, so long as it is without pretence. It is not simple ignorance, but the affectation that so often accompanies it, which provokes contempt. The Rabbi Aquiba said, "Stultum omninò ferre quàm semistultum facilius est, et ignarum omninô quàm semidoctum."

These remarks will give a general view of my system. Let us now consider the various subjects — History, Biography, Poetry, &c., and show with what authors, and what method, each line of study should be pursued. Only, I intend not to prescribe for the sound and vigorous patient, or for the unwearied man of letters, but for the delicate, weak, and sickly appetite, which requires humouring and coaxing at first to bring it to health and strength.

Chinese scholars are divided into two classes,

says a traveller: those who read only, and those who understand what they read. This distinction may be drawn nearer home. Those who read, and those who remember, are often different parties; and so also are those who remember, and those who digest. Readers who only retain facts, having minds like the article headed *Farrago,* or *Multum in Parvo,* in the newspapers, are not always the persons who, by digesting, classifying, and inferring, have a stock of really available information. I should be doing little if I did not teach so to read that we may first, remember what we read; secondly, digest it; thirdly, have it ready and available. "Say you so?" says a young friend, for whose guidance I am partly induced to write this; "then what I read must be little indeed; it must be a very short history at all events." Precisely what I was going to say. Read a very short History of England first—the Outline by the Society already mentioned. I know a child of ten years of age who learned this so thoroughly, that he could answer any question. I once defied an old college companion to puzzle him; and after receiving an accurate answer to twenty-three questions out of twenty-four, my friend wanted to know how it was possible for a child to learn so much. I showed the book—a well-chosen outline, too bare and meagre to be alone very improving — yet it contained all matters within the range of a child's comprehension. Fine painters tell their pupils, first draw a correct outline — let your anatomy be correct first; it is easy to fill in, and to colour afterwards. With this little history you have the figure — the bones; but we must galvanize this anatomy and add flesh, substance, vigour, and life; we must make "these dry bones live." Suppose this outline history represents the long stem of a tree; how are we to fill it up? It looks bare and naked at present, without leaves or branches. The pupil may begin to fill in just when he pleases, provided he takes care that the outline does not become erased, and that the whole figure of his tree is plainly before his eye from first to last. Every one according to his taste or ability may work out, and bring into bolder relief and more substantial form, any part he pleases. It is immaterial whether he proceeds up or down. Even the idle have a natural disposition to do even the most toilsome work in order to complete and connect little blanks which disfigure their work. Who has such apathy as to finish head, limbs, and breast of his figure, and then leave it, like the body of Tityus, with vitals doomed never to heal? The straight-forward way to fill up your tree would be to take up another larger history; not Hume's, it is too big as yet; but Goldsmith, first. The time required for learning these two Histories will be even less than would be required for Goldsmith's alone, without the guidance of these smaller works as an introduction. The parts which are substantially the same in all will be taken at a glance, and serve pleasantly to refresh the memory, rather than to exhaust the attention. We feel a secret pleasure in our studies when we meet with what we know; it shows we are improving, however gradually, to that state in which we may read whole volumes rather to judge and pronounce, than merely to be taught without discretion. Even Goldsmith gives little more than an outline; but, outline is a comparative term: he gives such an outline as deserves to be considered very substantial in comparison with the historical knowledge that most, even of those reputed well informed, really possess. "One half the world," says the proverb, "does not know how the other half lives." How few would like to confess the little that they really know — at least, the very limited number of correct replies they could at any moment sit down and write, for another's judgment, to questions which were within the capacity even of a child! Supposing ourselves born with minds literally like a blank sheet of paper, and that these tablets were required to be laid open for the inspection of our neighbours, who would not dread a discovery of the little that he knew, and the confused and indistinct lines in which that little was inscribed. Were the minds of many thus laid bare, all that at the moment remained for judgment would seem less the acquisitions of a life than the desultory reading of an hour. Oh! if the pale patient, blistered, bled, and reduced, could so read the mind of his physician — if the client with his estate in chancery could so pry into the narrow data on which his lawyer founds such broad conclusions — if those who dream of the unlimited powers of ministerial sagacity could so prove "with what very little wisdom the world is governed," many would agree that the goodness of Providence is in no way more remarkable than in this, that in the wise economy of creation, all disturbing causes are so nicely calculated and balanced, that busy man has even less power to do mischief, than he imagines to do good.

Let none despair because his knowledge seems little, if it be only accurate. The Germans, who so well understand practical education, say "nothing is so prolific as a little known well." Knowledge increases in a geometrical ratio. The total of the acquisitions of the mind is the continued product, rather than the mere sum, of all it contains.

A little sound and well digested historical knowledge will be always useful; but if the facts are mistaken, the deductions must be as false in matter as they are logical in form. All such arguments will be as absurd as the answer of a sum in arithmetic with an error in the first line. This inaccuracy accounts for the obstinacy of those called wrong-headed men. They are sure their reasoning is right; but as their facts happen to be wrong, they have only the advantage of "method in their madness," and blundering by rule.

This is a topic on which I am the more disposed to dwell, because many persons, really capable of knowledge, remain in ignorance from two causes. First, from an opinion that any available degree of information is beyond their powers. Secondly, because their neighbours appear to know so much that all they can learn will be nothing in comparison. Such diffident students should be consoled with the above observations, and taught to beware of shallow pretenders, and of men who always talk on their own topics. "You are surprised," said Talleyrand, "that I talk so well. Tell me, would it be no advantage to draw an enemy to your own ground, and only fight where your strength is concentrated and your position commanding? That is precisely my art." Men lose no credit by being often silent, if, when they speak, they speak to the purpose. Bacon refines upon this, and says, "He who is silent where he is known to be informed, will be believed to be informed where from ignorance he is silent." Again, Rochefaucauld observes, "The desire to seem learned prevents many from becoming such." If you study, exclusively devoted to the secret improvement of your own mind, and for the pleasures a well stored mind has ever at command, you will at the same time be taking the readiest means to "shine in society;" but if you seek the vain glory and opinion of others, you will sacrifice real improvement in the pursuit, and gain, at best, but the commendation of fools. "Let every man," said Lord Bolingbroke, "read according to his profession or walk in life. Suppose that a man shuts himself up in his study twenty years, and then comes forth profoundly learned in Arabic, he gains a great name; but where is the good of it?" There was an undergraduate at Trinity College, Cambridge, in 1829, who was famed for knowing the names, drivers, coach inns, times of starting and arrival, of most of the principal stages in England. The absurdity of this is too apparent to be imitated; but I will not say too great. There are many powerful minds at the present moment devoted to pursuits quite as unprofitable to others, and nearly as unimproving to themselves.

Another class whom diffidence deters from a literary course must be encouraged by the words of Sir J. Reynolds, addressed to the pupils of the Royal Academy; he says:—"The travellers into the East tell us, that when the ignorant inhabitants of those countries are asked concerning the ruins of stately edifices yet remaining amongst them, the melancholy monuments of their former grandeur and long-lost science, they always answer, 'they were built by magicians.' The untaught mind finds a vast gulf between its own powers and those works of complicated art, which it is utterly unable to fathom; and it supposes that such a void can be passed only by supernatural powers." What Sir Joshua Reynolds says of painting is true of literature. Those who understand not the *cause* of achievements beyond their own powers, may well be astonished at the *effect;* and what the uncivilised ascribe to Magic, others ascribe to Genius: two mighty pretenders, who, for the most part, are safe from rivalry only because, by the terror of their name, they discourage in their own peculiar sphere that resolute and sanguine spirit of enterprise which is essential to success. But all magic is science in disguise: let us proceed to take off the mask—to show that the mightiest objects of our wonder are mere men like ourselves; have attained their superiority by steps which we can follow; and that we can, at all events, walk in the same path, though there remains at last a space between us. Think of the wit of Hudibras! How wonderful the mind which could in the same page illustrate and throw into relief, as it were, by a single touch, distinct ideas, by reference to things of classes so different, that the fact of thought being employed about the one would seem to insure its overlooking the other! How strange that more witty things should occur to Butler while writing one page, and that bearing every appearance of an off-hand composition, than would occur to most men while writing a volume! Are these our thoughts? Draw back the curtain, and the phantom resolves itself into the common things of daily life.

"*The author of Hudibras*," said Johnson, "had a Common-place book, in which he had reposited, not such events or precepts as are gathered by reading, but such remarks, similitudes, allusions, assemblages, or inferences, as occasion prompted or inclination produced; those thoughts which were generated in his own mind, and might be usefully applied to some future purpose. Such is the labour of those who write for immortality."

Much as I admire Hudibras, I cannot help

believing that the reason so many of its imitators have failed is, that they endeavoured to meet at the moment a demand for wit which Butler had been a life preparing to supply. I have known men of little talent so ready, by the practice of a few months, with an inferior species of wit,—puns, that I see no reason why many men of superior talents should not rival Butler in a higher kind, if they only had recourse to the labour and method which, Dr. Johnson truly says, is the price of immortality.

See the miser in his lonely walk—his head down—his soul grovelling in the dust—all his senses intent on one narrow, sordid pursuit, money or money's worth;—look, he turns from the path on to the road:—"Is it? no, not a farthing, but a button—and no shank. Ah! buttons often leave their shanks behind." Still he takes it, and walks on. See again: "A tube—tin is it?—spout of something—may come useful one day—may find something it will fit: did once, two years after—fetched two pence." Look at him; scan that perversion of human kind, and say—were that man, old as he is, self-denying as he is, persevering and devoted as he ever has been, through many a toilsome day and restless night, were he a miser, not of pence but of ideas, or the coin of the mind,—were he equally capable of putting in his claim when none knew the rightful owner of one thing, of effacing marks of identity in a second, equally ingenious in converting a third, or in matching a fourth, what might not the same habits with the same limited faculties accomplish!

Again,—think of Sheridan. His speech on the impeachment of Hastings so completely ruled the spirits of his hearers that Pitt said, "All parties were under the wand of the enchanter, and only vied with each other in describing the fascination under which they were held." Mr. Windham, even twenty years after, said the speech deserved all its fame as the finest in the memory of man. Mr. Fox, also, in answer to a question of Lord Holland's, specified Sheridan's, on the Oude Charge, as the finest speech of his day. This would seem like genius—like inspiration. But, if Genius means, as in the common acceptation it does mean, a power that attains its end by means wholly new and unpractised by others, then was Sheridan's speech no work of genius. Moore describes him at the desk, like other mortal men, writing and erasing,—"Mr. *Speaker*," to fill up this pause, and "Sir," to fill up that; and confirms the opinion of Sir Joshua Reynolds—that the effects of genius must have their causes, and these causes may for the most part be analysed, digested, and copied; though sometimes they may be too subtle to be reduced to a written art. Sheridan stored up his wit like Butler. Some of his famous witticisms were found in his desk, written in many different forms—the point shifted, to try the effect, from one part of the sentence to another; and thus did he laboriously mould and manufacture what he had the readiness to utter as an impromptu.

I dispute not Sheridan's brilliant talents. I only argue that, high as they were, they were lower than the ignorant rated them. I would maintain that even the mightiest condescend to the same rules and methods of study by which the humblest are able to profit; and, amongst other ways and means,—to return from this digression introduced for my pupils' encouragement,—men of the highest endowments have practised and bequeathed Outlines of History, plans like my Trees of Knowledge, and Common-place Books.

Suppose then, you proceed to fill up your Historical tree with Goldsmith; you may either read it from end to end, and inscribe Goldsmith along the whole length of the stem, in order to have a more substantial outline than before: or, you may choose such reigns as happen to be interesting to you, and then record on the stem, "Henry VIII., or C. II.—*Goldsmith;*" and read the other reigns as curiosity dictates.—But, is it not the best plan to read a history through, and master all the difficulties? The best plan undoubtedly, if you can do it; that is, if you can not only read, but remember and digest the whole: but, if your mental constitution is unequal to the whole course and regimen, part is better than none: and there are very few young people who can profit by the whole of any history the first time of reading; so, why read what you are incapable of digesting?

The next question is, "How am I to proceed when I have read Goldsmith's History, or such reigns as suit my capacity?" Shall I read Hume and Smollett? Certainly not all the thirteen octavos, to forget the first before you come to the last. But, consider whether you feel so far interested in any particular part of history, that you are curious to read a more minute detail. If pleased with any one reign, or war, or negotiation; or, should the comments and observations with which men of genius have illustrated such portions excite your curiosity; turn to these portions in a longer history, in Hume or any other. The most profitable time to study any subject is while you feel a lively interest. Then, record on the corresponding part of your tree, "Hen. VIII. or C. II., — *Hume;*" and thus your tree will grow in strength and substance. But, that with every addition you may strengthen a particular part of your historical fabric, be sure you cast your eye over the whole work, to see that it yet remains entire. If you cannot readily run over in your mind the simple outline of the whole, you should refresh your memory with the outline history before you proceed to fill up.

Doubtless this advice must seem new: but the oldest things were new once; and all improvements must be novelties. Old usages and length of service appeal to our feelings; and wholesome customs are sometimes allowed the weight of laws: but if certain ways and means have stood the wreck, but not the test of time — if the good old tree beneath which our grandsires have gambolled has ever borne more leaves than fruit, time-worn but not time-honoured, then, root it up at once, and make room for those with which the science of to-day, collected from the failures of the past, enriches the rising generation. And certainly, as to the common ways and modes of study, "if *mode* it can be called where *mode* is none," judging by results, we can say little indeed in their favour. I ask any person of advanced years, "Could you call to mind more than one young person out of fifty who ever pursued private reading with a degree of method and judgment calculated to ensure success in the common avocations of life?" Hobbes of Malmesbury used to say, "If I had read as many books as other persons, I should probably know as little." And this philosopher is only one of many hundred witnesses, who, both by counsel and example, teach us "to read a little, and that little well:" such men think and count, not by the books they read, but the subjects they exhaust. Swift said that the reason a certain University was a learned place was, that "most persons took some learning there, and few brought any away with them, so it accumulated." Now, could it be said of our minds, that every habit tended to add, but nothing to take away, what a stock we should have at command! These rules, though new, are not untried; more than one of my friends have followed them, and proceeded with continually increasing interest, — the necessary consequence of a sense of steady and unintermitting improvement.

"Attend," said Gibbon, "to *the order, not of your books, but of your thoughts.* A particular work may suggest ideas unconnected with its subject; these ideas I pursue, in spite of any plan of reading."—Thus, Gibbon stopped reading Homer to refer to a chapter of Longinus, this suggested a letter by Pliny, and this again sent him off to Burke "on the Sublime and Beautiful."

Let us now suppose that by a course of methodical study you have filled up the greater part of your outline from Hume or some larger history: what now will be the extent of your knowledge? Will you be disheartened if you are told that you have nothing but an outline still? For this is scarcely an exaggeration. It is true that, in some periods, Hume may have given as full particulars as cotemporary authorities supply, or as the most scrutinizing curiosity desires; but, upon the greater part of events, all he gives is a mere outline or epitome of original annals. For instance, Froissart's Chronicle alone is equal in bulk to Hume's eight volumes, although it extends over scarcely an eighth part the number of years. Again, reckoning (and there is good authority for so doing) each Times newspaper of a double sheet as equal to two octavos, the news of the nation, apart from advertisements and trivial subjects, would make a history as large as Hume at least once a month. And if so, what a bare outline must eight volumes contain of matter which represents, not months, but centuries!

"Then on what an ocean we embark! Can we ever follow out so large a plan?"

Have patience. After mentioning many volumes of English history, I was going to add, not that there were so many to read, but so many from which to choose; and, of course, the larger the choice, the more easy to suit each variety of taste and inclination.

Without dictating the extent of your studies, I would show you how to make the little time you employ go as far as possible; for which purpose I advise a short outline of the whole, and a minute knowledge of parts; and for this reason: The sketches of the historian are like those of the artist. You may have, first, an outline which gives rather the shadows of men than the men themselves; you may have a broader outline, which still leaves every man alike; you may have the figures rudely filled up, giving substantial form and individual character, but still stiff and inanimate; or, lastly, you may have a faithful expression of impassioned agents, delineating an interesting passage of real life. Now, which would you prefer, — one good historical picture — say a panorama of the Battle of Waterloo, in which you could understand all the movements, positions, and manœuvres of one mighty action, which would serve as a key to every other; or, a long series of the usual battle-pieces, differing from each other in little else than in the artist's partiality for fire and smoke?

THE MOST VALUABLE SKETCHES ARE THOSE DRAWN BY CONTEMPORARIES. The leading events of history may be copied from age to age. Ingenious writers may ascertain the details of wars and treaties at a distant period of time: but contemporaries alone can draw characters, and amuse us with vivid portraiture. This was Johnson's remark on Robertson's histories. He said the characters in history must be fiction, unless drawn by those who knew the persons, as Sallust and Clarendon. Sir Joshua Reynolds remarked, that the distinctness of Robertson's historical characters was caused at the expense of truth, by exaggerating their more marked features. And Sir Robert Walpole, when, as Mr. Croker quotes, his son Horace offered to amuse him with reading, said, "Any thing but history—that must be false;" he meant to say, the imputed motives, finer springs of actions, and minute detail of concurrent causes, were, for obvious reasons, so inscrutable to historians, that he cared not for their works.

Wherefore, in preference to a dry outline enlivened only by fictitious circumstances and plausible reasonings on doubtful data, read the history of a limited period, written by men who had some opportunity at least of knowing what they wrote.

This mode of historical study is supported by high authority. Bacon remarked, he should like a history formed of the genuine works of all the writers of their own times, arranged, and, if requisite, translated, but not abbreviated. "For compilers," said he, "are the very 'moths of history.'" Consider what was passing in Bacon's mind when he made choice of this expression. History, as faithfully related by a series of writers, each detailing what he saw and heard, seemed to Bacon like a fine piece of tapestry, wherein were delineated figures that seemed to move and breathe in positions which told the whole story—who the victors—who the vanquished—the cause of the strife—the fire of the chiefs, and the struggles of the men. To such "cunning embroidery" we may liken the varied and vivid page of Froissart; but, when Hume comes in the character of moth the first, makes havoc of all colour and perspective, till no eye can distinguish between friend and foe—when Goldsmith follows as moth the second, eats up each remnant of distinctive character, and makes the living motionless as the slain—and when Pinnock comes, as moth the third, preys on what the other two have spared, and makes skeletons both of the dying and the dead—surely such shadowy sketches of things that were, cannot so far give the character of the past as to make it what all history should be, the mirror of the future — "the lessons of philosophy teaching by example."

"Original authors," says Southey, "are the bees that make the honey, compilers are the bears that rob the hives."

With this picture present to my mind, I call Goldsmith's history an outline — a skeleton: it contains topics under which you may very conveniently arrange ideas derived from other writers. But to be contented with such an outline alone is like taking the trouble of providing yourself with a frame of pigeon-holes for historical papers, and collecting no papers to fill them. For, to say that such epitomes alone give distinct ideas, is absurd: only suppress the names, and then if we ask which is Oliver Cromwell, and which is Wellington, we may well be answered, like children at the peep-show, "Which you please."

Since the voluminous histories in common use, such as Hume and Smollett, pass over matters with so light a touch, it follows that readers who confine themselves to such compositions, pursue rather the shadow than the substance of real knowledge. And this is a remark which Coleridge might as truly have made on the writings of Hume as on those of Gibbon, of whom he said, in his "Table Talk," that he passes along from height to height, so as to convey more the idea of romance than of history, and shows nothing of the wide flats and valleys of real life.

Indeed it cannot be supposed that Hume, or any other single writer, could investigate the memorable achievements of sixteen hundred years. How his fingers must tire ere he could unfold all the time-worn records of ages past! How his eyes must swim over the black-lettered Chronicles! Think how the many volumes which, as Hallam says, are rather the property of moths than men, would try his sight and test his patience, before he could give their meed of fame to Romans, Britons, Danes, Saxons, Normans. Well might Edmund Burke say he found Hume not very deeply versed in the early part of British history. The powers of the mind, like the waters of the sea, though vast and deep, are limited to bounds they cannot pass; and when highest in one part are lowest in another. And such was the complaint of Lady Mary Wortley Montagu, after making an attempt to rival the many tongues of all her household at Pera, from whom, be it known to all housekeepers of these degenerate days, she was doomed to hear the same excuse ten times told in ten different languages! The practice of one language had a tendency to diminish her aptitude for another; and her English was falling into decay. Burke said that Hume admitted to him, that from the early historians he derived no increased satisfaction to lead him on to deep research; and Burke considered himself a competent judge, having gone through all the early authorities. The reign he thought most carefully composed was that of Charles II.

And here we may notice a vulgar error, that Smollett wrote "a Continuation of Hume." The truth is, that Smollett wrote a History of England from the time of the invasion of the Romans. It is not one of the least of the curiosities of literature, that the fame of Hume should so completely have eclipsed that of Smollett as to overlay all that part of his work which could possibly enter into competition with his own. Even a writer in the "Edinburgh Review," in October, 1839, observed,—"Smollett has made a sorry figure by *continuing* the History of England."

Then the conclusion of all this is, that we must actually make out History for ourselves?—Yes. This is the legitimate conclusion from all my reasoning, that though what is called History is of some small value, inasmuch as it keeps the terms and forms of knowledge from passing into oblivion, still, it is composed more of names than things, rather shadowy than substantial, and greatly inferior to what an intelligent reader may easily be led to collect for himself. You must choose between these maxims: — "Every man his own historian," or "No man an historian at all:" take which you please. I am not guilty of making the difficulty, only of stating it; though real difficulty there is none: the only trouble consists in making choice of proper authors, or proper parts of them.

But here let me meet the old objection — "We have been always advised to read books through from end to end." The only consistent meaning of this advice is, to read no books but such as are worth most careful reading. The principle is good; but if taken literally, you would read dictionaries through, or cyclopædias, which is absurd; as indeed Dr. Johnson once remarked, in talking of a letter from the Rev. Herbert Croft to his pupil: —

Johnson.—"This is surely a strange advice. You may as well resolve that, whatever men you happen to get acquainted with, you are to keep to them for life. A book may be good for nothing, or there may be only one thing in it worth knowing: are we to read it all through?" It is well known that the Doctor said he never read any book through but the Bible. Adam Smith said, "Johnson knew more books than any man alive;" and Boswell innocently remarks, "He had a peculiar facility in seizing at once on what was valuable in any book, without submitting to the labour of perusing it from beginning to end."

To draw a correct outline first, carefully preserving and retracing it from time to time, while filling up according to inclination or ability, is the method I propose to explain and illustrate; and though I am now showing its application only to History, I shall presently explain its adaptation to literature generally, as a means of avoiding confusion, and marking progress alike in every subject.

"Well, then," said J. C. (a friend who will excuse my citing his case), on entering my study one morning with long sheets of paper, "here are my outlines. I have drawn the trunk of my tree: now for the leaves and the branches."

"Leaves and branches must be drawn in proportion to the maturity and vigour of the tree; or, to speak less figuratively, you must consider your curiosity, taste, and inclination. The strong food of the full-grown man may not agree with the child."

The taste of all readers may be regarded as threefold:—

One class of readers requires excitement, and that kind of interest which it is the part of the novelist to supply. Their favourite books are of the nature of the "Newgate Calendar" and

"Terrific Register." They read for the pleasure of conjuring up horrid scenes in their imaginations, and enjoying that sense of comparative security which the poet Lucretius has so sublimely noticed. If it be true that—

> The stage but echoes back the public voice—

if, that is to say, the current theme of every novel and romance shows the public taste, as plainly as the cut and colours in the dressmaker's window show the ruling fashion, we can readily discern one of the oldest favourites of a very large section of the literary circle,—I mean in homely vernacular "Hanging Stories." "God's Revenge against Murder" was the title of one of the earliest books ever printed. Punch and Judy, with the gallows and the public functionary, is one of the oldest shows; nor at any fair in the country does it find a more fearful rival than "Maria and the Red Barn," or any "most barbarous and inhuman murder, with the ghost of the unhappy victim." George Barnwell, and many other plots, too exciting in their very name to allow of very fastidious criticism as to their composition, have contributed to supply the same demand with the same commodity, in different forms, down to the present day. And now, in the plot of every novel, whether there be or be not

> Dignus vindice *nodus*,

a murder and the hangman seem as common a resource as a broken heart or the blacksmith of Gretna Green, in the novels of our younger days. Mr. Gibbon Wakefield, about ten years since, wrote an interesting pamphlet "On Crime in the Metropolis;" in which he says that by comparing the statements of a large number of prisoners in Newgate, he ascertained that inveterate thieves rarely failed to be present at an execution, not so much for an opportunity of picking pockets, as for the pleasure of excitement, which, he says, by the very exciting nature of their lawless pursuits, thieves soon become too callous to derive from any ordinary source. There is something true to nature—painfully true, in these words, and something very like the case of many novel readers, who bring themselves to that morbid state, that they are only to be touched by an appeal to their most vulgar sympathies! Oh! well did Shakspeare know the human heart when he crowded together all the stirring topics of Othello's history. There is many a young lady of whom we might say, that when serious things are talked of, like Desdemona,—

> Still the house affairs would draw her thence;

but, to a tale like Othello's, she would

> Come again, and with greedy ear
> Devour up my discourse.

Myriads there are both of men and women, who will read only for excitement. This stimulus is exhibited by authors in various forms and different quantities. The best employ it like the sweetening or spicing of a draught, to cheat the full-grown child into taking that which ministers to health. I allude not to certain writers who mix things sacred with profane; still less do I allude to writers who adopt the marketable form and title of a novel to publish their views of political philosophy; but I refer with great respect to a few novelists who have the goodness and the talent to contrive by three small volumes to rivet the attention of many an idle youth, and for a total space of some twenty hours, or more, wean him from that

> Which Satan finds for idle hands to do;

and in its stead provide for twenty hours a wholesome exercise for the finest sympathies of the heart. Still, when this wholesome recreation fails, literary pastimes of a mere negative character are not to be despised: because, they answer the purpose of keeping worse thoughts away, and sometimes lead on the student, step by step, till he reaches the purest sphere of intellectual existence. The first of the classes into which I divide readers we will regard as resembling Desdemona: they would have all narrators of Othello's caste, and would read of—

> battles, sieges, fortunes;—
> . . . . of most disastrous chances,
> Of moving accidents by flood and field;
> Of hair-breadth 'scapes i' the imminent deadly breach;—
> . . . . of antres vast and desarts idle,
> Rough quarries, rocks, and hills whose heads touch heaven;—
> And of the Cannibals that each other eat,
> The Anthropophagi, and men whose heads
> Do grow beneath their shoulders.—

A book with this page of Shakspeare for its table of contents, would probably be a general favourite with the subscribers of every circulating library in the kingdom; for, the majority of readers are not much above the excitement class. Their state of mind is by no means healthy, I allow; still, the lowest order of intellectual is preferable to mere physical resources. A book containing but little good has kept many a youth from company productive of positive evil. The excitement and gross immorality even of the worst of the old-fashioned novels is a less pernicious stimulant than lounging night after night with a cigar to the billiard-room. Not long since I heard a father say, "If I could only see my boy reading Tom Thumb, I should be happy: that would be a beginning: but, he avoids a book as if it had the plague." The habit of seeking amusement from books is so truly valuable in limiting the sphere of youthful temptations, that a parent should encourage it at almost any cost. Children should be taught that books are as natural a source of entertainment as tops and balls.

A quondam acquaintance who tried in vain for nearly seven years to take a degree at Oxford, observed ludicrously enough, "Books were never put in my way; when I could scarcely read, my guardians sent me to Rugby. My grandmother did once offer to make me a present of the 'Seven Wonders of the World,' or some such book, but I told her I should like the money instead, so she gave me neither. Now, I am trying for some situation under Government, but very few will suit me. Head work in an office is out of the question. Something like Commissioner of Woods and Forests, or any *out-of-door work* would do exactly!"

This is very laughable, but very sad. Think of the tedious hours of such a person's in-door life in rainy weather, from breakfast to luncheon, — to dinner — to supper — to bed. "Would it were evening!" "Would it were morning!" and in this state of mere vegetation, without the energy of life, many a man has existed who had all the natural qualifications for a sphere of usefulness, if his parents had been only satisfied to give him stories suitable to his childish taste.

In paying so much deference to those who read for excitement, I only act on the principle that to keep a child quiet we must give him such toys as he is in a humour to play with. Children (in mind) are found of all ages; and, as Aristotle says, "whether young in years, or young in character, matters not for the present argument:" children often attain to the so-called years of discretion without being able to run alone. A youthful taste must be indulged in its own way, and gradually led on by timely encouragement, and by the influence of superior minds, to mingle works of valuable information with those of more thrilling interest. Thus, from criminal trials (and who has not read the Newgate Calendar?) youths may acquire much information of the principles and practice of the laws of their country; trials for murders may lead to trials for treason, and cotemporary history; and thence, as the mind matures, they may learn to reflect on the state and progress of society. In short, whatever be the taste of a youth, it is better he should read in his own way, with certain obvious exception s than not at all. "What?" I may be sure some will say, "is that which ministers to love of excitement and a morbid appetite for subjects which are vain and profitless, and take up time never to be redeemed — is this to be recommended for youth?" No — not in the abstract, but as a choice, which so commonly presents itself, of manifest evils. The mother of a large family once observed, "Some object to novels and story books as irreligious, because exciting. I have four very high-spirited, though very excellent sons; if I lock up Robinson Crusoe from my George, and the Waverley novels from the other three, how *am* I to prevent them from turning the whole house out of window the first wet day; for they *will* read nothing else?" A few days after, a sensible physician told me he had a patient who could digest nothing but lobster salad. "Now," said he, "men with one idea would starve him first, and plead the rules of their profession afterwards." So, some who minister to the mind, instead of giving the child childish things, try to force an appetite for what they call instructive reading: the consequence is that they nip in the bud the slow-growing but healthy plant, which, with careful nurture, would have borne good fruit in due season.

Sir Walter Scott must be admitted to be one of the greatest benefactors of modern times. His writings are wholesome, generous, and ennobling. He gains the ear of those who would never hear anything half as serious from any one else. Bishop Heber was a great admirer of Scott's works. We learn from his Journal that he read Quentin Durward on his voyage, and said no other man but Scott could have written it.

Some men make shots at truth with only one idea at a time. They can manage one barrel, but not two. "Books," they remind us, "can never teach the use of books," as Bacon said: and therefore what? Why, therefore, they argue reading is of little good. Whereas, the legitimate conclusion is that, therefore, reading and observation, theory and practice, should go together. Reading multiplies experience: the vision of the unlearned is limited to his own little circle, his own country town, and his own few years of discretion. The man of reading, however, may have gone round the world with Captain Cook (*animoque rotundum percurrisse polum*), have soared among the stars with Newton, may have penetrated the earth with Buckland, or explored the caverns of the deep with Cuvier and Linnæus. The life of the one is three score years and ten: the other has outlived the age of Methuselah, and with vivid recollection to the last.

Class the first, therefore, comprises readers of youthful taste. Their appetite is for the rare, the dainty, high-seasoned viands. When instructive subjects are proposed, they soon find "house affairs to draw them hence," and must be amused, like Desdemona, before they will "seriously incline, and with greedy ear devour up my discourse." When one of this class sits down to a book of sterling worth, he looks at his watch, prepares his marker, smooths down the page, knits his brow, turns his back to the window, and begins. The first page is read with great attention, and, per chance, the second: he turns over the third, and, in a few minutes, finds his eyes nearly at the bottom; how they got there he knows not, for his thoughts, he feels, had gone off at a tangent from the top. These truant thoughts are soon recalled, obey for a page and a half, and then are off again—how *remarkable!* Who has not felt this mental phenomenon, and said, "How strange! I was so resolved—I wanted to attend, but my *mind* does *so* wander." Only consider these two words—"*I* and *my mind;*" most people think *they* and *their minds* are one and the same thing, but they seem as different as *I* and *my dog,* for my mind and my dog are equally prone to wander in spite of me—equally run off after anything that suddenly breaks upon my path; both evince an equal eagerness to chase anything but what I prepare to pursue. But there is a way to make my dog obey me, to change his wandering nature, to lie down when I say "down," passing without a glance all game but what I choose to hunt; all this I can do by *gradual discipline.* Let every man make the trial, and resolve that his mind shall become as tractable as his dog, by the same watchfulness and judicious exercise. He must not be severe with it at first, nor task it beyond its opening powers. The dog will never take the water if you begin by throwing him in—use gentle encouragement, and avail yourself of each earliest indication of maturing strength. Thus, you may continually extend the sphere of activity, improve the nature of mind as well as matter, and promote the readers of class the first to class the second, and, in due course, to class the third, which I will respectively describe.

The second class consists of those who study biography, or some branch of natural philosophy, who desire to improve, and can endure present toil for future profit. Let us draw a comparison between this and the former class. Tales of excitement cloy—the appetite becomes dull, till the bloodiest of all bloody murders does not make us *creep*—every headless spectre at midnight resolves itself into a shirt and red garters—no giant seems more than a dwarf after the monster who had a whole rookery flying out of his beard, and every ship-wrecked crew are at once foreseen either to be divided among sharks and cannibals, or else made more comfortable than if nothing had happened, by some home-bound vessel. Every species of battle, murder, and heroic exploit is soon familiar, and therefore the topics of my first class of readers are easily exhausted. But works of history, of fact not fiction, are ever varied and ever new. They expand the mind and continually enlarge the sphere of interest. If the first class of students visit the Polytechnicon, or Adelaide Gallery, they will saunter about for a few hours, return home, and say, with much composure, "Now we have seen it," as an unanswerable argument against visiting the same objects again. A visitor of this order of intellect accompanied me one day, and the two things which made most impression on his mind were a new bit for a runaway horse and a chair for surgical operations. Nothing arrested his attention for a moment but what was already familiar to him. A little patience and exertion of mind, with the courage to confess ignorance and ask questions, would, in many instances, have increased his knowledge of principles, and invested the mysterious wheels in glass cases with all the interest of the patent snaffle.

A few days after I met a young friend in the Polytechnicon, who had been there day after day; what he saw in the morning was a continual incitement to study in the evening; thus his curiosity was no sooner satisfied than hungry again, and literally "grew by what it fed on." My second class of readers study on the same principle. Dissertations on taxation and other points of political economy which occasionally occur in history, to some are dry and profitless; but they take the first opportunity of reading an article from a Cyclopædia on this very difficulty, find it far easier to understand than its repulsive name led them to expect; and, ever after, when they meet what once only convicted them of ignorance, they eagerly grapple with it, assured of all the pleasures of conscious superiority and improvement.

But, the third class of readers are of a higher order still: as the first like Fiction, and the second Fact, so these like Principle. To examine into causes and consequences is one of the highest exercises of the human mind, and one attended with the purest pleasure. Fiction delights us for the moment with imaginary scenes; History gives more lasting satisfaction by the realities of life; but the study of principles or Science is like extracting the essence or culling all that is profitable from both, and laying it up in a convenient form to be ever useful, ready, and available. Suppose a man found himself one of many hundred servants in a large factory or house of business, he would naturally desire to know something of the rise, progress, and future prospects of the system in which his own prosperity was involved. Fiction would tell what things *might be*—History would tell what things *had been*—but Science, in investigating the principles of the system, would, by comparing present with past, reveal what things *would be*. Just such a system is the complicated machinery of human society; such servants are its members, and such is the knowledge which the study of principles can impart. Homer's seer was a man deep in principles: "things which were and had been," taught him "things to come."

Again, the subjects of the three classes of readers may be the same, but each reads with a different purpose, gathers a different knowledge and exercises a different power of the mind. The butterfly flits over every flower-bed and stores up nothing; the spider gathers poison, but the bee honey. So, the lover of fiction reads a novel for the excitement and interest of the story; the lover of history reads the same novel to learn the manners and customs of the day; the lover of science and principles seeks to quicken his observation, and increase his knowledge of the human heart. And this would suggest the remark, that the value of every book, moral or intellectual, depends on the object with which it is read. The same volume may be made to minister to a morbid love of excitement, or to increase knowledge of the past, or to aid a noble contemplation of the present or the future. The child pulls off the lid of the kettle for sport, the house-wife for use, but young Watt for science, which ended with the discovery of the steam-engine.

Tastes and faculties differ — all are capable of improvement — and with good counsel most persons may learn to prefer the higher to the lower exercise, till the most exalted proves the most delightful, and our pleasures and interests coincide.

Bishop Sanderson said, "It was no less than a miracle of knowledge that men might attain to, if they proceeded thus distinctly in reading authors and pursuing knowledge."

I will now proceed to recommend books for each class respectively. Would that I could insure that the highest order of works should be preferred; or at least that those of a lower kind should be invested with an improving character by the high purposes which their readers aspired to promote. But to advise readers to study nothing till they feel a taste for works of the highest character, is like saying "never enter the water till you can swim." To hope to confine ourselves to books pure and unexceptionable, not only in their general tendency, but in every word and sentiment, is like hoping to join in none but the purest and most perfect society. So rigid a rule in a world like this would lead to monkish seclusion and narrowed faculties, with a better name, though worse influence, than intercourse the most unguarded would exert. If we may not read Shakspeare lest we learn improper language, we should not walk in the streets for the same reason; but the body would suffer from want of exercise in the one case, so would the mind in the other.

The first and most numerous class of readers, whose chief object is rather present amusement than future profit, should of course, when two books are equal in interest, make choice of that which is more improving. Therefore, one rule for a choice of books is to prefer those which almost all well-informed persons are presumed to know; books therefore which most frequently furnish apt sayings to quote, and positions to illustrate. "Æsop's Fables," the "Arabian Nights," "Robinson Crusoe," most of the "Waverley Novels," and plays of Shakspeare, "Don Quixote," the "Pilgrim's Progress," "Goldsmith's Vicar of Wakefield" and "Deserted Village," "Gray's Elegy" — these works are frequently quoted; if unacquainted with them, we should feel greatly at a loss almost every time we read a newspaper, enter a picture gallery, or converse with a man of ordinary fertility of mind.

These books serve in society as a common measure or standard for the easy interchange of thought. "Quixotic," for instance, is quite a common word. Allusion to vivid scenes and leading principles in these works serves for the transfer of ideas, just as letters of credit for the transfer of money. A knowledge of this circulating medium gives all the facility to conversation, that quoting the rule in "Shelley's case," or "Campbell *versus* Johnson," gives to an argument in a court of law; it saves explanations as tedious as recurrence to first principles.

To these books, add the voyages of Captains Cook and Parry, Basil Hall's Travels, Voyages to the North Pole, and Whale Fishery, Southey's Life of Nelson, Life of Napoleon in the "Family Library," Gulliver's Travels, Scott's Tales of a

Grandfather, Johnson's Rasselas, and Boswell's Life of Johnson.

Here is a short, but varied and most comprehensive, list for beginning. I should say, for beginning your choice. They may not all suit the taste of the same reader, and I freely allow you the privilege of laying down any book you do not like, and taking up another. More than one of these books has formed the taste — more than one has determined the fortunes — of thousands. "Southey's Life of Nelson," said an anxious mother, "I have put on the top shelf, out of my boy's way. His cousin Harry sends home fine accounts of mast-heading, and in windy weather too. All comes of Nelson's life — the child never thought of going to sea till that book turned his head."

There is a tide in the affairs of men,
Which taken at the flood leads on to fortune.

Certainly, there is a period when the mind of youth is critically poised, when

A breath may make them, as a breath has made,

and marred them too. The nursery game of deciding professions by straws, long and short, or the head of a stem of grass — "tinker, tailor, soldier, sailor, apothecary, thief" — ridiculously but truly represents the feather-weight which turns the scale of youthful destiny.

The Vicar of Wakefield in German, read by Goethe in childhood, gave, says Mr. Forster, a tone and character to that great poet's mind and feeling for life. To Ricaut's History of the Turks, read at Harrow, Byron ascribed his interest in the affairs of Greece, as also the oriental colouring of his poetry.

"The Beggars' Opera" was long prohibited, for fear it should encourage pickpockets: another book we could mention, which an officer of Newgate, after contradiction, persisted in saying that Courvoisier told him suggested Lord Russell's murder; and though that book has not been prohibited, still the evidence of a gaol chaplain of Liverpool showed it to be, in the form both of novel and melodram, a shocking incentive to the rising generation of thieves. "It is certain," says Falstaff, "that either wise bearing or ignorant carriage is caught, as men take diseases, one of another; therefore let men take heed to their company." Sir David Wilkie's touching picture, "Distraining for Rent," says Mr. Bulwer, in his "England and the English," remained long unengraved, from an opinion it would inflame popular prejudice against the landed interest.—"Books suggest Thoughts, thoughts become

Motives, motives prompt to Action. Man is a complicated piece of machinery: hundreds of nerves and muscles must act and react for the slightest turn of the body; yet, the very wind of a word, a casual hint or association, can set the whole in motion, and produce an Action—actions repeated form habits, and determine the Character, fixed, firm, and unalterable for good or for evil. So, the delicate hand of a princess can launch a man-of-war, and the voice of a peasant bring down an avalanche.

The reason I am desirous to give a varied list is, because there are few books which suit every taste. Gray saw little merit in Johnson's Rasselas; and Johnson was equally blind to the beauties of Gray's odes. Neither Moore, Byron, nor W. S. Landor could appreciate Chaucer. "Obscure and contemptible!" said Byron—though Southey admired Chaucer even more than Spencer. Byron called Shakespeare an impostor, and said he was sadly overrated. Byron throughout all his letters never quotes Shakespeare with admiration. Byron "detested" paintings, even those of Rubens and Murillo. Sir W. Scott's indifference in the Louvre is testified by Sharpe the engraver. Lord Eldon cared neither for painting nor music, and said, in the great Opera trial, he "would not give five shillings to hear Madame Catalani sing for six months!" That very popular song, which Burns said was in his best manner, "Scots wha hae wi' Wallace bled," was thought inferior both by Wordsworth and Mrs. Hemans. Dr. Parr said Sir Walter's popularity would not last. The poems of Ossian, which so many have admired, Johnson thought any man could write when he once hit the strain; and Edmund Burke declared they were intended to try English gullibility. Dr. Wolcot, better known as Peter Pindar, ridiculed Dryden's Alexander's Feast, and maintained, in a most humorous criticism, that it was positively absurd. — While tastes and opinions so far differ among the learned, I may well allow great latitude to the choice of the youthful reader.

It is a great error to wait for some fancied season of uninterrupted leisure before we enter on any new study. Alison's History, and Lord Campbell's Lives of the Chancellors, are the fruits of hours stolen from a most busy life. Erasmus spent his life in travelling from kingdom to kingdom in the vain pursuit of patrons and preferment; still, in the few hours available for study, he contrived to write more than many in such circumstances would expect even to read. The judicious Hooker had his sheep to tend out of doors, and a scolding wife within — a fair lady who, like the matter-of-fact spouse of Albert Durer, mistook profound meditation for dreamy idleness — but nothing could mar the "Ecclesiastical Polity." Melancthon, also, had his troubles, as Fuller* relates; for "a certain Frenchman found him dandling his child in the swaddling clouts, and in the other hand holding a book and reading it."

The secret is, that, to men of well-trained minds, interruptions are not hindrances: while debarred from literature, they draw on the resources of their own thoughts; and when at length the long-wished-for book is opened, it is devoured with an avidity all the greater from the delay.

A few books may furnish very many ideas, or instruments of thought; and only a few ideas well arranged and brought to bear on one point will clear away difficulties which a host of disorderly powers would fail to remove. Show an uneducated man a book, and he will say, "Who can remember all those Letters?" Tell him there are but twenty-four — he will still wonder at the many Words: say that the words, too, are limited in number, and that a knowledge of a system of inflection and composition solves many difficulties, and he will understand that the labours he reckoned by millions exist by tens. As with Words, so with Ideas. In most books ideas are few and far between. The distant forest which, to the inexperienced botanist, seems to abound in trees, numerous in kind and almost infinite in number, proves as he enters it to contain but one single species, each widely branching, with expanding limbs and luxuriant foliage; so, the study of one gives a knowledge of all. The power of recognising any old and well-known truth in each variety of garb, of stripping it of every accident and ornament, of studying it in its simplest form, and then investing and combining it anew, and setting it up in a useful and efficient attitude — this power is one of the most valuable results of human learning, and more to be envied than a memory fraught with the most varied stores of reading. The one possesses, but the other coins. Butler, the author of the Analogy, said, "Whoever will in the least attend to the thing will see that it is not the having of knowledge, but the gaining of it, which is the entertainment of the mind."—In every part of life the pleasure is in the pursuit, not in the possession. And if

> The worth of anything
> Is just as much as it will bring—

in happiness as in money — if that is true of the end which is said of the means, then we may deny that "a bird in hand is worth two in the bush," and prefer "an estate in expectancy" to one "in possession," though the worldly-wise maintain the contrary. Pursuits of literature are like the chase. Whether we exercise our feet or faculties, mount a hunter or a Pegasus, start a fox, or an idea, the fun is over when we have run it down, or, it has "got to *earth.*" The young men in Æsop's fable unconsciously cultivated their vineyard and improved their own strength and industry, while they dug for an imaginary treasure. So, many a student is insensibly storing strength while he seeks for knowledge. The classical maxim "to follow nature" is good indeed, when we can discern what nature says, and fish up truth from the bottom of the well, or rather, sift it from the rubbish, which, while truth was yet upon the surface, ignorance heaped upon it. Still, with all the darkness and difficulties of man's benighted state, there is an instinct he may safely obey, and one which, both in physics and metaphysics, disputations of science, *falsely so called,* have done much mischief in thwarting. This at least is true of my present subject — Study, and Curiosity as its guide. This instinct of Curiosity, an "appetite that grows by what it feeds on," urges many a youth to turn over and over the same favourite tale, while a host of the usual advisers cry out, Waste of time — pray read something new. " And, is he to obey curiosity and inclination to this extent?" Why not? a book cannot continue to fix attention unless it continues also either to impart or elicit new ideas. If the same passages make the same impressions, the book will be laid aside: but, if they make new impressions, the reader is learning to regard the same scenes at a different angle, or to shift the component parts, till they form, like the same pieces in the kaleidoscope, a variety of pleasing combinations.

A distinguished literary character of the present day was often found in childhood lying on his little bed, where none were likely to seek him, reading " Robinson Crusoe." " Only reading Robin — only Robin," was the constant excuse for all absence or idleness, till his friends augured that the future man would be a very different character from one who has done much to preserve the most valuable part of English literature. As a child he was devoted *to one book.* He has since been a man of one book. Shakespeare has been his favourite author. The rest of his reading has been determined by an ever-present desire to correct, illustrate, and restore every trace of that immortal bard. His course of studies being dictated, as we have advised, by his own curiosity and inclination, was peculiar. For instance, at the time of Sir

Walter Scott's death, he had not read one of the Waverley Novels.—"But would he not be afraid of betraying this deficiency in society?" He could find many a precedent to bear him out. Sir James Mackintosh had not read Shakespeare's minor works when forty years of age. Mr. Wilberforce used to say he would read no modern poetry till he was tired of Homer and Milton. Dr. Johnson had not read Othello when he wrote Irene, and visited Iona without seeing Staffa, though the Duke of Wellington went thirty miles out of his march to see Schrivanabalogol, "the big Indian," whom Chantrey said he could beat.

Look on that picture and on this,—"Coleridge's mind," said Southey, "is in a perpetual St. Vitus's dance—eternal activity without action. At times, he feels mortified that he has done so little; but this feeling never produces exertion. 'I will begin to-morrow,' he says, and thus he has been all his life long letting to-day slip. He has had no heavy calamities in life, and so contrives to be miserable about trifles." Charles Lamb, also, said to Coleridge, "I grieve from my very soul to observe you in your plans of life, veering about from this hope to the other, and settling nowhere. Would that the dancing demon may conduct you at last in peace and comfort even to the life and labour of a cottager!"

A friend, on looking over these pages, now asks me, "But is there no danger that men of one book, however honourably we hear them mentioned, should be ignorant of every other subject of conversation which does not bear upon their favourite topics?" Certainly the mind requires variety; still you may pursue one system, choose one class of authors most suitable to your own peculiar talents, and prefer to be sound in a limited sphere, to being superficial in one more extended. I would recommend every young man to make choice of his book — Shakespeare, Milton, Bacon, Clarendon, Burke, Johnson's Conversations in Boswell; or, to those of a thoughtful habit, I would say, take Butler's Analogy and Sermons, bind them up in one thick volume, on which write WISDOM in gold letters, and begin to read it through every New Year's Day. One sterling author, to call "my book," ever most conspicuous and most at hand, read, re-read, marked and quoted, standing on the shelf, if not "alone in his glory," at least surrounded with pamphlets, manuscripts, and authors to illustrate it — this will do much to form the mind; this will teach us to think as our favourite author thought, to aspire to the same precision of expression, the same purity of taste, loftiness of views, and fervency of spirit. This will give a high standard of excellence, chastening us with humility, while it fires us with emulation. *The one thing needful*, and the Holy Volume, which teaches all things pertaining thereto, must of course be uppermost in the thoughts of all. I shall content myself with observing that one of my fellow-collegians, highly distinguished both at Winchester and Oxford, made the Bible not only the subject of his serious meditations, but a book to illustrate and a literary resource in his hours of recreation. It was the pride of his mind to be a living index or treasury of Biblical literature.

The best guides in the study and the choice of English literature are, as general advisers, Hallam and Berrington, who have written the History of Literature, and Dunlop, who gives the History of Fiction. For Poetry, Johnson's "Lives of the Poets," Campbell's Essay, and Aytoun's "Poets of the Nineteenth Century." Pick your way, by help of the table of contents, through these books, and read the works recommended on the spur of your appetite. Also, look through the Lives of Southey, Campbell, Scott, and others. See what they admire; and "rectify" your taste, and "clarify" your judgment, by their purer standard.

Whenever we feel unusually entertained with a work, it is natural to inquire for other works by the same author; and, though his other compositions bear no very inviting titles, we may still hope that he has made them the vehicle of the same order of ideas. Bishop Berkeley betrayed the same train of reasoning in his "Thoughts upon Tar Water," as in his "Principles of Human Knowledge." The verses in the celebrated "Pursuits of Literature," a book which gives a page of satirical observations to a line of text, were said by George Steevens to be "mere pegs to hang the notes on." And so, at the present day, a book with the name, size, style, and letter-press of a novel, will often prove to be the insidious form in which science, political or theological, is homœopathically exhibited and disguised.

Defoe wrote, besides "Robinson Crusoe," the "History of the Plague of London," in which his fertile imagination, guided and assisted by a few authentic incidents, has placed before our eyes a series of pictures nearly as vivid as that of Crusoe himself when starting at the unknown foot mark upon the sand. You might also be tempted to read Defoe's ghost story of the appearance of Mrs. Veal, prefixed to the second edition of the English translation of "Drelincourt on Death," as also the "Life of Defoe," in Sir W. Scott's prose works (vol. iv. p. 267.), where we have an outline of the story, and the circumstance that led to its fabrication. The first edition of this translation had but an indifferent sale; Defoe ingeniously contrived to render it popular, by prefixing the story of a ghost which appeared and recommended the book; the consequence was that those who had not been persuaded to read Drelincourt by any man living, were yet persuaded by a recommendation from the dead. Drelincourt's admirable work first drew my attention as I read an allusion to the story of Mrs. Veal, in Boswell (iii. 194.). I therefore added it to my list of "authors characterised and recommended," in which I enter any accidental notice of works of interest, as I shall presently describe.

But I think I hear some censorious reader say, "Why tell us where to find ghost stories? Proceed at once to things worth knowing." This is precisely the point to which I wish to show that subjects the most trivial may be made to tend. I was going to observe that Dr. Johnson, like every one else till a comparatively recent time, was ignorant that this story of Mrs. Veal was a fiction, and said, "I believe the woman declared on her death-bed it was a lie." So, a fabricated story had a fabricated contradiction. Does this supply no lesson as to the Credulity of man, and the Uncertainty of human Testimony—two topics well worthy of a man of reflection to illustrate? What can be more requisite as a foundation of all learning than a clear knowledge of the extent to which human testimony has erred; and how far favour, affection, association, prejudice, and passions of all kinds render man liable to yield too ready and too general an assent to partial evidence? Let this subject be pursued by readers of a speculative turn; and, even from common stories and anecdotes they will derive no less profit than entertainment. Consider the extraordinary impositions which have been practised in literature, and the controversies to which they have led —that of Lauder, for instance, in 1747, who by an essay in the "Gentleman's Magazine," tried to prove that Milton had borrowed from Latin authors of modern date. A great many scholars were actually deceived before he was detected by Douglas, afterwards Bishop of Salisbury, who showed that passages which Lauder pretended to have found in the poems of Massenius and others, were really taken from Hogg's Latin translation of Paradise Lost! Dr. Johnson was so far deceived as to write a preface and postscript to Lauder's work. An account of this imposition is found in Nichols' "Literary Anecdotes of the 18th Century," a work to be read while inclination lasts, and no longer. This limit should be particularly observed with books of anecdotes or miscellany, and the multifarious reading which Biography supplies. It must not be supposed that mere dipping into a chapter here and there will convey all the advantages of sound study: only, after gleaning all which interests at one time, the rest may be reserved for an occasion of more extended curiosity. I do not like to hear a man say, "Rasselas, or the Vicar of Wakefield, is a work of genius, but I have not read it since I was young." The second reading of a good book is often more profitable than the first. The same truth has many meanings: it has one voice for the wise — another for the unwise. It pleases the vacant mind by the knowledge it imparts; it pleases the full and fertile mind by the force it gathers from numerous associations, and by the new ideas it elicits, as also by making mere shadowy impressions distinct. A good book may be ever new, so long as our own minds continue to gather from it new strength to develope, and new images to combine.

But to return to the topic of human testimony, we might read the "Confessions" of Ireland, who, as Malone was speculating on undiscovered MSS. of Shakespeare, forged "miscellaneous papers and legal instruments, under the hand and seal of William Shakspeare;" also "Vortigern," a play, which he pretended was written by Shakespeare, and which was actually performed at Sheridan's theatre, and only condemned by the double meaning which Kemble's sneer gave the line —

And when this solemn mockery is o'er.

Many men in literary circles were deceived. Dr. Parr acknowledged "the forgery beat him." Warton said of a prayer which was also among the forgeries, though written off-hand by Ireland when only seventeen years of age, that it surpassed in sublimity any part of our Liturgy!

I must not omit Chatterton, who imposed on many literary persons by forging poems, and ancient records and title-deeds, which he pretended were found in St. Mary Redcliffe Church at Bristol. Horace Walpole, with the help of Gray and Mason, detected the forgery; but Walpole's letter to Chatterton proved he had once been deceived. Afterwards, a line of Hudibras was discovered among this ancient poetry; — still, considering this deception was practised at the age of sixteen, and that the poetry is pronounced by Southey "the finest ever written at so early an age," Dix's "Life of Chatterton" will be found a work of lively interest. Dr. Johnson said, in his peculiarly unsympathetic style, "It is wonderful how the young whelp could have done it." Coleridge's Monody on the death of Chatterton evinces a widely different feeling.

Again, George Psalmanazar, born 1679, in the south of France, pretended to be a heathen native of the island of Formosa, and invented a new language, which he called the Formosan, and into which he had the boldness to translate the "Church Catechism." This remained long undetected by the learned, while his "History of Formosa" passed through two editions. His "Auto-biography" is deserving of credit. Johnson said, "I scarcely ever sought the society of any one, but of Psalmanazar the most. I used to find him in an ale-house in the city: latterly he lived as a very good man, and died a sincere Christian: — his 'Auto-biography' was a penitential confession."

On the same topic of the strength and weakness of the human mind, we may mention the controversies about Homer, "Epistles of Phalaris," Ossian, Junius, Chevalier D'Eon, Man with the Iron Mask, "Voyages of Damberger," Eliza Canning, Johannah Southcote, Mary Tophts of Godalming, the Cock-lane Ghost, and Jugglers' Feats, as related by Eastern travellers. If any person entertains curiosity in these matters, "Sketches of Imposture and Credulity," in the "Family Library," and Sir Walter Scott's "Demonology and Witchcraft," will supply abundant interest.

"But surely this is a strange selection." Granted. But I do not name these subjects to the exclusion of others, but principally to show that youthful taste indulged even in its own caprices will involuntarily lead to a kind of knowledge available in the season of maturer judgment. I would also illustrate the advantage of always bearing in mind one useful subject, which every hour of reading and reflection may contribute to illustrate. Every mind has a host of wandering thoughts, which unbidden come, and unregarded go, only because they want a ready standard round which to rally.

A subject like that of Abercrombie, "On the Intellectual Powers and the Investigation of Truth," would surely be a laudable employment for the talents of the greatest genius; and would not this course of reading, childish as it may seem, supply facts too valuable to lose? How often have some of these cases of deception been cited by the avowed enemies of the Gospel! Who can say that he may not feel himself called upon to give the same serious attention to the history of these impostors, as Paley, in his "Evidences of Christianity," has given to the subject of fictitious miracles, and for the same purpose?

Here, my friends, let me remind you that from "Robinson Crusoe" I have wandered to the

"Evidences of Revealed Religion;" and though I did not see the point at which I should arrive, I felt confident of eventually showing that, with Curiosity as your guide, your route will afford you no less profit than interest, whatever be your starting point. The ever-recurring questions, "Where is the *use* of this?" or "the *good* of that?" may well be met with the reply, that many things are eventually useful, though not immediately convertible; and that prudent housekeepers say, "Keep a thing three years, and you'll find a use for it." But I must be careful not to give up a commanding position, because it is convenient to meet a feeble enemy on lower grounds. Let us, therefore, remember that in a well-stored mind to which, as Herschel says, "a thousand questions are continually arising, a thousand subjects of inquiry presenting themselves, which keep the faculties in constant exercise, and the thoughts perpetually on the wing, so that lassitude is excluded from life, and that craving after artificial excitement and dissipation of mind, which leads so many into frivolous, unworthy, and destructive pursuits, is altogether eradicated from the bosom;"—in such a mind, there is *a use*, indeed: there must therefore be *some good* in whatever reading conduces to form it. This argument, I say, asserting not the sordid money reckoning of the hireling but the enlarged estimation of the Christian, who values literature as it lessens the temptations of earth, and slopes the path of heaven—this is the true and impregnable ground of defence against the sneers of the friends of so-called utility and expediency. Still, as we delight in foiling insignificant cavillers, not only on our own grounds but on theirs, I would ask them, if they would have seen *the use* of Newton's pondering over a falling apple; and yet it raised his thoughts to the laws which govern the revolution of the planets in their orbits. Would they not have joined in the ridicule of *swing-swangs,* which did not prevent Robert Hooke from reviving the proposal of the pendulum as a standard of measure, since so admirably wrought into practice, as Herschel remarks, by the genius and perseverance of Captain Kater? Would they not have joined in the laugh at Boyle, in his experiments on the pressure and elasticity of air, and asked Watt, as I before mentioned, *the use* of playing with the kettle, and yet all can see *the good* of the steam-engine? Then think of blowing soap bubbles, by which the phenomena of colours has been studied; to say nothing of where could be *the good* of playing with whirligigs, the simple means by which, a few years since, a society of philosophers were investigating certain principles of optics, as exemplified in the clever toy called the Magic Disk. A scientific friend (an F. R. S.), a short time since, intent on geological discovery, sat down one sultry day, with a hammer, to break stones by the road-side. A fellow-labourer, employed by the parish, looked on with amazement, till he saw some fossils selected from the heap, and then said, "Why, Sir, I suppose they give you something for them?" "No," said my friend, "they don't." "Then, what can be the good of them?"—This poor fellow was quite as enlightened as many intellectual paupers, who, when their money is as low as their wit, may break stones too.

Cultivate literature for its own sake, not for profit; though, profit may incidentally spring from it: this most charming of all pursuits is the most desperate of all professions. Southey, Charles Lamb, Rogers, and Campbell, among others, emphatically warn us that disappointing and sickening is the toil of those who woo the Muses rather for their fortune than their charms. Money is only paid for things in actual demand; and that genius which is in advance of its age and writes for future generations must not expect to be paid by this.—"A man would as soon sit down to a whole ox as a whole Epic now-a-days," says Lord Jeffrey; and, to compose not according to the impulse of fancy, but the demands of the trade, and not what you can write best, but what will sell best, — the very idea of this drudgery will paralyse the energies of any writer. And what a chapter in literary history might be made on the poverty and persecution of men of genius: Simon Ockley, author of the "History of the Saracens," said he was writing the Lives of others, and could hardly live himself. Cervantes at times wanted bread; Camoens died in an hospital; Tasso would have thanked us for a candle to write by, and Ariosto could not have afforded to help him; Corneille had a present from Louis XIV. when dying of want; Otway was starved; Collins, partly from the pressure of want, ran a howling madman through the aisles of Chichester Cathedral. Dryden, Johnson, Savage, and Goldsmith have all been in want of a dinner; poor Sydenham died in a spunging-house, and it was in sympathy for him that the "Literary Fund" was first instituted, on which, in an earlier age, Rymer, Spenser, and Le Sage might all, from poverty, have had a claim. Then fancy John Milton wasting his sublimity in a school, Chantrey carrying milk-pails, Stephenson in a coal mine, and Sir J. Paxton, a gardener's labourer!

The unknown author of "Fleta" has recorded by its title that that learned law book was written in the Fleet; but a prison formed the study also of Buchanan, and of Grotius, besides Boethius, whose "Consolations" seem as congenial to the place as poor Dodd's "Prison Thoughts." From a prison also issued the works of Sir Walter Raleigh, Lydiat, Selden, and Sir W. Davenant. It was in a prison that Cervantes wrote "Don Quixote," that Voltaire wrote his "Henriade," De Foe his "Robinson Crusoe," and John Bunyan, the "Pilgrim's Progress."

So far I have supposed that a juvenile taste has led my reader through a course of study, which in a note-book, of the kind I shall presently recommend him to keep, would stand thus:—

Memorandum of Reading.—Read "Robinson Crusoe," which suggested "History of the Plague," and "Defoe's Life," by Scott, in which was quoted Defoe's "Preface to Drelincourt," concerning which I consulted Nichol's "Literary Anecdotes." *To be read,* Nichols, again and again, at future periods. This specimen of *literary imposition* suggested reading the life of Chatterton; also Psalmanazar's, Ireland's, and Lauder's forgeries. The credulity of the wisest men was a topic which made me curious to read "Sketches of Credulity and Imposture," as containing an outline of all notable instances, to which I find so many allusions; and also Scott's "Demonology," which I was told gave a common-sense explanation of supernatural appearances. Query.—Was Dr. Johnson superstitious? Must read more of Boswell.

MEMORANDUM OF KNOWLEDGE.—Learned the extent to which fiction may resemble truth—the fallibility of human judgment—that men of the greatest genius are not above the prejudices of their day. The nature of evidence—the many causes which hinder the investigation of truth. To read about fallacies, human understanding, laws of evidence, blunders and pretensions of critics, with a view to illustrate these topics; to attend to the historical accounts of all popular deceptions, criminal trials, and the like.

These memoranda are recommended as Aids to Reflection; also, to teach how to digest all the knowledge we acquire. "Heaping up information," says the author of "Woman's Mission," "however valuable of itself, requires the principle of combination to make it useful. Stones and bricks are valuable things, very valuable;

but they are not beautiful or useful till the hand of the architect has given them a form, and the cement of the bricklayer has knit them together."

Let us now take, from the list assigned to the first class of readers, a second book, that we may see how the same method and principle of combining and digesting applies to other amusing subjects. Consider the "Travels" of Captain Basil Hall. His third series gives a brief but clear outline of the History of India, from the year 1497, in which the Portuguese discovered the route by the Cape; the formation of the East India Company; war with the French; the Black Hole of Calcutta; Lord Clive; Hyder Ali; Warren Hastings; an interesting account of the system on which British India is governed; Tippoo Saib; Cornwallis; Wellesley; writers and cadets; a most interesting account of Bombay and the wonders of Elephanta (Series ii. vol. iii.), and Ceylon; the stupendous labour of making Candelay Lake; the voluntary tortures of the superstitious Sunnyasses; how widow burning was abolished; the immense tanks; the "big Indian" Shrivanabalagol, a statue seventy feet high, cut out of a hill of granite; descriptions of canoes, and inventions, strange habits, and customs of a variety of nations. Basil Hall's "Travels" in America are written in the same style, equally combining amusement with instruction. After reading these interesting volumes, and following the course which I should suppose your inclination would suggest, your note-book would bear, as I judge from my own, some such entry as the following: —

MEMORANDUM OF READING. — Read Basil Hall's "Travels;" mention of Warren Hastings; suggested to read a few pages of Miller's "George III.," about the impeachment of Hastings; also Macaulay's "Clive," "W. Hastings," which suggested life of Sheridan in Biographical Dictionary. Burke's "Speeches," recommended on the same subject, and Nabob of Arcott — read both. To see more of the meaning of "Charta" and "Company," H. W. promised me that five minutes' reading in my Cyclopædia would inform me; also that I might find the same by the index to Blackstone's "Commentaries;" found much more in Blackstone; also "India" in Cyclopædia, and had a general view of the whole subject. Must observe Daniell's Indian drawings as very near reality. H. W. says the Museum at the India House, in Leadenhall Street, and the Naval and Military Museum, near Whitehall, may be visited with advantage. Rev. W. Ward's book on the "Literature and Customs of the Hindoos," recommended; also Sir W. Jones's

"Letters"—picked out a great deal from both; also from Robertson's "Ancient India," showing what was known to the ancients about India, and about Phœnicians: advised to read Ezekiel, c. xxviii.; very curious—about ancient commerce and navigation—read of Tarshish, Ophir, Elath, and Eziongeber, Palmyra, Arabians, Genoese, and Venetians.

MEMORANDUM OF KNOWLEDGE.—Feel more confidence, as well as curiosity, about India. Can converse with and draw out my Indian friends to advantage. Know more about the ingenuity and power of man. Must compare pyramids, railways, and Indian tanks. Did not know there was so much curious knowledge in O. T. Quote II. Maccabees, ii. 23. Excellent on the use of an abridgement. Begin to observe the natural productions, manners, and customs of the Book of Job. Read some of the "Scripture Herbalist" about the plants and trees; also looked into "Natural History of the Bible:" surprised at finding so many curious things which never struck me before. Herschel's proof (Nat. Phil. p. 61.) of the insignificance of the labour which raised the great pyramid, compared with the weekly expense of steam power in our foundries.

I should now consider that I had given my class of readers their full share of attention, were it not that, profiting by the example of Molière, who used to judge of the probable success of his comedies by the degree they excited the risible faculties of his old housekeeper, I read these pages to a young friend, and was told, "that it is not so easy to find the answers to the various questions which we should like to ask in reading travels; for too many authors assume that what is familiar to themselves is familiar to their readers."

This remark leads me to speak of the use of Cyclopædias, Gazetteers, Biographical Dictionaries, and other books of reference.

We just mentioned India; East India Company; Clive; Hastings; Cornwallis; Wellesley; Writers; Cadets. On each of these heads you may consult the "Penny Cyclopædia," which excels all others in the variety of its subjects. You can read each article, more or less attentively, according to the degree of interest which casual notices of those topics in books or conversation have excited. When you have read them all, cast your eye again over the article on India, and you will feel that the several parts of your newly-acquired knowledge have a propensity to "fall in," as the drill sergeants say, and find their proper places in the main line which this sketch of Indian history has marked out. And probably allusions to Tippoo Saib, Hyder Ali, Brahmins, Buddhism, Caste, and other subjects, will lead you to read the separate articles upon these topics also; and, I will venture to promise you will rise from your studies with feelings of considerable satisfaction. Having once mustered courage to plunge into the ocean of learning, if you cannot swim at first, you will acquire a sense of your own buoyancy, and more easily resolve to try again. When the splashing and floundering is over for the first time, you will feel some confidence in society, and listen to catch a hint from the greater advancements of others. Many a boy would never have learned to swim, had it not been for some companions who tempted him just to try one dip. Many a man would have gone through a whole life subject to that creeping sense of inferiority, which is the every-day punishment of ignorance, had not some literary companions led him to take the first step, which carried him so much further than he expected, that he was emboldened to try a second, and at length to join the busy throng, in which powers unknown, because untried, made him first and foremost. With this beginning in Indian history, take another Cyclopædia, the "Britannica," or "Metropolitana," and look out for the same articles. Then look for India in a Gazetteer, and the names of men in a Biographical Dictionary: to these articles are usually added the names of authors from whom more information may be derived. By this method you may soon make an extensive collection of facts. I say *of facts,* for sound, mature, well-digested *knowledge* is not the growth of a day: facts to the mind are like food to the body; digestion and strength depend on the constitution, mental or physical. After reading long histories, or lives of distinguished characters, most young readers find that they rise with a knowledge more confused than accurate, and that even certain plain and obvious questions, such as the age at which certain men attained celebrity; at what times particular changes happened; what circumstances led to certain events, and other things of interest, escape observation, from the many pages over which the required information is interspersed. These the compendious articles of a Cyclopædia, or Biographical Dictionary, are peculiarly suited to supply; before commencing a biography in two or three volumes, read a short outline; this prevents your thoughts from wandering and enables you to keep the thread; and for this purpose outlines are always useful. Also, keep books of reference at hand, and turn at once to the name of any unknown character introduced.

Again, Magazines and Reviews often contain concise accounts of campaigns, political questions, and the present policy and interests of different nations. Nor must we forget, that, with the exception of Novels, Magazines are now nearly the only channel by which an author can publish his opinions with the least prospect of remuneration; so, a compendium of facts, and series of reflections, which would once have made a plausible appearance in two volumes octavo, are now cut down to the length of a single essay in the "Edinburgh," or "Quarterly," and gain no little vigour from the pruning. The chief value of the Magazines is, that they give us the benefit of early information. Bacon says, that "Reading makes the full man, and Conversation the ready man;" and Johnson says of Conversation, that it supplies only scraps, and that we must read books to learn a whole subject; then, Bacon goes on to say, that "Writing makes the exact man." The digesting and arrangement of knowledge are two points which should never be lost sight of: the use of a short compendium will tend to that clear view and that habit of exactness which writing more fully promotes.

Besides cyclopædias, gazetteers, biographical

dictionaries, and magazines, there are many other works like the magazines furnished with indices, and readily available as books of reference. I have already mentioned Blackstone's "Commentaries," which, though I cannot speak of it as a work of general interest to the young, contains, as a glance at its index will show, many things to solve questions which arise in the study of history. Again, biographies are good books of reference: about the Reformation, the lives of Luther, Knox, Calvin; about the Methodists, Southey's "Life of Wesley;" about the slavery question, "The Life of Wilberforce;" about military matters, the lives of Marlborough, Sir T. Picton, Wellington, Napoleon; about naval affairs, Rodney, Earl St. Vincent, Nelson, Lord Exmouth, — severally contain much information, to which an index or table of contents will direct. You have only to inquire, what celebrated men are connected or cotemporary with the matter in question, and you will generally find that their biographies contain their opinions, and enough of the history of their times, to make their opinions intelligible. Of all biographies none is so valuable for a book of reference as Boswell's "Life of Johnson." During the middle of the last century, nearly every conspicuous character, or memorable incident of that and of many preceding ages, passed successively in review before the severe judgment of him, who was confessedly one of the wisest of men, and his opinion has been faithfully recorded by a biographer, of whom a writer in the "Quarterly" has truly said, "It is scarcely more practicable to find another Boswell than another Johnson."

One of my young friends again asks, "Does all my learning go for nothing? I have read many books, but know none accurately; still I feel a degree of confidence when their contents are the subjects of conversation." Your time cannot have been entirely thrown away; this confidence is worth something; you have gained at least the habit of reading: if you stop where you are, knowledge without accuracy is like an estate encumbered with debt and subject to deductions. But it is fair to hope, on striking a balance, something will remain; or, even if bankrupt quite, it is well to have, as they say in the mercantile world, a good connection and habits of business; in other words, to have a general acquaintance with authors, and all the stores they severally supply, and also to have habits of application to begin again with greater advantage. So, I would console my many young friends who are in this predicament with the assurance, that they have probably made a useful survey for future operations, and worn down so many rough edges, that, in retracing their former steps, they will have more time to look out for objects of interest, and fewer obstacles to daunt their energies.

I shall now proceed to treat separately of all the principal divisions of knowledge, such as History, Poetry, Philosophy, Theology, and the Fine Arts. Complete essays on these comprehensive subjects will not of course be expected from one who addresses himself to the young and inexperienced, and whose chief ambition is to be useful. The maxim of the poet is only fair: —

"In every work regard the writer's end,
Since none can compass more than they intend."

PART II.

CHAP. I.

ON THE STUDY OF MODERN HISTORY.

THE first glance at the following pages might lead my readers to think I intended to imitate Dufresnoy, who, after laying down a course of historical study, mildly added, "the time required is ten years." But I stipulate for no length of labour; but only that you shall employ your usual hours of reading, few or many, with the method here proposed, and on such subjects as suit the peculiar bent of your inclination. Thus in one year you may achieve more than the majority of your neighbours will achieve in ten; so many are those who read without any system or definite object in view, but carry on a desultory campaign like that of the Greeks around Troy, who, as Thucydides says, were foraging when they ought to have been fighting, or there would have been no ten years' siege. The following chapters contain many subjects, and each subject contains many divisions, that every reader may select according to his taste. Works are recommended to suit every capacity, requiring different degrees of industry and talent: also, the works are so chosen and so arranged, that every hour expended shall bring its hour's worth. "The many-aproned sons of mechanical life," of whom Burns speaks, may spend their Saturday's evening according to these directions, and learn something complete, with a beginning, middle, and end, in full assurance that, when they have more leisure time, they may go on adding and enlarging, without pulling any of their work to pieces. The University Student will find standard works, and a course of reading, sanctioned by the first judges of literary labour: in twelve hours a week, stolen from his Ethics or Differential Calculus, the Collegian may attain a considerable accession of that kind of knowledge which will save him from the reproach of being deep in the past while ignorant of the present, and of that knowledge which is indispensable for advancement in public life.

I have not the slightest fear that any student will abandon this course of reading when once he has fairly tried it. The first step is all I ask. A clergyman of my acquaintance chanced some years since to take up "Tom Telescope," a little book on Astronomy: from this, as from a centre, the rays of his curiosity shot forth on all sides: and he is now a man of great scientific attainments.

One of my most intimate friends was induced to study Grecian history on the principle here recommended, of beginning with an outline and filling in by degrees. Encouraged by his unexpected progress, he has since, by the same method, attained a considerable knowledge of numerous subjects.

But now for the study of history: and first let us suppose you decide on a branch of modern history, and would begin with

THE HISTORY OF GREAT BRITAIN.—Your first step would be to read some History of England through. A man of disciplined mind, long used to laborious application, should read Hume, Smollett, Adolphus and Hughes's Continuation, and Dr. Croly's George IV. "And how long would he be in gaining a satisfactory knowledge, such as Niebuhr possessed of Gibbon, when he defied a friend to puzzle him from the index?" The successful candidates for high university honours, achieve nearly as great a work as "getting up" Hume and Smollett in the last month preceding their examination. And since many pages in each of those volumes need not be very accurately remembered by the unprofessional reader, all of the above works would be satisfactorily perused in one month's real chamber study. "Indeed!" some young lady will exclaim, "why, a single volume employed me more than that space of time." I can easily believe it, and will prescribe for your case next.

The outline History of England by the C. K. Society, in 140 clear, lively, duodecimo pages, is suited for every man, woman, and child.* Even the hard-headed scholar will find this outline useful to give a comprehensive view of the whole. Only, let him not stop here. Parr's History of England will be found most useful in tracing the gradual progress of the country in wealth and civilization. Keightley's History, in 2 vols. duodecimo, or Goldsmith's, may be read next. It will be easier still, to read the little History again as far as Henry VII., and the rest in Keightley: next, read in Hume any reign, war, or negotiation, which excites your curiosity; and thus strengthen the stem of your Historical Tree as much as you please. That you may have the satisfaction of tracing its gradual growth, make a memorandum on the simple drawing by which this tree is represented, just as the works of Rapin, Lingard, and other narrators of the same events are wholly, or partially, read to combat or corroborate the views of Hume.

* Gleig's Series is better still.

So far then you have been instructed how to gain a more or less substantial outline of English history. But, to be full and copious on every point — to strengthen every link — and to master every topic of so long a line, is not much more practicable than to man the wall of China. Like a good general, be content to concentrate your forces on one point at a time. The intermediate parts, when left by themselves, will prove less formidable than they appear, and will readily give way as you become a more practised assailant. So far, you have reconnoitred the general face of the country: tne next thing is *to select one portion for a more searching and minute examination.*

The leading principles of this selection are,

First, to be guided by your own taste and curiosity. Sail with the current of your nature, if you would traverse the wide ocean of truth.

Secondly, to consult your own necessities, and read whatever will be useful in business or insure confidence in society. Read what others read. Conversation is often more improving than books; so, read to profit by conversation. To profit by a visit to Paris, you must learn French. To profit by a visit to London, or by joining any particular society, whether of men of business, men of science, or men of literature, you must study the thoughts and topics of each society.

You will otherwise feel as much out of your element as a sheriff's chaplain when dining with the judges on circuit.

Thirdly, to read subjects which afford most matter for reflection. To be wise is the surest way to seem wise. Read those subjects which involve most principles. Principles are the most handy, convertible, portable, and prolific of all species of literary property; therefore,

Fourthly, read one good comprehensive account of a revolution, protracted war, or other ever-recurring phenomenon of human society. Thus, gain so intimate a knowledge of one that you may anticipate the chief characteristics of all. This was the secret of Edmund Burke's attainments. His letter to Lord Charlemont, at the commencement of the French Revolution, is considered to evince almost the power of prophecy. Niebuhr also, deep in principles, had studied Roman history till he ventured to assert, after a lapse of about 2000 years, an opinion of the early constitution of Rome in direct contradiction to classical authorities. By the recovery of some lost books of Cicero "De Republicâ," his conclusion was proved correct. One of my friends was assured by Niebuhr, that before he had read the summary of a lost decade of Livy, he wrote down an outline of what that decade must contain.

Another illustration of how far a little good intellectual coin may be made to go, is afforded by Gibbon, chap. xxxi., in which he conjectures the history of the unrecorded years between the withdrawing of the Romans from Britain and the descent of the Saxons.

These are the leading principles on which you should select "a strong point" in history; and on which I have selected, by way of example and illustration, the following portions:—

1st, The early history till about the time of the Conquest.

2dly, The era of the Middle Ages, including the feudal system, chivalry, and the crusades.

3dly, The beginning of modern history, marked by the art of printing, the use of gunpowder and the compass, the discovery of America, and the development of the colonial system.

4thly, The civil wars.

5thly, The Revolution of 1688.

6thly, From the accession of George III. to the present time.

I will now consider these eras separately, and ~~point out a course of reading upon each:~~ and,

I. On Early English History.— This portion will afford amusement to one fond of antiquities. It would constitute a good preparation for any university student going to the bar; still it is a portion which is only to be recommended to students of mature understanding.

Now, reader, what is your object? If you only wish to thicken and strengthen the lower part of your Historical Tree by other outlines of early history to run parallel with those already laid down, read a short sketch in Tytler's "Universal History," vol. iv. "Family Library:" also "The Romans in Britain," and "The Anglo-Saxons," forming one volume of the "Family Library:" to which the more voluminous reader may either add or prefer Turner's "History of the Anglo-Saxons," or, which is the shortest of all, Hume's "Appendix on the Anglo-Saxon Government," and Kemble's "Anglo-Saxons." Besides, or, instead of all these, read Mackintosh's "History of England," vol. i. The very profound inquirer may also refer to the authorities quoted in the foot-notes. Chalmer's "Caledonia," treating of the Roman period, is recommended in Professor Smyth's lectures,—lectures well worthy the attention of every reader of modern history. On the Roman period read also Tacitus's "Agricola;" Murphy's translation was recommended by Edmund Burke, as one of the best in our language. There are also translations of Cæsar and Suetonius, which should be consulted. Dr. Smyth remarks that

Gibbon, c. xxxi., supplies by ingenious conjecture the history of the years between 400 and 449. On the Druids, read the account in "Cæsar;" also a concise history in Southey's "Book of the Church." The history which treats of them most fully is Henry's "Britain," b. i. c. 4., where we have their history, manners, learning, and religion. For the progress of religion in those early times, read Southey, Mosheim, Milner; a few pages in each, to which the dates will be a clue. The reasons for believing St. Paul came to Britain, and the first promulgation of the Gospel, is given in "Peranzabuloë," an interesting account of an ancient church found buried in the sand on the coast of Cornwall. Tytler recommends Carte's "History," vol. i. b. iv. § 18., as containing an admirable account of Alfred the Great. The "Encyclopædia Britannica," "Metropolitana," Rees's and the "Penny Cyclopædia" (which I shall quote as "the Cyclopædias") also contain comprehensive articles on Anglo-Saxons, Alfred, Bede, Druids. Those who have access to Camden's "Britannia," to which many of the authors already recommended are greatly indebted, may satisfy the most eager curiosity. Camden, in 1582, travelled through the eastern and northern counties of England to survey the country and arrange a correspondence for the supply of further information. His "Remains" (of a greater work on Britain), was published 1605. Camden's reign of Elizabeth is recommended by Hume, as one of the best compositions of any English historian. Leland's "Itinerary" is also recommended to the curious. Camden made great use of it. In the reign of Henry VII. Leland was empowered by a commission under the Great Seal to search for objects of antiquity in the archives and libraries of all cathedrals, abbeys, priories, &c., and spent six years in collecting materials for the "Archæology of England and Wales."

I limit my recommendations as much as possible to books which may be easily procured. Many other eligible works I omit; because, with these directions, any reader may ascertain the value of nearly every work within his reach. Almost all of the above works quote authorities, and contain incidental remarks on the sources from which more extensive information may be easily derived.

To those who have a real love of learning let me observe, that Ingulphus, secretary to William I., wrote the "History of the Monastery of Croyland," with many particulars of the English kings from 664 to 1091. William of Malmesbury wrote most laudably, as he said, "not to show his learning, but to bring to light things covered with the rubbish of antiquity," a history of Old England from 449 to 1126; also a Church History and Life of St. Aldhelm. The venerable Bede, early in the eighth century, wrote an Ecclesiastical History by aid of correspondence, and that before the penny postage, with all the monasteries in the heptarchy! All these works have been under the hand of the compiler and the spoiler; that is, as Bacon would say, the moths have been at them: but away with these dilutions and drink at the fountain.

II. THE MIDDLE AGES. — This comprehends the Feudal System, Chivalry, and the Crusades.

This era may be also profitably selected by university students and men of liberal education. A knowledge of the feudal system is of the first importance. Chivalry and the crusades must be examined more particularly in respect of their causes and effects on civilisation.

On *the Feudal System*, read a chapter in Blackstone's "Commentaries," vol. i.; also Tytler, b. vi. c. 2.; and Hume's second "Appendix." The scholar should read also Roundell Palmer's "Prize Essay on the Clientship of the Romans." Dr. Smyth strongly recommends the account in Stewart's "View of Society." Robertson's Introduction to "Charles V." is very valuable. Attend particularly to the proofs and illustrations at the end. Bacon's "Henry VII." I can strongly recommend; also part of Montesquieu. My readers must not take fright at seeing so many books on the same subject. Most of my references are only to a few pages out of several volumes, and these easily found by an index or summary. Learn the facts and arguments of one treatise thoroughly during hours of study, and the rest will be easy enough for "hours of idleness." No light reading rivets attention so much as any dissertation on those topics about which study has excited a spirit of inquiry.

On *Chivalry*, as well as the feudal system and the crusades, Hallam's "Middle Ages" is of the first authority. Mill's "History of Chivalry" is much admired. The very popular author, Mr. James, has written the History of Chivalry, as also the lives of Richard I. and the Black Prince, from which much information may be derived. He has also written on Chivalry and the Crusades. These works, as well as Horace Smith's "Tales of the Early Ages," combine amusement with instruction. On Chivalry read also Gibbon, ch. lviii. Of Gibbon let me say, once for all, that as a man he is guilty of having turned aside from the line of his history to shake that faith which, with all his scepticism as to its divine original, he would have been the last to deny to be the richest earthly blessing. But as a historian, Gibbon is regarded with admiration by all learned men. Even Niebuhr praised the depth of his research, and the clearness of his views. Blackstone speaks with great respect for his learning. The accuracy of his facts and the sagacity of his conclusions, where his infidel prejudices are not concerned, are indisputable.

Of the *Crusades*, a good short account is given by Tytler's "Universal History," book vi. c. 9. Read also the Introduction to Robertson's "Charles V.," and search his notes and illustrations, for they give a ready clue to the best sources of all matters relating to the middle ages. Lastly, read the articles in the Cyclopædias, upon the Feudal System, Chivalry, and the Crusades; and consult, generally, Brande's "Dictionary of Science, Literature, and Art."

III. THE PERIOD OF THE REFORMATION, and the commencement of modern history.

On *the Reformation in England* read Southey's "Book of the Church." Those who have little time may read the small volume on the Reformation in the "Family Library." Consult one or more of the Cyclopædias. Dr. Smyth's "Lecture" is very useful. Lives of the Reformers will make a profitable variety. Select also the appropriate parts of Short's "Church History," Milner, and Mosheim. The labour will be less than you would suppose: an accurate knowledge of the narrative of one virtually exhausts the difficulties of all. While these authors give a true Protestant account, Lingard's "History of England" will show what can be said by a Roman Catholic, and in Hume's "History" you see the subject treated by a man who cared for neither party. Read also Sir J. Mackintosh's "Life of Sir Thomas Moore." Burnet's "History of the Reformation in England" is allowed to be a very full and authentic account. It was written in 1679, at the times described by Sir Walter Scott in "Peveril of the Peak." For the Reformation in Scotland, compare Robertson's and Scott's "Scotland." Dr. Smyth strongly recommends Dr. M'Crie's work. Add the life of Knox, and selections from Fox's "Martyrs."

On *the Times of Henry VIII.*, and indeed on every other period, consult Miss Strickland's "Queens," also "The Pictorial History of England," especially for a view of the state of society. Think of the times when more than 70,000 criminals were executed in a single reign. In these days, says Fuller, we read, "the common sort of people were not much counted of, but sturdy knaves were hung up apace."

On *the Discovery of America*, the most easy

and entertaining reading will be Robertson's "America," and the "Life of Columbus," by Washington Irving.

Heeren's "Colonial System and Modern History," is chiefly valuable to more profound readers. Read also Sir J. Mackintosh's "Life of Sir T. More," and the same subject in Lord Campbell's "Chancellors." The Lives of More, Wolsey, and Bacon, are truly interesting.

Another portion of English History for extensive reading, is

IV. The Period of the Civil Wars.

Begin with Hume's "Charles I. and the Commonwealth." Dr. Smyth's "Lecture on the Civil Wars" will draw attention to the leading points, and direct your reading. Then, the practised student will take Clarendon's "Rebellion." Sir W. Scott recommended it to his son as a book replete with wisdom, in a style somewhat prolix, but usually nervous and energetic. For many readers it is too long; but since its author combined a power of striking portraiture, and an intimate knowledge of the human heart, with deep political wisdom, and since he stood in a position which gave a general view both of grand movements and secret springs of action, the work of this stanch friend of Church and State is one which no man of literary taste must long delay.

to read. Harris's "Lives of Charles I. and Cromwell" will give the views of a Dissenter and a Republican. See also Forster's "Lives of the Statesmen of the Commonwealth." The notes to these Lives show great research, and are longer than the text. Carlyle's "Letters of Cromwell," is a book which, in Carlyle's own very able though affected style, is designed to show that Cromwell was rather a self-deceiver than a hypocrite, and not the unqualified reprobate he is too often represented. Godwin, in his "Times of Charles I. and the Republic," follows on the same side. Neal's "History of the Puritans" is reckoned good, and as fair as could be expected from one of their own party. But Milton on the popular, as Clarendon on the royalist side, is the great cotemporary authority. The utmost allowance must be made for the partiality of Clarendon and the strong prejudices of Milton. Milton's Eiconoclastes, "the Breaker of the Image," appeared by order of Council in answer to Eicon Basilike, "the King's Image," a book written just after the execution and in the king's name, but in reality by the pen of Dr. Gauden, Bishop of Exeter, at the command of Charles II. on the Continent, in order to keep up the spirits of his friends in England. Eiconoclastes is the best of all Milton's prose works. It has more inspiration (to use a figure of Burke) than the Sibyl of Carlyle, without half the contortions. The curiosity to read the king's book was so general that 48,000 copies were sold; and that in England alone, in an age when about 1000 copies of Shakespeare had served for forty-one years, and 3000 copies of Paradise Lost were thought an unprecedented sale for the first eleven years. Mr. Macaulay regrets that Milton's prose works are so little read, and says they deserve the attention of every man who would become acquainted with the full power of the English language. "They abound with passages superior to the finest declamations of Burke —a perfect field of cloth of gold. The style is stiff with gorgeous embroidery." The first volume of Macaulay's "History of England" gives a clear and masterly summing up of all that could be said against the king. This, with Miss Strickland's "Life of Henrietta Maria," will interest even the dullest reader. The deep reader has only to follow out Macaulay's authorities. Burnet's "Own Times" is certainly quite what Dr. Johnson termed it — most entertaining chit-chat of a man who went everywhere, and talked to every one. The first part of Burnet, containing the result of his personal observation, is the most entertaining. "Hudibras," with Gray's "Notes," and Dryden's "Absalom and Achitophel," may be read in connection; as also Sir W. Scott's "Woodstock." Miss Aikin's "Charles I." is very ably written. Short's "History," as well as Southey's "Book," will show the state of the Church. Read the "Memorials of Whitelock," a lawyer whose opinion was taken about ship-money, who served in the parliamentary army, and was appointed one of the council of state. Also "Memoirs of Holles," who was a play-fellow of Charles I. in his childhood, head of the Presbyterian party, lieutenant of the parliamentary forces, and raised to the peerage by Charles II. The "Memoirs of Ludlow," another leader of the Republicans, are full of interest; as also are those of Hutchinson. The "Life of Monk" most read is that by Dr. Gumble, his chaplain, who once served on the republican, but afterwards wrote on the royal side. Dr. Smyth recommends Guizot's "Times of Charles I."

The "Diary" of Samuel Pepys, Secretary to the Admiralty in the reigns of Charles II. and James II., extending over the years of the Restoration, the plague of London, and the fire of London, are invaluable illustrations of the manners of the 17th century.

V. The Revolution of 1688.

Dr. Smyth's twentieth "Lecture," vol. ii., will

serve as a guide, marking an outline and quickening observation. When Keightley's "History" has given an accurate knowledge of the course of events, Ward's "Essay" will tell you all that can be urged in support of every theory: the opinions of Blackstone, Mackintosh, Hallam, and Russell are concisely stated and considered. Burke's opinion will be found in his "Letters on the French Revolution." Burnet's "Own Times" is in favour of William, to whom he was chaplain. The "Diary of the Years 1687, 1688, 1689, and 1690," by Clarendon, son of the Chancellor, is in favour of James II. Sir D. Dalrymple, much respected by Dr. Johnson and his circle, published "Annals of Scotland to the Accession of the Stuarts," recommended by Dr. Smyth, as also are the "Memoirs of Sir J. Reresby." Hallam's "Constitutional History" should be consulted; also the "Stuart Papers," and memoirs and letters of all contemporaries. The "Memoirs of Evelyn," who held office in the reign of James II., are very curious. Belsham, Tindal, and Ralph, who is much recommended for detail, and also Somerville, have written the general history of the days of the Revolution. For more directions, read Smyth's twenty-second "Lecture" on William III. Above all, read T. B. Macaulay's "History from James II."

Macaulay's History is a work of genius: vivid, stirring, and graphic. It surpasses all other histories in this; that Mr. Macaulay asked himself, apparently, of the bare skeletons which fill other histories, the question of the prophet—"Can these bones live?" And in his hands live, indeed, they do, clothed with the distinctive form and quickened with the energies of real life. His imputed faults are, to most readers, virtues.—"He writes like an advocate:" therefore with all the force and liveliness of a lucid and brilliant address, imparting the intensity he feels.—"He writes like a novelist:" therefore he does not leave the most amusing topics out; actually remembering that where he ceases to interest, he will cease to be read. As to "partial selection" or "misrepresentation of facts," the answer in the "Edinburgh" should be read as well as the accusation in the "Quarterly." All good Churchmen are advised to read Chancellor Harrington's "Reply to certain Passages on the Church."

VI. From the Accession of George III., in 1760, to the present Time.

Begin by reading this part of history in Goldsmith; then take Miller's "George III.," characterised in the first chapter. Select according to your own curiosity. The account of each opening of parliament, and the exact state of parties, for instance, may be useful to some, though most interesting to the determined talker of politics. The contents of each paragraph are given in Roman characters, so that you may readily "read and skip," a practice which I shall discuss presently. Since Miller contains little else than a continued epitome of the newspapers, it may be read with the same indulgence as a newspaper. The "Lives of George IV." and "William IV." have been published on the same principle by the same publisher. Bind the three volumes together, with a flexible back, mark the date of the events of each page on the top, and you will thus have a most ready and valuable book of reference, with abstracts of public speeches and documents, besides state trials and matters of deep curiosity. The other continuous histories of George III. are, Belsham's, to the year 1793, and Adolphus's. Mr. Hughes's "Continuation" is greatly to be recommended. The "Life of George IV.," by Dr. Croly, may be read as a novel. Lord Londonderry's is a brief and most interesting account of the war in the Peninsula. The "Annual Register" is a very valuable series of records. It has employed the pens of very able men: Edmund Burke wrote the historical parts for thirty years, beginning in 1758; and for years after it was written, under his direction, by Ireland. The

"Gentleman's Magazine" is a work of equal authority. It afforded Dr. Johnson his chief employment and support in 1738 and many following years. The "Annual Biography," as well as the "Edinburgh Review," "Quarterly Review," and "Blackwood," will most pleasantly and profitably supply and strengthen many a link in your chain of reading. It were scarcely too much to say, that if we make good use of the cyclopædias and periodicals above mentioned, we shall not require many other modern publications.

From Lord Brougham's "Statesmen" we may gain a great accession to our knowledge of later times, of which we will make three sub-divisions.

1. *From the accession of George III. to the French Revolution.*

In this period fill up your outline with the "Annual Register" and "Gentleman's Magazine," and then read the "Life of Burke;" that by Prior may serve, but it is not very good. Read Dr. Johnson's "Taxation no Tyranny;" also *his* "Parliamentary Speeches;" positively *his*, for he did not report but composed them, as you may see in a few most amusing pages in Hawkins' "Life," pp. 122—129., quoted in Croker's Boswell, i. 169—172. Read the "Life of Washington"—one of the shortest is that in the "Family Library;" also the lives of Chatham,

Pitt, Fox, and Franklin. I need not always specify which biography is considered best. Biographical dictionaries and cyclopædias often contain useful, though concise accounts. Do not be dismayed because you see works in four or five octavos each on your friends' tables. Choose books which *you* feel that *you* can remember, not those which others appear to read. Junius's "Letters" are so often quoted, that you should know something of them. The authorship is discussed in Brougham's "Characters," vol. i., and in Macaulay's Essay on "Warren Hastings," as well as in "Sketches of Credulity and Imposture." A late biographer of Lord Lyttelton makes as strong a claim of authorship for his Lordship as was ever made for Sir P. Francis; and Mr. Smith, the Editor of the "Grenville Papers," has prefixed to them a long dissertation on the claims of Earl Temple to this equivocal honour.—The capture of André by the Americans, and his trial and execution, are often mentioned.

Original letters of the Kings of England have been published by Sir H. Ellis, also by J. O. Halliwell.

2. *On the French Revolution and the revolutionary war.*

When familiar with the outline from the

general histories, read the two first volumes of "Scott's Napoleon," which shows the long train of causes; then, if the other volumes are too long, read Napoleon's Life, 2 vols., "Family Library." Segur's Russian Campaign is as interesting as any novel. Proceed with the Lives of Burke, Sheridan, and Wilberforce; and the Life of Erskine, in the "Lives of Eminent Lawyers," in Lardner's "Cyclopædia." The actions by sea are related in Southey's "Life of Nelson," and some in the Lives of Earl St. Vincent, Howe, and Collingwood; and the actions by land in Southey's and Napier's "Peninsular War," the "Life of Sir T. Picton," and "Despatches of Wellington." You may add, of course, memoirs of any contemporary public characters. Then "pick your way by help of the table of contents" through Alison's famous History. His own Epitome, one small volume, is excellent as a brief History of this eventful period; but a sixpenny volume of the Religious Tract Society is the very best compendium of the "French Revolution" I have ever seen.

3. *From the end of the War to the present time.*

Alison has commenced this part of History, and Miss Martineau has given us two interesting volumes, which may be highly recommended, as well as Maunder's "Treasury of History" in which the events of more recent times are detailed at considerable length. The "Annual Biography," "Annual Register," and periodicals, are almost the only source of information. The "Penny Cyclopædia," and articles in Chambers' "Library," give very late news: other information must be sought in the latest memoirs of distinguished characters.

The practice of "reading and skipping" is so liable to abuse, that I must qualify it with a few observations. READ WITH A GIVEN OBJECT IN VIEW, AND SKIP NOT ALL THAT IS DIFFICULT, BUT ALL THAT IS IRRELEVANT. Many books may be read like a newspaper, which we search for information on certain points, passing by every article unsuited to our peculiar taste and curiosity. Bacon says, "Some books are to be tasted, some few chewed and digested." A book is like a guide, whom we leave when he has shown us what we want, not at all ashamed of not following him to his journey's end. For instance, if you wished to read ten different accounts of the Reformation, after reading one attentively, you would see at a glance that a second contained whole pages of facts which you already knew, and which you would therefore skip, unless you wished to refresh your memory. In taking up a third account you would find many, not only of the facts, but of the arguments, the same; and by the time you had read a fourth or fifth, you would look rather to the table of contents than to the pages, and turn only to the parts in which you expected more particulars. Again, the Lives of Nelson, Howe, Earl St. Vincent, and others, I remarked, would give information about the British navy. Reading with this view, you would skip whole chapters about the wars in which these admirals were engaged, if you had read them elsewhere, or intended to read history at some other time. The detail of naval and military manœuvres may be read by those of military taste. In corroboration of this advice, let me add the following quotations from Dr. Smyth's "Introductory Lecture:"—

"This (method of reading parts of books), it will be said, is surely a superficial way of reading history. But we must either read books of history in this manner, or not read them at all. The more youthful the mind, the more hazardous the privilege thus allowed of reading pages at a glance, and chapters by the table of contents. But the mind, after some failures and some experience, will materially improve in this great and necessary art—the art of reading much while reading little."—To indulge in the practice merely to evade difficulties and humour idleness, is like picking the plums out of your cake: you cloy the appetite, and what were otherwise a treat will prove tasteless and insipid.

The above remarks on English History, being laid before one of the young friends for whom they were originally intended, drew forth two observations:—"First, do not be afraid of making it too plain to your readers, that all your many lists of books form one long bill-of-fare to suit all ages, appetites, tastes, and constitutions. Make it plain that some dainties are for an acquired taste, some for the strong, others for the weak. Explain clearly that there is more than a supply for one person—that, in short, any one person might be supposed to pass the greater part of his life before he would undergo all the changes of mind and body requisite to enjoy every variety of dainty you have set before him. Secondly, write one short, easy, and amusing course, to teach a good outline of English History to readers who, like myself, have little leisure and less industry, but are yet ashamed to be ignorant of what others know."

Then read the first sixty pages of the duodecimo "History" by the Society, which will tell as much as most persons know, to the end of Henry VII.'s reign. Read Goldsmith's "History of England from Henry VIII. to George II.," and the rest in Keightley's "History," and the three-halfpenny sheet of Chambers' Journal, which gives the history from the accession of George III. to the present time. In this outline you will find not more than you may accurately remember; and if your only ambition is to know as much as the average of your neighbours, be sure that a clear and unbroken outline, with every event assigned to its proper time, place, and persons, will give you a greater command than if you possessed the confused and ill-assorted stores which form the largest "floating capital." However, in condescending to provide for wants so limited, I am led by the hope that you will eventually feel disposed to make such outline clearer and broader by additional knowledge drawn from other sources.

In the HISTORY OF MODERN EUROPE the principal points are the seven following:—

1. The Decline and Fall of the Roman Empire.
2. The Revival of Learning.
3. The Religious Wars in the Low Countries.
4. The Thirty Years' War.
5. The French Revolution.
6. The History of America and the West.
7. The History of British India, and our other Colonies.

The student's object will, of course, be to learn

an outline of all these divisions, and to gain a thorough knowledge of one division at least.

These seven divisions are not all that are worthy of attention, nor do I attempt to name all the authors who throw light upon them, but only to give such assistance, that the reader may select other portions of history, and other authors for himself. And this observation applies to every subject on which I treat.

First, *On the Decline and Fall of the Roman Empire*, the great authority is Gibbon, whom I have before characterised. Milman's edition is the best for sound readers; for students of little leisure, there is a compendium in one volume. The History of the Decline and Fall is also given in the second volume of Lardner's "Cyclopædia." The article in the "Cyclopædia Britannica" is very comprehensive; but the best of the short accounts is in Tytler's "Universal History."

For an account of Mahomet, read his "Life" in the pamphlets of the Society for the Diffusion of Useful Knowledge; and read a little of Sales' Koran, with the introduction; and, above all, Carlyle's account of Mahomet in his "Hero Worship." White's Bampton Lectures on the precepts of Mahomet are quoted with respect by most writers. Another esteemed authority is Ockley's History of the Saracens. Tytler (book vi. ch. 1.)

writes briefly but comprehensively of Arabia and Mohammedanism. For the establishment of Christianity in the Roman Empire, read Tytler (book v. ch. 4.); read also ch. 5, 6, 7. on the last period of Roman History, and to learn the genius and character of the Gothic nations. The Franks, the Feudal system, Charlemagne and his successors, the Normans, and the rise of the secular power of the Popes, are all points of history deserving attention, and most easily to be learned from Tytler (book vi. ch. 2, 3, and 4.).

The Germans, their genius, laws, and customs, may profitably be read in the translation of Tacitus's "Germany." Dr. Smyth, in his second Lecture, strongly recommends Butler on the German Constitution. This Lecture treats on the laws of the barbarians, and will serve as a useful guide to University students and men whose minds are disciplined and used to deep study. On all of these points, Gibbon may be consulted by means of the index or summary.

"Then you do not take it for granted we shall read all Gibbon?" will be the exclamation of some University student in the ardour of his first term.—Enter, my good friend, the first bookseller's shop, and ask him how often, in taking in exchange Gibbon and other voluminous authors, he has found the leaves cut or soiled

;hroughout. When you have passed from col-.ege rooms to "lodgings out," and thence after :he days when, from being one of many *candi-lates* (so called from white cravats and whiter 'aces), you gradually find the *incubus* removed, :he last button of your waistcoat less tight, and ,vhen you have ceased to fancy yourself Tityus, ,vith something kennelling in your diaphragm ınd preying on your vitals—when, in short, the ;ight of your "*testamur*" has made you your-;elf again, and has sent you into the country, ,vith time to learn that college and college ways ınd notions are to the bachelor of arts what ;chool seemed to the undergraduate—from that :ime, the leisure hours of life will be found "di-'isible with a remainder" by very few sets of ;welve octavos. So, beware of a plan too exten-;ive to execute. Did you ever see a pudding nixed? Well, the way is this—take first a little lour, and then a little water; stir it well, till quite smooth, then add a little more, first of one, ınd then of the other, stirring and mixing, till quite free from lumps; but should you, in your ıaste, throw in a second handful of flour before the first is well mixed, all the stirring of all the cooks who ever delighted in perquisites, will not prevent the said pudding from being lumpy and indigestible. So the food of the mind, like the food of the body, must have due time for each accession to blend, to amalgamate, and to digest.

Secondly. *The Era of the Revival of Learning.* Supposing that millions of guineas long buried in some miser's garden were suddenly dug up by country clowns, who little knew the value, some would be trampled under foot and lost; but if one hundredth part were restored to circulation and use, the result would be a sudden stimulus to all the buyers and sellers of the villages round. Such was the increase of spirit and activity which followed the sacking of Constantinople by the Turks; when, though 120,000 MSS. are said to have perished, yet many were carried away to other nations by scholars who knew more of their value than the degenerate Greeks. This event happened in the middle of the 15th century; but Dante and Wickliffe, more than a century before, and then Petrarch and Boccaccio, who had exerted themselves to bring to light the great authors of antiquity—the former discovering the Epistles of Cicero, the latter bringing Homer from Greece to Tuscany—gave a promise of the general reviving of learning. A knowledge of this momentous era may be derived from the beginning of Hallam's "History of Literature," and part of his "History of the Middle Ages;" also from two chapters of Gibbon (the 53rd and

66th); from part of Roscoe's "Leo X." and "Lorenzo de' Medici;" also from the introduction of Robertson's "Charles V." Mosheim's "State of Learning in the 13th and 14th Centuries," is much recommended. Read also, especially, the "Life of Petrarch;" Vaughan's "Life of Wickliffe;" Lives of Dante and Boccaccio, in Lardner's "Cyclopædia." Read Shepherd's "Life of Poggio," who early in the 15th century searched the monasteries for ancient MSS., and found Quintilian, and some of the speeches of Cicero, besides Silius Italicus, and many of the later writers. To these add some account of the art of printing; and, for other sources of information, observe the authorities quoted by Hallam and others.

Doubtless all these sources have been searched, and their stores reduced to a portable and readily accessible form by the Cyclopædias and Biographical Dictionaries; for, as literature accumulates, it would become unwieldy, were it not that a constant demand for the gold without the dross operates with general literature as with laws and statutes; that is to say, it stimulates a supply of treatises and abridgments, which, like legal digests, contain enough for general use, and point out the sources of deeper knowledge.

Thirdly. *The Era of the Reformation* will

cause me to refer to some of the authorities connected with the Reformation in England. Milner and Mosheim treat this period in the general course of Church History. But the one book allowed to supersede all others, is the late translation of D'Aubigné's work. It is written with much warmth and unction; its great merit is, that the chief personages are allowed to speak for themselves, and speak to their hearts' content. This book contains about 1800 closely printed pages octavo. Intelligent readers, who have not time to read the whole, will find it easy to omit parts without losing the thread of the narrative.

Robertson's "Charles V.," Coxe's "House of Austria," and two chapters of Roscoe's "Leo X.," all bear on the same subject. The History of Printing and the Revival of Learning are of course closely connected with it. With all due praise to Luther and his friends, we must not presume that the most prominent are always the most efficient instruments in the hands of Providence. The men who like Petrarch and others, contribute to the expansion of the human mind, and thus lay the train and provide the fuel, may be more useful, though less glorious, agents than those who merely add the spark. The barbarism of the Turks in disengaging and setting free the pent-up spirits of Constantinople, might not have done less service to the cause of Christ, than the never-failing faith and courage of those whom every true Christian to the end of time must admire. The truth is, God rolls along the still untiring stream of time; and whether its surface is ruffled by a ripple or a whirlpool — whether it bears on its wide bosom the curling leaf or rifted oak — whether the licentious poets of Italy or the faithful scholars of Germany are struggling in its dark and mighty waters, still it onward moves, for purposes transcending mortal knowledge. "We see in part and understand in part." Those mighty efforts on which man prides himself, as if complete and valuable in themselves, are often but the minutest links in one great providential chain, reminding us of those clustered myriads of coral cells by which the little insects conspire unconsciously to raise a resistless barrier to the angry lashings of the Indian Ocean.

The Essays of Sir James Stephen, reprinted from the "Edinburgh Review," are truly valuable, especially those on Ignatius Loyola and the Port-royalists. Taylor's "Loyola" also contains an excellent account of the Jesuits. Coxe's "Philip II." and Grattan's "Netherlands" give an interesting account of the religious wars in the Low Countries, than which there is no finer subject for contemplation in any part of Modern History.

Dr. Smyth's Lectures on the Reformation will be found very useful, as also Ranke's History of the Reformation, which has been admirably translated into English by Mrs. Austin.

The Reformation is considered by Heeren the chief event which marks the commencement of Modern History; the other events which distinguish it from the History of the Middle Ages are the discovery of America, and the consequent development of the colonial system, the influence of the art of printing, and the improvement in the art of war by gunpowder. The era of the Reformation, therefore, will be a good point from which to begin a course of reading: this is the era at which Heeren commences his Modern History, a work I would strongly recommend to any collegian who desires a good course of modern reading to accompany the classical and mathematical studies of sixteen terms in the seclusion of college rooms.

Fourthly. *The Thirty Years' War* is well deserving the attention of all who have studied the Reformation. The detail of this portion of history is intricate; its principles and secret springs of action give much scope for that reflection which distinguishes the mere reading, from the study, of history. "The whole interval of about one hundred years, from the days of Luther to the Peace of Westphalia, must be considered one continued struggle, open or concealed, between the Reformers and the Roman Catholics." This is the language of Dr. Smyth, whose 13th Lecture will afford considerable assistance.

The most important part of this interval is the Thirty Years' War; the other parts are filled chiefly with its causes and consequences. The best book for a commencement is the Life of Gustavus Adolphus, in the "Family Library." After this, read Coxe's "House of Austria," and, lastly, Schiller's "Thirty Years' War."

Fifthly. *The French Revolution.* Mr. Alison's work is now almost universally allowed to supply what has long been wanted — a general history of the state of Europe during these momentous times; and I am happy to advert again to his epitome in one volume. For, Mr. Alison's work is very voluminous, and, like all long histories, it should be regarded as a general view and running commentary; the judicious reader will yet desire to examine the evidence of eye-witnesses, and to weigh and compare a variety of opinions. The true use of books is to give facts and arguments. After hearing evidence and counsel on both sides, every man who reads to any purpose will be his own judge, and decide for himself. The man whose mind is stored only with the conclusions and judgments of others is like a man who collects a set of rules and measures which he has not the art to apply, and at best only can attain to "truth in the wrong place." Therefore read parts of Miller's "George III." from 1789, for an epitome; then either the whole of Scott's "Life of Napoleon," or the first and second volumes, for the causes of the revolution. This was written "in one year of pain, grief, sorrow, and ruin." It was sold for 18,000*l.*, and, says Mr. Lockhart, "none of the pamphleteers could detect any material errors." The accounts of Carlyle, Mignet, Thiers, and Madame de Stael are much recommended. The Memoirs of Talleyrand, Fouché, La Fayette, the Prince of Canino, and every character of the times, are among the very best sources. The index of the "Edinburgh" and "Quarterly" will also be a ready clue to the most able dissertations. Few books relating to the revolution are reviewed without serving as a theme for an essay on the times. Sydney Smith, one of the originators of the "Edinburgh," says, the use of a review is to give a man who has only time to read ten pages the substance of two or three octavos. Burke's "Letters on the French Revolution" is a book which no English scholar should fail to read. Mackintosh's reply gives the other side of the question. The flow of Burke's language is like that of a mountain torrent rushing impetuously down over crags and rocks; that of Mackintosh resembles a stream smoothly gliding through ornamental grounds. Thomas Campbell said, that though the greater part were lost, any ten consecutive sentences would show the hand of a master as plainly as the genius of a sculptor is discerned in the mutilated marble of Theseus. If to these volumes is added the criticism on Alison's History in the "Edinburgh Review," the reader will have a fair knowledge of this momentous question. Add the French characters in Brougham's "Statesmen of George III." and Dr. Smyth's second course of Lectures, which treat exclusively on the French Revolution. If you read Carlyle's French Revolution, read it last; because it supposes much previous knowledge. Carlyle's writings are only to be recommended to advanced students.

Two subjects only remain to be mentioned in connection with Modern History — India, and the Colonies and America.

Of British India I have before spoken. Hall's Travels contain a lively sketch of its history. Gleig's School Series and the Cyclopædias give epitomes more or less concise, but each sufficient for general purposes. The history of British India in the "Family Library," and a volume of "Martin's Colonies," will also be a ready source of knowledge. Either of these works, as well as parts of Miller's "George III.," will give *facts*, which, as they cannot be known too well, so they cannot be taught too simply. For the policy, principles, conclusions, and connection of effects with causes, read Mills's or Malcolm's "India," or both. I say *both*, because it is little trouble to read the second treatise when you *know* the first—not when you have merely *read* the first. Inexperienced readers who cannot readily grapple with books of this kind, and really *know* them, should choose others. Musicians tell us to play easy pieces first; for it will take less time to learn one-and-twenty pieces of music if each is more difficult than the next preceding, than to learn only the one which is most difficult without the gradual discipline of the remaining twenty.

Mr. Macaulay's "Clive," and "Warren Hastings," are two choice essays, and should be read in connection with Edmund Burke's Speeches. These speeches were delivered when Burke was nearly sixty years of age; his "Essay on the Sublime and Beautiful" was published when he was only twenty-eight; yet it has been observed as very remarkable that Burke displayed far more poetical imagination in his speeches than in this essay, though written at an age and on a subject better suited to exercise imaginative powers. The name of Hastings reminds us of the "enchanting power" which Pitt allowed to the eloquence of Sheridan on Hastings' trial. But the oratory of Sheridan was like the music of Paganini, which died with him. The oratory of Burke reminds us of many a musical genius who has left the world a written record of that harmony of soul, which he had neither the voice nor hand to express. Burke's speeches, and indeed all his writings, are what Thucydides would term *κτῆμα ἐς ἀεί.* Burke had the same kind of knowledge of what things were natural, what artificial, what things belonged to the individual, and what to the species in the body politic, as a skilful physician possesses respecting the human frame. As anatomy and practice have taught the one, analysis and observation have taught the other. Burke is one of the chosen few who, like Thucydides on the plague of Athens, and like Shakespeare on every subject, have shown that what is true to nature is true always. Writings of this class exactly exemplify the saying of the Wise man:—"*The thing that hath been, it is that which shall be, and that which is done is that which shall be done.*" And if any man says, "*See this is new,*" let him look in the writings of such men as Burke, and he will find the case foreseen, the rule provided, and his wisdom forestalled, and that "*it hath been of old time which was before us.*" The best of all Burke's speeches to read, as Mr. Prior, in his "Biography," observes, is that on the Arcot debts; yet Pitt and Grenville agreed, while it was being delivered, that it was making so little impression on the House, that they need not answer it.

On the ancient state of India, read one volume by Robertson, with notes and illustrations referring to other valuable writings.

The Life of Clive will give much information on the events of the last century; while the Lives of Sir T. Munroe and Lord Wellesley will give later times. Heber's Journal is an elegant composition; but it is principally valuable to the traveller in Hindostan. The same may be said of the Duke of Wellington's Indian Despatches. Every man of the least curiosity must prize a record so suited to give the impress of the great mind of its author; still I would allow much weight to the words of my friend, Captain B——; "The proper persons to buy the Duke's 'Despatches' are cadets. You cannot make them a more appropriate present. Every man deserves to be cashiered who pretends to serve in India, without reading every despatch, letter, and memorandum." Read the work of Sir Alexander Burnes, and also the work of the Hon. M. Elphinstone, of which Sir R. Peel said, in the House of Commons, that it was a book of deep learning, of the first authority, and the latest information.

On AMERICA, read Robertson's history of the conquest and early settlements, a simple but most deeply interesting narrative; Prescott's is the best account of Mexico. On the curiosities of Mexico, any catalogue will refer you to many accounts, with prints showing memorials of the long-lost arts of that most remarkable people. Inquire also for similar works on Peru; and examine the curiosities collected in the British Museum. I lately saw a Peruvian mummy in Dublin, at the College of Surgeons. Dr. Johnson said, that a man who travels must take out knowledge with him, if he would bring knowledge home. This is as true of visiting collections from foreign countries, or reading books which describe them, as in visiting the countries themselves. While reading we should think of things to examine when we visit a museum, and while visiting a museum we should think of new questions to be solved when we return to our reading. Catlin's work, illustrated with numerous plates, on the North American

Indians, is well worth perusing; as also is the review of it in the "Edinburgh." Several similar books have lately been published, describing matters of the greatest curiosity in North America. Cooper's "Deerslayer," "Pathfinder," and his novels generally may here be recommended. On *Canada* and *Newfoundland,* read Martin's "Colonies" or articles in the Cyclopædias. On the *United States,* Basil Hall's "Travels" give much information about the working of the democracy, and may be classed with the Journal of Mrs. Butler (once Fanny Kemble), the American Notes of Dickens, and the Sketch by Mrs. Trollope: but beware of mistaking caricature for fact, or lending yourself to those writers on American customs who are bent rather on holding up their peculiarities to ridicule, than their better qualities to imitation. But, by far the best and most instructive work that has been published in England on the United States, is Mackay's "Western World."

The preceding observations on Modern History, I trust, will be found sufficient. Martin's "Colonies" will convey the latest information on Malta, Gibraltar, and the rest of our settlements; while the general history of the continental nations is given in the cyclopædias as fully as most readers require. Concerning France, the Life of

Richelieu and others, with histories of kings, or reigning families of most interest, may easily be selected, arranged, read, and digested, according to the principles already explained.

The study of history and general literature is like the study of law: that man reads to most advantage who makes such a selection from the ponderous records of the past as enables him to bring most to bear at a given moment, to support an argument, or refute an adversary. Old people are apt to form most exalted notions of the literary advantages of the rising generation. They think that difficulties diminish as books increase; whereas, in furnishing our minds, as our houses, more is expected in proportion to our facilities. The term *well-informed,* is not less a word of comparison than the term *rich.* A modern schoolboy, says T. B. Macaulay, knows more of geography, than Strabo. True: but he has not the merit of being equally in advance of the knowledge of his cotemporaries. However much the labours of the learned may slope the way, the temple of knowledge may always be represented on a hill enveloped in a mist: the ascent should be drawn most precipitous and cloudy at the bottom, with crowds of travellers, dull, heavy, discouraged, and bewildered; while, towards the top, the slope should be gradual, the travellers few and far between, looking better both in health and spirits, and the mist clearing away, till the one happy man on the summit is in a flood of light, and cannot take off his hat to huzzah for the sun in his eyes. Fancy would add sign-posts, with "Beware of man-traps"—"Try no short cuts"—"The best road lies over the hill." In the foreground, swarms of little children, of pantomimic proportions, might be selling penny guides to many an eager purchaser; while one or two sages might be standing aside, presenting a chosen few with lectures of a far less tempting appearance on *patient and methodical study.*

CHAP. II.

ON THE STUDY OF ROMAN HISTORY.

THE first question which would occur is—Upon what ancient authorities is the History of Rome chiefly based? The following: Livy, Dionysius of Halicarnassus, Polybius, Diodorus Siculus, Appian, Dion Cassius, Varro, Cicero, Sallust, Cæsar, Velleius, Tacitus, Suetonius, Plutarch, and Cornelius Nepos; these are the principal classical authorities. The Scriptores Hist. Augustæ,

Procopius, and others, are comparatively little consulted, except by men of the research and enthusiasm of Gibbon.

These authors I mention, because their names so often occur, that any young person would do well to employ an hour in reading a short account of them from a Biographical Dictionary. I would also show how arduous is the task of becoming profoundly learned in every part of Roman History. De Thou wrote 138 books on the continental broils during the last half of the 16th century; but, before he began, he knelt down and offered up a prayer, that he might accurately and impartially execute a work to which, from that moment, he resolved to devote his life. Gibbon was twenty years composing the Decline and Fall of the Roman Empire. It would have taken many more years to add the history of its rise and grandeur. To men of such genius we leave the original authorities; without entering the mine ourselves, we will be content with such specimens of the buried treasures as their researches bring to light.

I must now address myself to two separate classes of readers; first, to young men preparing themselves as candidates either for Scholarships or classical honours at the universities; secondly, to young ladies, and other general readers, who have only learning and leisure sufficient for a shorter course.

To speak of the first class — *youths at school*, or *with private tutors*, if well directed, may read much to advance them at college. The mode of reading history which they must adopt is peculiar. They have not only to fill but to form their minds, and to satisfy not only themselves but examiners. Others may be less careful of facts, when they have gathered principles, and preserve the kernel without the husk; but candidates for honours must exhibit a knowledge of principles, which they can only do by having facts available and ready at command. A college examination is conducted by written questions which serve as pegs on which to hang your knowledge: but should you confuse even the names of historical characters, you will lose the chance of displaying your attainments, although your mind is stored with the deepest reflections on the Roman policy or constitution. The first thing, therefore, to consider is, that you can never be said to know any more history than you can accurately write out, with time, place, and circumstance. Read, therefore, on the method before described, which I shall call the expansive principle. Begin with committing to memory an outline; then fill in no faster than you can make good your ground.

Thus you will always be ready to be examined to the extent of your reading, and will rear such an historical edifice as will admit of continual addition and enlargement. This advice is more simple than obvious. Many a University student has passed his time collecting materials which were at no single moment, from first to last, in a state to be put together; and that, even supposing that the disorder of his mental store-room did not render it impossible to find or to identify the many separate pieces so laboriously collected. Wisely did Sir Egerton Brydges advise our occasionally "bringing out our own conceptions," and computing not the pages read but the knowledge stored, and thus "intellectually taking stock." In 2 Maccabees, chap. ii. verse 23. are curious remarks on historical abridgments.

Your first book should be "The Outline of the Roman History," in Gleig's Series. This little book is very ably executed by Professor Browne. It traces the Romans as they gradually spread from a corner of Italy over nearly all the known world, and gives the chief dates, characters, and events. When this outline is known thoroughly, it will serve as a *memoria technica*, to connect and facilitate the recollection of more minute detail. For, the difficulty in history is to remember not the principles and general impression, but who said this, and who did that, and when or where particular actions occurred; and, in an examination, you can only show that you know anything by giving a clear and accurate account. Horace Walpole said, "I was forced to quit Dow's Hindostan, for the Indian names made so little impression on me that I was every minute reverting to the former page to find about whom I was reading." Let an outline, then, be impressed deeply on your memory, so that you may have one Roman picture ever hanging before your mind's eye, to serve as a historical map of the country. One plan I found very useful was, to draw out the leading historical facts on a sheet of paper, divided into vertical columns, each column comprising one century. Then by drawing across them four black horizontal lines, I cut all the centuries into quarters, and the sheet into departments. I found it easy to remember the contents of each department, or the position of each fact on my paper, and thus I had a clue to dates and a long series of events. When this outline is perfectly familiar to the "mind's eye," proceed to fill it up according to your taste and inclination. The usual examinations for Scholarships require an exact knowledge of the commonly received accounts of historians rather than that critical research into particular portions which is required of the candidates for Classes. In reading for a Scholarship, you should prepare for writing historical essays, which will be read with reference to two points: first, your Accuracy; secondly, your Reflection. For Accuracy, the observations respecting the outline history will be sufficient. For Reflection, you must read a brief account of the whole, rather than a more copious compilation of part, of the Roman annals. And for this reason; — to show Reflection, you must draw comparisons between the events of different periods. Should you confine your studies to one period only, this may chance not to be the subject of a single question, and then all your industry will lose its reward. I should therefore advise you to take Keightley's "Roman History," or that by Schmitz. The chief points to remark are these: —

1. The successive changes in the form of government, their effects, and causes;

2. The gradual rise of the plebeian power;

3. The conquests and accessions to the Roman dominions.

Trace also each distinguished character through his whole career, so that you may be prepared to write the life of any party proposed.

During my early studies I had a friend with whom I used daily to discuss parts of history;

and in these peripatetic lectures, as we used to call them, the glorious exploits of the good, as well as the high-crimes and misdemeanors of the bad, formed the subject of very animated controversy. Vivid and lasting were the impressions which these discussions produced; besides, inconsistencies were detected, and explanations sought, which would not otherwise have occurred. What you read by yourself you may doze over, and your mind may wander just where attention is most required; but you can hardly converse on a subject without reflection. Bishop Sanderson said, "I learnt much from my Master, more from my Equals, but most from my Pupils."

At college, it was agreed between three friends (myself and two others), that whenever we met we should endeavour to puzzle each other with a question on Herodotus. The continual exercise of recollection and attention to which this mere frolic gave rise, rendered us wonderfully accurate in that portion of ancient history. I would strongly recommend some such diversion to pupils in the upper form of a school. Imagine: "Which way did Hannibal cross the Alps?" "Yes, but you can't tell the route of Napoleon." "I can, and next week I give notice I shall puzzle you with the retreat of the Ten Thousand." In one half-year Keightley might be learned from beginning to end. Schmitz will then be easy reading. Some questions have been published, which are useful to try your knowledge, provided only you read at least twenty pages, and never look at the questions till you have thus prepared a portion for self-examination: for, to read with questions before you is a most pernicious practice; all original reflection is superseded, and everything but the mere subject of the questions escapes notice. When perfect in Keightley, take Smith's' "Dictionary of Greek and Roman Antiquities," and read attentively about Consuls, Tribunes, Interregnum, Plebeians, Clientship, and every term of office or dignity in Roman History, and remember Mr. Rich's dictionary with 2000 woodcuts of ancient arts and customs! The five numbers of the Roman History, by the Useful Knowledge Society, are highly useful to scholars, especially the chapter on the Credibility of Roman History. The article in the "Encyclopædia Metropolitana," on the same subject, is very good, as also are some remarks which you may find by the index in Hooke's "Roman History." Certain lives in Plutarch may be read in connexion with Roman History. The articles on Livy, Rome, and the names of offices and magistrates in Anthon's Lempriere, are also good. This will be enough to say to candidates for Scholarships. When perfect so far, they may take a hint from the few remarks I have to offer to—

Candidates for Classes.—These students I must refer to what I have said in my "Student's Guide to Oxford Honours;" at the same time that I add, that the early part of Roman History, which is allowed to be the most difficult, has now been treated by Dr. Arnold. Malden's "History of Rome" is also used by candidates for honours. What is required at Oxford, for the final examinations, is a thorough knowledge of portions of Roman History, from the original authorities, rather than a mere outline of the whole. Indeed, a writer in the "Quarterly Review" asserts that there probably are not three men in the whole University who know any more of the later periods of Roman History than can be derived from English compilations. The Oxford examinations in Roman History, even for the highest honours, are chiefly confined to the first and second decade of Livy, with (as indispensable) Niebuhr's History, about two books of Polybius, to complete the history of the Punic war, and half of Tacitus. To illustrate these books, it is usual to read portions of the Roman History and Biography in the "Encyclopædia Metropolitana."

Lord Eldon, in his advice to his grandson at

Oxford, said, "After long and great experience, I never knew a young man who had indulged too much in amusements at Oxford to the neglect of very diligent study, who ever afterwards in life graced his friends, family or country: and I never knew one who signally devoted his time at Oxford to study who did not in aftertime become an ornament to his family and country." Therefore *general readers* and *ladies* I advise to begin with the "Outline History" before mentioned, and to learn it thoroughly; then to read parts of Keightley or Schmitz on the Punic wars, or any other events which curiosity suggests. Regard the outline as a map of the Roman empire, which you must daily consult to show you exactly whereabouts you are. Men of well-formed minds will readily observe all the changes in the constitution; young ladies, and others, in whom general curiosity and imagination predominate, can amuse themselves with the "most disastrous chances," and the many tragical positions, in which Roman story abounds. Those who frequent theatres should see the Roman plays, Coriolanus, Julius Cæsar, and others. Much talent and industry is employed in the principal theatres, in providing scenery, dresses and decorations, critically correct and true to the time and place in which each plot is laid. Certain sets of

Roman engravings will answer the same purpose. Our appreciation of Roman History greatly depends on terms and descriptions bringing before the mind's eye scenes and customs as they really existed. Swallow-tailed coats, livery servants, a regiment of champagne bottles, fan-bearing young ladies, and ice-presenting young gentlemen, must not rise in our imagination when we read of a Roman supper; neither must every shower of rain in Rome be associated with umbrellas, Mackintoshes, and cab-stands. To prevent these modern from marring ancient views, the accounts of Pompeii, Herculaneum, and the late discoveries in Etruria, will much contribute; as also "The last Days of Pompeii," by Bulwer; "The Fawn of Sertorius;" "Pericles," a Tale of Athens: "Charicles," an illustration of the private life of ancient Greeks; "Gallus," the same of ancient Rome. "Macaulay's Lays," a work in which the printer, binder, and engraver have conspired to aid the effect of the poetry, will fill the dullest with the spirit of ancient Rome. The bold engravings of Piranesi make so deep an impression on the imagination, that the buildings of the mighty city will ever after be present to our imagination. A small edition of Adam's "Roman Antiquities," and Smith's "Dictionary of Grecian and Roman Antiquities," contain many engravings; but, for the pencil, all such works yield to Rich's dictionary. With these works on Roman Antiquities, readers of the most ordinary curiosity will find their attention riveted to a variety of articles, describing how that mighty people ate and drank, and bathed, and slept; to say nothing of how they debated, went to law, and fought; and the daily routine of their private life.

These works will make a pleasing variety while reading Keightley's or Schmitz's History. Similar entertainment may be profitably derived from Fosbroke's "Treatise on the Arts, Manners, Manufactures, &c., of the Greeks and Romans." I can also recommend "A History of Rome, from the earliest Times to the Founding of Constantinople," drawn chiefly from Schlosser's history, two small volumes of Lardner's Cyclopædia. Mr. Merivale's History of the Empire is also much commended; and his "Fall of the Roman Republic" supplies a gap which has been long acknowledged to exist in school literature.

So far I have only recommended one Roman Outline, price 9*d.*, and one History, price 12*s.*: and these, as I said of the histories of England, are mere skeletons; when you have a competent knowledge of them, and have perused the works on Manners and Customs, proceed at once to the original authorities;—to the Punic wars in

"Livy's pictured page," which Clarendon took as his model; the Catiline Conspiracy, which Johnson allowed to contain historic portraiture, because Sallust knew the characters; Tacitus, the philosophic annalist, who gives facts and principles, the secret springs and the great movements, in the same sentence; Plutarch, first the lecturer, and afterwards the proconsul, of Trajan, who studied at Athens, and travelled through Greece and Egypt, the favourite author of Lord Chatham and Napoleon, each of whom would almost have said of Plutarch, with Theodore Beza, what, in substance, a writer in the "Quarterly" said of Boswell, "that if we were obliged to throw all the books in the world into the sea, this should be reserved till the last." Think of each time-honoured genius: how gladly would we invite him to wine and walnuts, and try to draw him out; and shall we not read his works when elegant translations are in almost every library? Have we not the curiosity even of the daughter of a country post-master, who eagerly claims the perquisite of a peep at the letters of the great? We are not obliged to read one of these works through, but let us cease to regard them as sealed books. We may take a translation of Cicero's "Letters," and see what he had to say to his wife and family, and what to the public, of those most eventful days. If we retain a knowledge of the general history, these authors will serve to fill up the outline, and every new idea will find its place, and tend both to pleasure and to profit.

Dunlop's "History of Roman Literature," in 3 vols., and Schlegel's "Lectures on Ancient and Modern Literature," 1 vol., are standard works, deemed almost indispensable for those emulous of classical honours. Such works, however, can give only the mere terms and sounds of knowledge to that large majority of readers who are unacquainted with Greek and Roman writers.

A few hours devoted to the article on Rome, in "The Penny Cyclopædia," will be enough to give a fair insight into the constitution as developed by Niebuhr.

Of Cicero and his times, which are topics equal in interest to any part of Roman History, Middleton's "Life of Cicero" is the great authority. A very good short account, by Mr. Hollings, is published in the Family Library. The Cyclopædias also contain compendious articles. Macaulay's "Survey of the Greek, Roman, and Modern Historians," published in the "Edinburgh Review," is very useful. The "Tour to the Sepulchres of Etruria in 1839," by Mrs. Hamilton

Gray, will be entertaining and instructive to most readers—to the classical scholar especially.

Of Niebuhr's history, I have only to say that it is highly valuable to good classical scholars, but unintelligible to most English readers. They may read a review of his work, both in the "Quarterly and Edinburgh Reviews."

Eustace's "Classical Tour" will profitably relieve and vary the study of Roman History. But, never be the slave of books: the *pale* student reaps little profit for his pains. When fatigue begins, improvement ends: to say nothing of "exhausting our capital" of strength. The best scholars at Oxford are often the best cricketers—The "Cricket Field" (reviewed as the "Isaac Walton" of another sport) we are proud to say is now the standard work on our National Game. So play Cricket, Fish, Shoot, have some diversion—not a mere milestone-measured walk. The Jesuits insisted on the mind of each student being unbent after two hours' study; holding, with Seneca, that "continued labour deadens the soul." Socrates found diversion with children; Cato, with a social glass; Tycho Brahe, in making instruments of science; Descartes, in gardening; Granville Sharp, in boating; Samuel Clarke, in gymnastics; Sir Henry Wotton, Paley, and Sir H. Davy, in angling. *Mens sana in corpore sano!* How many forget the latter part, and, like Sir W. Follett, ruin the lamp that holds the light! When the head attempts a tyrannous despotism over the body, the stunted limbs and exhausted members soon "refuse the supplies" of healthful energy, and bring down the usurper from his throne. A fall or a fit of sickness, says Pascal, may bankrupt the ablest understanding. Addison regrets that Pascal spoke feelingly, and observes "Pascal contracted an ill habit of body, and the history of his life is one continued account of his soul struggling under innumerable pains and distempers."

CHAP. III.

ON THE STUDY OF GRECIAN HISTORY.

THE "Outline History of Greece," in Gleig's Series, is the first book for the candidate for Scholarships, by which I mean all young men who are desirous of improving their last year at school, or under a private tutor. Thirlwall's Epitome of his larger History in one volume, will be the second book. The whole of the "Outline History" should be learned almost by heart, as I said before of English and Roman History. In Keightley you may be contented to read only as far as the death of Alexander the Great: the remainder you may leave till almost every other part of Ancient History is exhausted. Nine out of ten of ordinary advisers would tell you it was indispensable that you should read the whole of the Grecian History, by Mitford or Thirlwall (8 volumes each), and the valuable work by Mr. Grote. The time for reading Mitford, in my opinion, is gone by: the best part is the Life and Times of Alexander; and this I had rather read in the Biography by Williams, in the "Family Library." Thirlwall's History, as also Grote's, are masterly performances; but the question is not what is creditable to the writer, but what is profitable to the reader. When your mind is prepared to realise, and make your own, any parts of Grote's history, then read those parts, but those parts only. You will ask to what preparation I allude; I mean that Grote classifies facts, extracts principles, and makes comments. The preparation requisite to profit by his writings is therefore threefold: first, to be familiar with the facts which he quotes; that is, to take at a glance any sentence from Herodotus, Thucydides, or others, and feel a curiosity to know whether he has anything more to say of it than you already know: and if you have never seen the sentence before, any remarks upon it must be a burden to your memory, without assisting your understanding. The second preparation is to be used to compare some, at least, of the sentences which Grote classifies; for then, and then only, will you be improved by that increased quickness of observation, and that ready comprehension of all the bearings of facts, which a good history should serve to promote. The historian, like the judge, should sum up, arrange, and weave into one plain story, all that falls from competent witnesses; while the reader, like a juryman, should decide, not by the leaning of the judge, but by the bearing of the evidence. It follows, then, that besides being first conversant with facts, and, secondly, having viewed facts in connection, the third qualification is a competence to form an independent judgment upon them. Few persons, I admit, enjoy this threefold qualification for the whole of any history; still a mature mind can weigh and decide on one page, understand enough to assent to a second page, and suspend judgment on a third. But I am at present addressing youths whose minds are not matured, and who are required, by the university system, to read history rather to form than to fill the mind, and rather for discipline than information. But on this topic I must refer to my "Student's Guide," which, I have the satisfaction of knowing, one of the most experienced examiners has long been recommending for the guidance of his pupils. And for all information on the manners, the lecture-room, and the studies of the Universities, I need not scruple to say that the head master of one of our most distinguished schools recommended the "Collegian's Guide," or "Recollections of College Days," as the very book to prepare the minds of youths leaving school for college.

Keightley has also written a small Elementary History of Greece. Before either of these publications, there appeared a History of Greece, by the Useful Knowledge Society, which was first submitted to the revision of Dr. Arnold. This contains about 300 double-columned pages; the first 150 of which comprise all events to the death of Alexander. Thirlwall's Epitome is a very good book: but "Greece to the end of the Peloponnesian War," in the Encyclopædia Metropolitana, by Sir T. N. Talfourd and others, shows the valuable results of combined talent.

The student who has followed my advice so far, may read the lives of Pericles, Nicias, and the other Grecian characters in Plutarch. Above all, he should learn most accurately every event in chapters 94—117. of the first book of Thucydides, which treat of the interval between the Persian and Peloponnesian wars: here, part of Grote's Greece will be the best commentary. Let the student read this portion till he can trace every step in the rise of the Athenian supremacy.

I have now given as long a course of Grecian History as any youth can be expected to know perfectly, before he enters the university: I would add more, but I have not forgotten my own college days, and all the instructive retrospect I have often enjoyed in comparing notes with old friends, Very great designs, and comparatively very small achievements, enter into the confessions of every student. Young persons are always sanguine; and when they once are betrayed into forming too large a plan, the work is wanted long before the two ends meet. Books require time for reading, time for reflecting, and time to digest; that is, to blend with our system, to become part of our mental implements, and to serve as a common measure and every-day standard of thought.

It is worth remembering, that a man never learns the use of instruments, whether mental or physical, so readily or so thoroughly as when he has few of them. The rude implements of the Indian have surpassed the machinery of Manchester. "John Hunter's head," said Abernethy, "was like a beehive;" not that he meant to say it was all in a buz, but that it had a separate cel' for every store. The modern Attic bees are in a hurry to gather the honey before they have prepared the combs. My advice is, to read, on each subject, one outline, again and again, till you have once formed the cells: you may then sip of ever flower in the wide field of literature — fill withou confusion, and preserve without loss.

To candidates for university honours I hav little more to say on Grecian History. I mus again refer to some general remarks in "The Student's Guide." Since 1836, the year in which that work was written, we have been favoured with the works of Keightley, Thirlwall, Grote and Wordsworth. Of the value of the three last, if read judiciously and in a spirit of inquiry, we can hardly say too much. The general error of Oxford classmen is, confining themselves too much to the books they propose for examination. The mind requires not only relief but variety, which Wordsworth's "Greece," a book of entertainment and of lively interest, is well calculated to afford. Eustace's "Classical Tour" is of similar value to the readers of Roman literature. I would also suggest translations of Arrian, Pausanias, Xenophon (especially his smaller treatises), and almost every original authority which comes to hand. Far from intending to overtask your mind, I advise you to read more or less, to select the amusing, or to toil through the intricate, according to the principle I have already vindicated of being guided by taste and inclination. While the subjects of your regular classical studies form the cells, translation will furnish stores to fill them. The history of Greek literature (Encyc. Met.), price 7*s.* 6*d.*, by the Bishop of London and others, is truly valuable.

Many classical scholars will be ashamed to acknowledge that they have any occasion to read translations. But, when critical knowledge of the text, and an accurate recollection of the matter of sixteen or more Latin and Greek books are required, very little time can remain for reading the many works required to illustrate them. These, therefore, I propose to read by the medium of translations. Surely it is as worthy of a scholar to read a translation of Xenophon, as any English History which gives the narrative of Xenophon, not only translated but condensed. Many talk of reading Greek like English; but there are very few men who can read other languages, least of all Greek and Latin, with as little effort as their own. Bring any silly pretender to the proof; lay before him the first column of the Times, and the first page of the Oratores Attici, and challenge him to a trial. The truth is, there is a kind of short-hand reading, by which we catch the sense of a sentence, without seeing more than one word in a line. And will any one pretend that he can skim over Plutarch's Greek, as readily as Langhorne's translation? Sound scholars may mark passages in translations to read in the original; and these translations of contemporary authors form a better commentary than any English essays I can recommend.

English translations are chiefly useful to the classical student in two ways. We will leave entirely out of the question how readily translations explain difficult passages of those authors which are read in the original; we will not argue how much translations may contribute to elegance, and how much they often do contribute to idleness, sapping the foundations of all sound scholarship; but, the first use of translations to classical students, is to enable them more thoroughly to appreciate those historical compilations to which they are obliged to trust for a large part of ancient History. Let every student of Grecian History keep a well-read, "marked and quoted" copy of Thirlwall's Epitome; let this form his outline, or, as Abernethy would say, "his series of cells;" and during his leisure hours let him amuse himself with marking on the margin any part of Plutarch, Pausanias, or other writers, whom he identifies as Thirlwall's authorities. With a little reflection he may see that Thirlwall has said too much on one point, too little on another, and has not chosen the best illustration or argument in support of a third. This exercise of judgment is very improving: it is more improving to think, though we sometimes think erroneously, than to follow blindly, like a traveller who observes only what his guide points out. The student should gradually extend these marginal notes and references; for they will agreeably mark his progress. How many a classical anecdote passes traceless through the mind, because we want a cell for it—because we have no such common-place book in which to set it down! The value of facts, as of figures, is determined by the series in which they stand: and nothing is more likely to render us alive to their value than the constant comparison which translations will suggest, between some seemingly unimportant observation of Plutarch and the value which the same observation assumes in the hands of Thirlwall, by elucidating the social or political institutions.

The first time we read Herodotus it seems like a collection of stories; at the second reading we begin to trace the connection; till, gradually, the mist clears away, the scene becomes distinct, and large sections of the ancient world open to our view. Another suggestion for expanding the mind, and teaching "How to observe" (the title of a clever volume by Miss Martineau), is, to read Herodotus through once, without assistance, and a second time in connection with Heeren's "Researches into the Politics, Intercourse, and Trade of the principal Nations of Antiquity." Heeren, like those who travel into comparatively unknown countries, is rather apt to be led too far, by an endeavour to bring to light curiosities commensurate with his toil, and is accused of drawing conclusions rather more extensive than his premises; but this is only saying, that in reading Heeren, like every author, you should hear his opinions, but still judge for yourself.

Again, translations open to us the only true source of the manners, customs, and general spirit of past ages. Niebuhr has revealed great part of the Roman constitution; but, as to the habits of life, topics of conversation, and subjects of thought which filled up the twenty-four hours of every day at Rome or at Athens, there is still a wide field for discovery. The books on Antiquities, by Smith, Rich, Adams, and Potter, convey mere fragments, and are no more to be compared to the perusal of the original authors, than the scraps of information from a tourist's guide-book are to be compared to the well-digested knowledge of an observing traveller. "For this knowledge of antiquity," said Niebuhr, "the materials lie widely scattered; every scholar must collect and arrange as many as he has the industry or the ingenuity to discover; and in putting them together (like the pieces of some ancient pavement, to form one consistent pattern, delineating ancient life) the mind receives a most invaluable exercise."—Supposing you wished to know the spirit of the last century and the general state of society; history would tell you perhaps that a taste for literature, or sense of religion, were less general than at the present time. By such vague and negative testimony, diluted in a flood of words, with the mere names of "men eminent for piety or learning," do historians (always excepting Mr. Macaulay) convey impressions which they have derived from memoirs and private letters written by the most distinguished characters of their respective times. Consider, for instance, the letters of Lady Mary Wortley Montagu; think not only of their general tone and spirit, not only of the social influences and sphere of action which those letters betray; but think of the state of society, when a lady of rank could complain in a letter to a friend, that so deplorably ignorant, so devoid of all but folly and vanity, were the minds of the young ladies of fashion, that they were more open to sophistry, and more commonly turned atheists, than even the professed rakes of the other sex; and, instead of that modesty which should teach respect for married persons, they really laughed at them, as having prudishly fettered themselves by an obligation with which the world had become wise enough to dispense. Equally great is the difference between the vivid and truthful impressions produced by translations of Xenophon or Cicero, and the vague remarks and "impotent conclusions" of modern writers. In short, if you would rather listen to "thoughts that breathe," in "words that burn," from a traveller telling his own story, than to a spiritless version second-hand; if you would be better satisfied with hearing truth drawn by instalments, and with all the reluctance of the seven teeth of King John's Jew, from a lying witness by a sharp counsel, than with reading a report of the same trial in ten lines; if you would enjoy all the strife of tongues, and time-beguiling interest of a debate in the House more than the summary in a country paper a week after; then must you also prefer picking your way through translations of the classics, and culling the choicest sweets and flowers, according to your own taste and appetite, to any essays on manners and customs, and any of those meagre descriptions to which we may well apply the words of Byron,

"'Tis Greece, but living Greece no more."

"I consider," says Jeremy Taylor, "that the wisest persons, and those who know how to value and entertain the more noble faculties of their soul and their precious hours, take pleasure in reading the productions of those old wise spirits who preserved natural reason and religion in the midst of heathen darkness, such as Homer, Euripides, Orpheus, Pindar, and Anacreon, Æschylus, and Menander, and all the Greek poets; Plutarch, and Polybius, Xenophon, and all those other excellent persons of both faculties, whose choicest dictates are collected by Stobæus; Plato and his scholars, Aristotle, and after him Porphyry, and all his other disciples, Pythagoras, and especially Hierocles and all the old Academics and Stoics within the Roman school."

Consider, in the classical records of the wisdom of antiquity, the faint glimmerings of life and immortality, which it remained for the Gospel fully to bring to light; consider the evident yearning of the souls of men for knowledge; consider the history of unassisted reason, which describes, in the feelings of every heart, such discord as plainly showed the need of a Revelation to teach the uses and relations of the several parts of the complicated machinery of man. Keep these points in view during classical studies. Read in Thucydides how Nicias, amidst all the dangers of the

Sicilian campaign, tells his soldiers "his hope and comfort is to reflect that he had always dealt honestly with his neighbour, and been mindful of his God,"— how Euripides says that "the man who has his God for his friend, has the fairest hope of prosperity;" and Pliny, that "it is God-like in man to show charity to man, and this is the road to eternal life." Read more of the same kind in Plato's Phædon, describing the last hours of Socrates, and also in Xenophon's Memoirs. In the Greek tragedians, Humility is so inculcated as to show that the minds of the Athenians were fully possessed by the feeling that the man who did not ascribe his prosperity to the hand of Providence, but showed a proud and unchastened spirit, was in danger of severe visitations; while, under the all-prevailing fear of Até, we may discern that the Athenians were less incredulous than many in later times of the truth of the threat, that the sins of the fathers should be visited on the children unto the third and fourth generation.

To general readers and ladies, my advice is to use the outline history and the works of Keightley, and study according to the method explained with the History of Rome. They may be satisfied with reading, first of all, to the death of Alexander the Great. To fill up their outline they should read the Grecian characters in Plutarch, and dip into

Xenophon's "Retreat of the Ten Thousand," and "History of Greece," which begins where Thucydides leaves off, near the end of the Peloponnesian War. It is quite certain, for reasons already published in the "Student's Guide," that Xenophon took up the pen exactly where Thucydides laid it down; and the difference between the style of the first two books of the "Hellenics," and the rest of Xenophon's writings, implies an attempt to continue the manner as well as the matter of Thucydides. On the Peloponnesian War, and the state of Greece for half a century preceding it, read a translation of Thucydides by Mr. Dale. Attend particularly to the curious specimen of historical criticism in the first twenty chapters; to all the speeches; the plague of Athens; the sedition of Corcyra; the siege of Platææ; and read attentively from the beginning to the end of the Campaign in Sicily. Beloe's Herodotus contains the materials of a very large part of ancient history. For the Life of Alexander the Great, read the work of Arrian, to whom the younger Pliny addressed several of his epistles. Arrian's history is founded on the Memoirs of Aristobulus and Ptolemy Lagus, who served under Alexander. A Life of Alexander by Williams, in the "Family Library," is well written. Gain an accurate knowledge of the route at the north of India; this will give an interest to Oriental travels lately written; especially those by Sir A. Burnes and Masson, as also that of Vigne, whose conjecture, that Cabul is the same as Cau-Pol (*Καυκάσου πόλις*), is, as Professor Wilson allowed, highly probable. The speeches of Demosthenes "On the Crown," and his three "Philippics," as well as that orator's life by Plutarch, may well be read in connection with the History of Philip of Macedon. I should also recommend the "Œdipus Tyrannus" of Sophocles, by Potter, the "Agamemnon" of Æschylus, translated by Mr. Sewell; and the "Medea" of Euripides, as highly serviceable to initiate the mind into the mysteries of Grecian fable. A lady of my acquaintance found the English translations of these tragedians sufficiently interesting to induce her to read every play. You may also pick your way through some of the dialogues of Plato, especially the "Phædon," and Gillies's translation of Aristotle's "Politics." As to the rest of Ancient History, instead of Rollin's "Ancient History," which, like Russell's "Modern Europe," tends, as I have generally observed, rather to the *confusion* than the *diffusion* of knowledge, read Heeren's "Researches both in Asia and Africa." This course of reading may seem long; but since I leave each person to select, more or less, according to the strength of his appetite and digestion, the course proposed requires less time and labour than Rollin's "Ancient History" alone. Pope's "Homer" I need hardly mention; so generally is it known and read by both young and old. See Johnson's criticism in his Life of Pope.

I will now conclude my observations on Grecian History and Ancient History generally, with remarks for the benefit of all classes of readers. The reason I extend my list of books, is to give more scope for variety of taste and inclinations, and not by any means to dispense with the rule, NEVER READ TOO MUCH TO READ WELL.

Egyptian antiquities deserve especial notice. Orpheus, Linus, Musæus, Amphion, Sanchoniathon and Homer, as well as Pythagoras and Plato, all visited Egypt. Solon, too, was assisted by the Egyptian priests: and it was in Egypt that Herodotus found abundance to gratify his inquiring spirit. From Egypt came the religion of the Greeks; and whatever in Grecian mythology seems to coincide with the Law and the Prophets, has been not unreasonably supposed to have been derived from the Egyptians, and by them from the Israelites. That the Egyptians did receive many things from those guardians of the Oracles of God, can indeed hardly be doubted.

Iamblicus, the preceptor of Julian, A.D. 360,

speaks of "the inscriptions on the ancient columns of Hermes, on which Plato and Pythagoras formed their philosophy. Now these columns existed in Egypt in the time of Proclus, B.C. 500; and on them were inscriptions according with the doctrine of the Trinity, as is ingeniously explained by Serle, in his "Horæ Solitariæ," who mentions also a name of the Deity "as near as translation can attain to *Jehovah*." If I add the columns mentioned by Procopius, found in the part of Africa where the Carthaginians settled, inscribed, "We are they that fled from the face of Joshua, the son of Nun, the Robber," the reader can require no further argument to show the interest which must attach to that land famed for wisdom in the days of Moses. Therefore, besides Heeren's "African Nations," Dr. Pritchard's "Egyptian Mythology" is a valuable work. Sir G. Wilkinson's "Private Life, Religion, &c., of the Ancient Egyptians," and published with 600 illustrations, a very valuable work, is of great interest; but Bunsen's Egypt is the latest, and in many respects unequalled.

Of Travels and modern writings for students of Grecian History, the best are Dodwell's "Historical Tour through Greece," Gell's "Itinerary," and Leake's "Travels." Müller's "Dorians" is only valuable to men of accurate classical reading:

university students should read it in connection with Herodotus and Thucydides. The articles on Athens and Greece, in the "Penny Cyclopædia," are very usefully composed. Müller's "Attica and Athens" has lately been translated by J. Ingram Lockhart. Stewart's "Antiquities of Athens," with seventy plates, is valuable. A slight glance at Mr. Wordsworth's "Greece," will show that it supersedes all earlier writers; for he has availed himself of the contents of all travels and works on Greece existing at the time he wrote. Flaxman's "Lectures on Sculpture," and the "Specimens of Ancient Sculpture, selected from different Collections of Great Britain by the Society of Dilettanti," as well as the Townley, Elgin, and Phigaleian Marbles, in the "Library of Entertaining Knowledge," should be consulted on the arts of Greece.

A "History of the Literature of Greece," by Müller, will be found in the "Library of Useful Knowledge." But, Col. Mure's work is by far the most complete treatise on the same subject that exists in English literature.

Lastly, I would recommend my readers to gain a clear knowledge of the length and breadth of the several parts of Greece, especially Attica; and to compare every measurement with that of some town or county of England.

I am only afraid that the variety of subjects and books already mentioned should tempt young persons to try too much. The first thing to consider is, for what purpose you are commencing a course of study. If to humour a literary ambition, to be thought learned, and to excite the wonder of the ignorant, then abandon this vile and degrading purpose, or your vanity will increase much faster than your learning. What you gain in head you will lose in heart; your mind will be filled, but not refined, and excite far more jealousy than admiration. Read, as Bacon said, "for the glory of your Creator and the relief of man's estate;" to improve your talents for running the race that is set before you; to prevent that periodical void within, which, like a vacuum, is doomed to fill, and that with gnawing cares and soul-debasing thoughts. Hear what Horace says,—the finest motto for a Bible:—

> "Et ni
> Posces ante diem LIBRUM cum lumine, si non
> Intendes animum studiis et rebus honestis,
> Invidiâ vel amore vigil torquebere."—I. Ep. 2. 37.

That is true of our faculties, which an old officer said of his men, that there was no such security for good behaviour as active service. The lusts of the flesh maintain "a long pull, and a strong pull, and a pull altogether," one way; and while reason, conscience, and religion are arrayed against them, the balance may be preserved. But when these guards are not on duty, or perchance are slumbering at their post, it is well if the history of the past, or some such innocent recreation, employs our memory, and engages our imagination; because, should these allies be gloating over old pleasures or devising new, they will be playing on such dangerous ground, that they may rouse up the enemy, and the citadel may be taken by surprise.

"He that loveth a book," says Isaac Barrow, "will never want a faithful friend, a wholesome counsellor, a cheerful companion, an effectual comforter. By study, by reading, by thinking, one may innocently divert and pleasantly entertain himself, as in all weathers, so in all fortunes."

In following out one course of reading, do not be impatient or disturbed because you do not seem to be advancing as rapidly as others. Among the many who desire to be thought literary characters, nothing is more common than an inclination to lock up the temple of knowledge and throw away the key; or, to kick away the ladder, that none may follow them.—So, beware of this class of literary impostors: their life is one continued lie: they pretend to know far more than they do know; and seek to magnify difficulties, and hint that things are not so easy as they seem, implying that a talent peculiar to themselves is required for their favourite subjects. In every department of knowledge the man really proficient is ever ready to communicate, and, forgetting all the difficulties he encountered, firmly believes he could teach his friends in half the time.

We should employ our minds with history, in the same way as we should have done had we lived in the times described. A man need not become a walking cyclopædia; neither are we more in honour bound to remember every circumstance of former reigns, than every event in last year's newspapers. We should read for the same purpose that we enter society, — to observe. The wisdom of the lesson may be remembered when the facts are lost; and the moral remain, though we forget the fable. The portions of history which enter into common conversation are limited, and experience will soon suggest the most profitable subjects for more accurate study. No man need be ashamed to say, when his memory is at fault, "this or that has escaped me; let me ask a question or two, and I shall be able to follow you." Few persons are so ill-bred as to introduce abstruse subjects into general society. If you join a party of antiquaries, you must expect antiquarian topics; but, in general society, no man of ordinary reading can be painfully at a loss for facts while he has the power of reasoning and reflection. Next to the improvement and entertainment of your own mind, your design should be to inform yourself on the general topics of conversation. Read about the North of India, Caffre Land, the Burman Empire, Australia, or any other part of the world interesting at the time present. To read only of the past, is to be always out of fashion, and as uninteresting as an old newspaper. Men of extensive reading find their chief advantage in this;—not that they remember all they read, but that they know exactly where to seek for information; and, a few hours' reading will at any time enable them to rally all their scattered forces on the topic of general conversation.

CHAP. IV.

HOW TO GAIN A KNOWLEDGE OF FOREIGN COUNTRIES. ADDRESSED TO FIRE-SIDE TRAVELLERS AS WELL AS OTHERS.

Readers of travels, as well as actual travellers, differ widely in curiosity and observation; therefore, as some tourists consult Guides and Hand-books to learn what galleries to visit and what sights to inquire for, others learn from Miss Martineau's late work "How to observe." As for those who must for the present be satisfied with the pleasures of anticipation, in planning tours and laying down the route they would like to take, should some happy contingency occur, — to these speculative voyagers over the wide waters of the round world, I will offer a few hints, showing how to gain as much knowledge as possible of foreign countries, even although, like the Vicar of Wakefield's family, "all their adventures were by the fireside, and all their migrations from the blue bedroom to the brown."

Basil Hall advises midshipmen to begin their career by "taking up a line;" that is, to aspire to some particular character; for seamanship, for science, generalship, or diplomacy; so, readers of travels should begin with choosing a topic which every volume may contribute to illustrate. Instead of turning over thousands of pages without an object, they should keep some one subject uppermost in their thoughts, so as to be competent referees on any question concerning it. Take, for instance, one of the following topics: —

1. The history of man, or human nature under every variety of climate or influence, whether social or physical; the savage, the slave, the freeman, the heathen, the Christian:

2. The wonders of creation,—the animals, produce; natural phenomena,—storms, earthquakes, or volcanoes, in every part of the world:

3. The arts and sciences,—literature, education, ingenuity, and points of superiority in different nations.

First. *As to the history of man.* This subject was chosen by Dr. Pritchard, whose learned work remarkably exemplifies how to collect and classify information. The author read all the travels he could procure, to illustrate the modifying influence of physical and moral agencies on the different tribes of the human family. From his work it appears that, however much may be said about the artificial and unnatural habits that civilisation produces, human strength, endurance, and longevity—to say nothing of the development of those capacities which are deemed the proper characteristics of man—are greater among civilised than in uncivilised nations. This is a fact which the most ordinary reader would be curious to know: I have therefore selected it from a volume of deep and subtle investigation, to show with what care and interest we may illustrate a subject seemingly of deep philosophy. Catlin's "Notes on the North American Indians," with 400 illustrations, contain a most curious history of our brother man. From these sources we learn that works of art, considered impossible under all the advantages of a civilised state, are every day produced by the simple instruments of untutored nations. After reading Mr. Catlin's travels, and visiting his collection, I happened to take up Bremner's excursion in Russia, and shortly afterwards Davis's and Gutzlaff's accounts of the Chinese, which induced me to visit the Chinese Exhibition in London. Let any reader consider the effect which must be produced on the mind by the following observations, relating to three races of men in distant parts of the world: First, Mr. Catlin showed an Indian bow which no turner in London could equal, and a cloth which astonished the manufacturers of Manchester. Secondly, Mr. Bremner stated that the Russians, with no plane or line, nor any other tool than an axe, will cut and join even edges with the greatest precision. And, thirdly, in the Chinese Exhibition appeared that varied collection of works of art too well known to need description. Again; how must the mind be opened and improved by comparing the different habits of life,—the food, the occupations, the character of these widely differing and distant nations. And how much more light will be thrown upon man's history, if in the life of Ali Pacha we read of the state of Egypt, and see how that prince of slave-dealers carries on, or at least sanctions, the annual negro-hunts. One who has not read of the horrors of this chase has yet to learn how far it is possible for human nature, left to the control of conscience alone, without the chastening discipline of a Christian community, brutally to make prey of the flesh and blood of his fellow-man. In the extermination of the Red Indians by the encroaches of the colonists of America, we learn more lessons of the same kind, though less cold-blooded and revolting. Borrow's "Gypsies in Spain," as well as his "Bible in Spain," which might as properly be entitled "Gipsy Adventures," together with the history of the "Thugs," or Indian Assassins, will all be valuable to those who think that "the proper study of mankind is man:" nor can any kind of reading afford more thrilling interest.

Secondly. *As to the wonders of creation and natural phenomena.* This, like the last, is a topic suited to every capacity,—to the philosopher, who needs no assistance, as well as to the general reader, who would beguile a winter's evening by gratifying his curiosity about the wide world and all things that are therein. Humboldt's "Kosmos" is a library in itself.

Thirdly. *The arts, sciences, literature, and comparative superiority of different nations* can also be studied by persons of various tastes and capacities. Some may compare the works of art and manual performance only, and see how little the pyramids of Egypt appear, in any thing but their uselessness, when compared with our mines and railways. The measurement of some of the tanks of India and the wall of China may be profitably remembered by reference to our docks, canals, water-works, gas-pipes, and other machinery. Again, those of maturer mind may regard rather moral and social, than physical grandeur; but my intention is directed to encourage and suggest the first attempts of a large class of readers, who are too diffident to believe they can attain the information which their friends possess. Many a naturalist, who has added a valuable collection to a museum, has attributed all his eminence to some accident which induced him to make a store of birds' eggs or snail-shells at school.

Cowley attributed his poetry to the chance perusal of the "Fairy Queen;" Sir J. Reynolds attributed his painting to Richardson's treatise; and Franklin imputed the cast of his genius to De Foe's "Essay on Projects." Nature implants, and education developes genius; but accident has much to do in directing it to suitable employments. Had not Gibbon sat "musing amidst the ruins of the Capitol, while the barefooted friars were singing vespers in the Temple of Jupiter, the idea of the "decline and fall of the city" might not have "started in his mind." Many an author who has enlightened the world has felt unworthy of the honours conferred upon him; because he attributes all his success to some chance suggestion which first directed attention to his favourite order of phenomena; and, because his discoveries seemed too obvious to be overlooked by any one who had collected the same class of facts under equal advantages. Men of genius will rarely believe an investigation to be impracticable to others which is so easy to themselves: still, a patient adherence to a mere mechanical system of study has often produced results which undoubtedly appear the work, not of industry, but of genius. "If I surpass other men," said Newton, "in any thing, it is in patient examination of facts."

One of my friends has a map of England, on which he has coloured each road he has travelled; every county of which he knows the habits of the people, or the produce and advantages of the soil. He has also marked with figures many of the towns, as being of the first, second, third, or fourth class, in respect of population. Such methods prove a strong incentive, both to deep research and methodical study; they forbid us to forget that we read, not to count volumes, but to store up knowledge. The maps we choose should be originally blank ones, representing terra incognita; a dark colour may also be appropriate. We shall thus be prompted to study, that we may dispel this cloud which broods over the face of the earth, and in its place diffuse some lively hue emblematic of the light of knowledge.

These few hints will serve as a sufficient clue to the shortest, safest, and most agreeable road to the knowledge which travellers can impart. Of all the works which may be skimmed, travels are those with which the reader may avail himself of this privilege with the clearest conscience. He is not bound to read of more than one passage from Dover to Calais, or of one ducking at the Line. The table of contents will generally point out the parts worth reading.

For those who prefer voyages of discovery, whale-fishery, and all the phenomena and wonders of the deep, the voyages of Cook, Parry, and Ross are to be preferred, because it is injudicious to remain ignorant of books which others know. Read Park's " Travels in Africa," for the same reason, also " Mutiny of the Bounty."

The " Lives of Drake, Cavendish, and Dampier, with the History of the Buccaneers," form one entertaining volume. The " Travels and Researches of Humboldt," being a condensed narrative of his journey in America and Asiatic Russia, is a work second to none. Besides these, "Eöthen" is the most compendious, and the best narrative of Eastern travel; and Warburton's "Crescent and the Cross;"—"From Cornhill to Cairo;" Stephens's "Central America;" Basil Hall's "Fragments of Voyages and Travels;" Charles Dickens's "America;" Sir F. B. Head's "Emigrant," and all his writings; Lyell's "Travels in North America;" Whiteside's "Italy;" and Borrow's "Bible in Spain," and "Gypsies in Spain." Here are ten works of more than usual talent. A common catalogue will supply numerous others of average interest.

As to manners, customs, and the general state of different nations,—these form more or less the subject of all travels; but more particularly of—

Catlin's "Letters and Notes on the Manners and Customs of the North American Indians;" "Travels in North America, and a Residence among the Pawnee Indians," by the Hon. C. A. Murray; "Life in Mexico," in the Foreign Library; Gardiner's "Visit to the Indians of Chili;" Davis's "Description of China and its Inhabitants," and Gutzlaff's "China Opened;" "Narrative of a Recent Imprisonment in China, after the wreck of the Kite;" "Ten Thousand

Things relating to China and the Chinese," by W. B. Langdon, Esq., curator of the Chinese Collection. This forms an epitome of the government, literature, trade, and social life of the Chinese. "Manners and Customs of the Japanese of the Nineteenth Century;" "History and present Condition of the Barbary States," with a view of their antiquities, arts, &c., by the Right Rev. M. Russell; "Nubia and Abyssinia," by the same author; Kohl's "Russia and the Russians in 1842;" "Excursions in the Interior of Russia," by Bremner, with an account of Nicholas and his court, and the horrors of exile in Siberia; "Journal of a Residence in Norway, in 1834," and "Sweden," by Samuel Laing. — All these works are of indisputable value, and contain much to interest both old and young.

For readers of mature mind, who can enter into historical disquisitions and historical reflections:—

"Notes (Moral, Religious, Political, Economical, Educational, and Phrenological) on the United States of America;" of this it is enough to say that it is written by George Combe; Smith's "Discovery of America by the Northmen in the Tenth Century;" Buckingham's "America;" the second series describes the slave states; Miss Martineau's "America;" a book of much observation and reflection; Sir F. B. Head's "Rough Notes;" the

"Pampas and the Andes;" Bishop Heber's "Journal" (very elegantly written, and generally admired, though few readers receive from it very lasting impressions); "Notes of a Traveller on the Social and Political State of France, Prussia, Switzerland, Italy, and other Parts of Europe, during the present Century," by S. Laing; "Mediterranean Sketches," by Lord F. Egerton; "Forest Scenes and Incidents in the Wilds of Canada," by Sir F. B. Head; Waterton's "Wanderings in the N. W. of the United States;"—describing the capture of rare snakes and birds; natural history.

For those curious about ancient cities, ruins, and remains of bygone days:—

"Tour to the Sepulchres of Ancient Etruria, in 1839," by Mrs. Hamilton Gray; Stephens's "Incidents of Travel in Central America, Chiapas, and Yucatan;" also his "Second Visit to the Ruined Cities of Central America." Norman's "Rambles in Yucatan; or, Notes of Travel through the Peninsula, including a Visit to the remarkable Ruins of Chi-chen, Kabah, Zayi, and Uxmal." Laborde's "Arabia Petræa, and the excavated City of Petra" (very interesting and curious); "Narrative of a Journey to the Site of Babylon in 1811; Memoir on the Ruins, with engravings — Remarks by Major Rennel

— Inscriptions copied at Persepolis," by Claudius James Rich, Esq.; also of a "Residence on the Site of Ancient Nineveh," by the same author; Layard's works on Nineveh; visit also the sculpture in the British Museum; Fellows's "Excursion in Asia Minor; including a Visit to several unknown and undiscovered Cities;" and his "Xanthian Marbles; their Acquisition and Transmission to England;" Kinnear's "Cairo, Petræa, and Damascus;" "Topography of Thebes, and General View of Egypt;" "Pompeii; an Account of its Destruction and Remains;" Professor Long's "Egyptian Antiquities;" and Bucke's "Ruins of Ancient Cities."

Fifthly. For readers of Classical and Biblical literature may be specified:—

Sir A. Burnes's "Travels to Bokhara and up the Indus." This may be read in connection with the life of Alexander the Great. Cramer's Asia Minor, Ancient Italy, and Greece, as also Lake's, are chiefly valuable to the more accurate students of the classics. Lake's "Northern Greece;" and "Topography of Athens and the Demi;" Lord Lindsay's "Letters on the Holy Land;" Robinson's "Biblical Researches in Palestine, Mount Sinai, and Arabia Petræa, in 1838;" "A Winter Journey through Russia, Caucasus, and Georgia, thence across Mount Zagross, by the Pass of Xenophon, and the Ten Thousand Greeks," by Migdan; Wordsworth's "Athens;" also "Ancient Greece," and Eustace's "Classical Tour," above recommended.

Sixthly. For tourists in Great Britain or on the Continent: —

A full and impartial catalogue of all the most approved works in every department of English literature is published annually by Messrs. Longman, containing, under the head of "Guides and Hand-books," a list of works for travellers visiting every part of England or of the Continent. In this catalogue the tourist will find pictures, hand-books, guides, and travelling directions of all kinds. But since Dr. Johnson wisely said that no traveller will bring knowledge home who does not take knowledge out with him, I would strongly recommend every tourist to inform himself of the government, constitution, resources, and general nature of the town, county, or country he intends to visit. The traveller should know what to look or inquire for: he should also read sufficiently to understand common allusions to such events of the day as every one with whom he converses will presume to be too familiar to need explanation. Let me strongly recommend young persons to avail themselves of all the Illustrated works they can procure, as the most fertile source not only of rational amusement but of serious instruction. With the productions of the pencil, as with those of the pen, the same methodical application and careful comparison are essential to real improvement. Panoramas are a great help to knowledge. Imitate Lord Kenyon, who, amidst all his judicial labours, was the first to visit every shilling show in London; and, beware of the erroneous supposition, that knowledge is only to be derived from books. The sculptor speaks with his chisel, and the painter with his brush — and speaks far more intelligibly, as to the visible creation, than the writer with his pen.

CHAP. V.

PHILOSOPHY, MORAL, POLITICAL, MENTAL — LOGIC — METAPHYSICS.

PHILOSOPHY, my young friends, may seem to you a very hard term, and you may feel disposed to pass by this chapter as wholly unsuited to your taste or talents; but, with a little attention, it may appear that to think and reflect, not only on what you see, but on what you feel, — in other words, to think about your own thoughts and emotions, and to examine curiously anything which seems remarkable in such thoughts, emotions or feelings,—you may find, I say, that this kind of study is not too severe, if you read a little at a time. And should you only try, the course of reading I have to propose, or indeed any one of the volumes, can hardly fail to produce a very sensible effect upon your mind. Have you never observed, that certain of your acquaintance are remarkable for giving a very favourable impression of their good sense and understanding to any person with whom they happen to converse, although only for a few minutes, and that too upon some topic which gives scope neither for general reading nor deep learning?

This mysterious influence, this weight of character, depends chiefly on the exact truth of our thoughts and the propriety of our words. "The truth, the whole truth, and nothing but the truth," should be the rule, even of the most casual of our daily remarks; and the degree of our conformity to this rule is the measure, mentally as well as morally, of our influence upon society. The world often pays homage to this truthfulness of thought and expression without knowing what it reverences. A certain plain and ssimple way of peaking, so generally admired, is nothing else but the language natural only to those who discern the exact truth of every question, — mean what they say, and say what they mean.

To seek truth for truth's sake has therefore been the laudable object of those called philosophers, or lovers of wisdom, both in ancient and modern times. To paint the surface of the human figure, we must know anatomy, otherwise there will be a want of ease and true expression. To speak correctly on our feelings, we must know the real nature of our feelings, or, Moral Philosophy; to speak correctly of our thoughts, we must know the laws of thought, or, Mental Philosophy.

On MORAL PHILOSOPHY, the most easy, plain, and intelligible work is that by Paley, which for vigour, freshness, ease, and perspicuity of style, as well as for aptness of illustration, is unrivalled; but many of its principles and definitions savour so much of casuistry that it is generally believed that Paley would have been incapable of writing so loosely at a later period of his life. This, indeed, is the remark of Professor Sedgwick, whose admirable lectures I should strongly recommend to be read in connection with Paley's "Moral Philosophy."

The moral essays of Johnson's "Rambler" and Addison's "Spectator" should next be selected;

and then such of Bacon's Essays as appear from their title to relate to this subject.

Chalmers's "Bridgewater Treatise" contains most ingenious illustrations, and is on the whole well calculated to give information in an amusing way. The style unfortunately is turgid, and contains many words "not found in Johnson." Chalmers's object was to prove how admirably our hearts and minds are suited to the sphere in which we live.

I do not presume that the same person will read all the volumes here recommended. Each can select such chapters as rivet his attention.

The following list is for those who have a more decided preference for philosophical works: —

Mackintosh's "Dissertations on the Study of Ethical Philosophy." This is an admirably comprehensive work, well suited as a guide to subsequent reading. For the same purpose, some recommend Beattie's "Principles of Moral Science," which have attained much celebrity, but less than "The Philosophy of the Moral Feelings," by Abercrombie. Those, however, who would go to the fountain, should read "Bishop Butler's Sermons:" this work is much read at Oxford, and forms a subject of examination for the highest honours. Dr. Chalmers and Sir James Mackintosh are both reputed to have said that nearly all they knew of moral philosophy they owed to Butler. The late Dr. Arnold also recommended Butler's Sermons as one of the few works we should never cease reading. Butler's reasoning is too abstruse for some minds. But, few persons, really desirous of improvement, can be at a loss for occasional assistance from men of sound education. I knew an instance of a young lady who read these sermons with her brother, that she might receive an explanation of every difficulty. Mrs. Somerville truly remarks, as an encouragement to her countrywomen to study science, that the degree of intelligence required to follow a theory is not to be measured by the genius originally required for its discovery. Dissertations most perplexing of themselves may be very easy when we have a friend to vary the terms and simplify the arguments. Many persons of sound judgment have declared, that if there were one book of human composition which, more than another, they felt thankful to have read, it was Butler's Sermons.

After Butler, Sewell's "Christian Morals" is a good book, if you read but one; and Abercrombie's "Philosophy of the Moral Feelings" is a work of deserved celebrity. It is written in a clear and elegant style. Abercrombie also is suited to those who have only leisure to read a little.

Sydney Smith's "Lectures of Moral Philosophy" are superior to any in point of entertainment.

John Foster's "Essays on Decision of Character" are admirable, and of the greatest interest to the class of readers now addressed; as also is Taylor's "Natural History of Society," in which are considered the origin and progress of human improvement.

Dr. Hampden's Article in the Encyclopædia Britannica, on Aristotle's Philosophy, will convey much well-digested information on ancient ethics. This, as well as Harris's Treatises on "Art" and "Happiness," is very generally read by Oxford classmen. To those who study Aristotle's Ethics, I speak advisedly, when I say, that if they would only select from the books here recommended all the chapters which treat on the same subjects as the several books of the Ethics, and if they would also accustom themselves to write Ethical Essays,—really *Ethical*, not Aristotelian,—they would have a better chance of University distinction, and would also enjoy the benefit of that mental exercise and those literary qualifications which Oxford honours should imply.

Political Philosophy.—Our duties as citizens form one part of Paley's "Moral and Political Philosophy," above mentioned. Bishop Butler's Sermon before the House of Lords, on the 30th of January, 1740, and also Burke's "French Revolution," albeit Fox said he disliked it as much as any writing by Paine, form an invaluable study for youth and age. The Right Hon. E. Burke's works are considered a treasury of political wisdom.

On Political Economy, the most easy and instructive reading for young persons is found in the Tales by Miss Martineau. I knew a young lady who read the whole series with the greatest avidity, although she was not generally fond of study. The leading principles of Adam Smith's "Wealth of Nations" are here shown in their operation in a village or other community, ingeniously and naturally represented, so as to present both cause and effect, the beginning and the end, of each impolitic system. Mrs. Marcet's Conversations are at least equally admired.

Miss Martineau has, like all other persons, male and female, who have the boldness to be original, been ridiculed, and in nothing more wittily than

"Femina tractavit *propria quæ maribus*."

Nor must her peculiar opinions, which give a harsh and ungenial tone to her writings, be forgotten; still, few persons are at once so deep and clear that they need disdain her assistance.

For men of reflection, Adam Smith's work must be the grammar and groundwork of political economy. Ricardo is also celebrated; but Mill's "Political Economy" is the best modern work. The "Westminster Review" speaks highly of W. N. Senior's treatise; but, for compendious information, the "Cyclopædia of Commerce," by M'Culloch, is a library in itself.

As supplementary to this branch of study, read "The Economy of Machinery and Manufactures," by C. Babbage; "The Cotton Manufacture of Great Britain," by A. Ure. On "Colonization and the Colonies," read Lectures by Herman Merivale; also, "Colonization, particularly in S. Australia," by Sir C. Napier; and Cornewall Lewis's "Essay on the Government of Dependencies." The works of J. W. Gilbart, General Manager of the London and Westminster Bank, consisting of "The History and Principles of Banking," "The Currency Question, an Examination of Evidence in Committee in 1840," and "Country Banks and the Currency, from Evidence in Committee in 1841," by G. M. Bell. Read also the Life of Horner, in Brougham's "Statesmen," and Papers in the "Edinburgh Review" therein recommended, written in 1802-3-4. On "Population," read Malthus, and the Reviews upon his Essay; also, "Political Economy," by the same, "Whateley's Introductory Lectures," "M'Culloch's Principles." Sewell's "Christian

Politics" contains some admirable observations. "Principles of Population," by Sir A. Alison, is the principal remaining work of note. Lord Brougham has also published his opinions on political economy. Francis's "History of the Bank of England," and his "Chronicles of the Stock Exchange," are highly interesting, especially to men of business.

Besides, or instead of any or all of these, the articles on Taxation, Rent, or any other part of political economy, may be studied in the Cyclopædias. This subject, indispensable as it is for understanding the news of the day, is generally considered to be a mystery which none but a chosen few can penetrate. If there is any one subject on which all should be informed, but almost all are ignorant, it is political economy. Many of the works above mentioned are suited to the most ordinary capacity; nor is there one of which most young ladies might not improve by the study of many portions. Young ladies reading Political Economy indeed! some will exclaim; and were there not some so silly as to laugh in the wrong place, this and many other books would be wholly unnecessary. It is not many years since reading of any kind was held ridiculous in women; but, happily, the opinion that ladies were designed for nothing nobler than "to suckle fools and chronicle small beer," as Shakespeare says, is less prevalent.

MENTAL PHILOSOPHY and METAPHYSICS.— Abercrombie's work on the Intellectual Powers is the best for those who can only read one book. Another work much more interesting to the general reader is Combe's "Constitution of Man;" at the same time I should recommend one of Combe's works on "Phrenology," and his "Lectures on Popular Education." Whether the reader believes in Phrenology, more, less, or not at all, the works of Combe and Gall are deeply interesting from the facts they contain. The Phrenologists, and Physiologists generally, write in a very lucid and pleasing style. There is no class of men with whom it is so easy to converse, and none who keep more to the point, nor are any more properly to be called clear-headed, than the Medical Profession. Gall's work displays great learning, and is valuable to every one who would know the history of human nature.

Locke's work "On the Conduct of the Understanding" is brief, and easily intelligible. This, as well as many parts of "Watts on the Mind," is well suited to young persons. Those who would dip more deeply into Metaphysics should read Locke's larger work, Harris's "Philosophical Arrangements," and Reid's "Essays on the Intellectual Powers of Man," to which is annexed an analysis of Aristotle's Logic;—these works alone will give a general knowledge of ancient Metaphysics;—then "Bacon's Novum Organon," Locke "On the Human Understanding," and the works of Thomas Brown and Dugald Stewart. However, it is not my purpose to attempt to lay down a plan for readers capable of profound investigations; I would only remind them of Sir J. Mackintosh's papers in the "Encyclopædia Britannica." His works have also been published in one volume.

Many works on Insanity are very interesting to the general reader—such as those by Munro, Mayo, and Willis. The facts on which the theories of every class of Physiologists are founded are so deeply interesting and generally useful, that they are supposed to be to some extent familiar to all persons of good education. In parts of Beck's "Medical Jurisprudence," as also in Dr. Taylor's book, much admired by the Profession, you will find an explanation of that insanity by which persons are legally irresponsible, as well as many interesting cases, in which medical science has promoted the ends of justice. Works of this kind, the unprofessional may read like a newspaper, remembering that they should dip into them with their minds as we would dip into a jar of steel filings with a magnet; more or less will adhere and be gathered up in proportion as the instrument has been previously charged.

"Pray remember," writes Southey to his son, "all other considerations should give way to health. A man had better break a bone, or even lose a limb, than shake his nervous system. Lord Mansfield advises only eight hours' reading a day for a student of law; and Sir M. Hale thought six hours as much as a man could bear; eight, he said, was too much." So read

POPULAR WORKS ON MEDICINE.—"Combe on the Constitution of Man" is very generally read by persons of all ages. Of late, so many men of eminence have been impressed with a conviction that health and life are daily and hourly thrown away through ignorance of the most simple principles of health, air, exercise, food, and general habits, that many works have been written, not only for the doctors, but for the patients. "Every man by thirty is, in his own case, either a physician or a fool," said Abernethy.

Thompson's "Domestic Management of the Sick-room," and, above all others, South's "Hint's on Emergencies," are well written, and intended for the guidance of those who would co-operate with the medical attendant, or supply his place before he arrives. I have known a case in which a life was saved by a lady having the sense to get a warm bath ready when a child had the croup; and a life lost by the ignorance of a wife, who pressed on her husband a plate of roast meat in a case of inflammation.

Dr. Holland's "Medical Notes" are very instructive. Read particularly an article in the "Quarterly," No. CXXX., on Dr. Holland's medical treatment, and the case of St. Martin in America. St. Martin had an open wound in the stomach, so that the process of digestion could be watched: many hundreds of observations were made on the digestibility of food and the influence of various habits both of the mind and body.

On GRAMMAR, LOGIC, and RHETORIC.—The Grammarian teaches the connection of words in propositions; the Logician teaches the connection of propositions in argument; the Rhetorician, the connection of arguments in persuasion. The most useful English grammar is that by the celebrated William Cobbett. He treats particularly of the points on which persons are most commonly deficient. As works of a more philosophical character, Harris's "Hermes," and Horne Tooke's "Diversions of Purley," are known to most good English scholars. The "Edinburgh" and "Quarterly" also contain several instructive essays, which may be found by the index of each.

Dr. Crombie's "Etymology and Syntax of the English Language" is also in high repute. Trench's "Use of Words," and Latham's "Structure of the English Language" may also be recommended. The scholar should devote one or two weeks to Vernon's "Anglo-Saxon Guide."

On Logic, read Whateley's "Elements," and a Treatise by Dr. Moberly, and "Edinburgh Review," No. 115. The Oxford student should make Aldrich his text-book, and use the treatises of Huyshe, Moberly, Hill, with Questions on Logic and Answers to explain Aldrich. Also Hampden's article on the Rhetoric of Aristotle, Woolley's "Logic" and select chapters of Aristotle's "Organon." Mr. Newman's "Lectures on Logic," delivered at Bristol, are much admired.

On Rhetoric, read Whateley's "Elements," Campbell's "Philosophy of Rhetoric." Scholars may read Cicero's "Orator," and Quinctilian; even the English reader may profitably dip into the translation of Aristotle's "Rhetoric;" and read Hampden's article upon it before mentioned.

Grammar, Logic, and Rhetoric, are subjects to be deeply studied only by those who are naturally fond of science. Still, no one can be considered well educated who has not read at least one treatise upon each of these subjects.

The best general History of Ancient Philosophy, Moral and Metaphysical, is that by Ritter. Mr. Lewes's "Biographical History of Philosophy," will be found an interesting introduction.

CHAP. VI.

ON THE FINE ARTS.

PAINTING, Sculpture, and Architecture, are three subjects on which nearly all persons of polite education, professional or unprofessional, feel compelled to conceal ignorance, if they cannot display knowledge. It is not my purpose to minister to the vanity of those who pick up the names of ancient masters or celebrated galleries, and affect to be connoisseurs: but, two or three simple directions for attaining the elements of criticism and a general history of art may be profitable in various ways. It will save us from that shame and confusion which we should otherwise feel when the fine arts form the subject of conversation; it will enable us to understand the elegant illustrations which authors commonly derive from the arts; it will qualify us to profit by the conversation of men of taste, giving a nucleus for gathering a new kind of matter, drawing forth a new power of the mind, and opening to us a never-failing source of the purest pleasure and refinement.

I may encourage the studious with the strongest assurance that, great as is the advantage of cultivating a taste and of acquiring knowledge of the fine arts, this to many minds is a work of very little time or toil. It consists more in observation than in reading; it consists in opening our eyes and ears with curiosity, on occasions in which they are too frequently closed or turned away. Indeed, so prevalent is the opinion, that we cannot judge of any picture, statue, or piece of architecture, without some qualities with which only a chosen few are endowed, that many possessing not less judgment, but more honesty, than their neighbours, confess, that for them to visit works of art is mere waste of time: they say they know what is pleasing to themselves, but cannot venture to express any opinion, because such matters seem not within the sphere of their understanding. But this is often an unfair estimate of their own capacities. With a little attention to the following directions, it is quite possible that they may prove even better qualified to give a sound opinion on works of art than many of the most confident connoisseurs of their acquaintance.

We will begin with PAINTING.

First. Request some friend of undoubted taste, who is fond of drawing, to accompany you to some extensive collection, and improve the opportunity according to the suggestions of the following anecdote:—

A youth of my acquaintance, who had been more than once in the National Gallery, without seeing the peculiar merit of any of the pictures, chanced to visit them in company with a professional painter of correct judgment and good common sense. He observed, on entering, that he knew nothing of the value of paintings, and would gladly receive a little general instruction. The painter told him to look at each picture attentively, compare it with what he knew of nature, and say honestly, not what others thought, but simply what impression it produced on his own mind. The opinions so elicited, proved nearly all to savour of truth. In some instances, the artist told him to consider if he was conversant with nature under the peculiar forms represented, and whether he knew how much lay within the sphere of art; at the same time observing that these two points would require a comparison of paintings, first with nature, and then with each other. With such hints and cautions was this youth restricted to judging on such points only as were within the range of ordinary judgment. If he felt encouraged by the frequent corroboration of his own opinions by those of the artist, he was yet more prompted to the full use of his faculties and open expression of his sentiments, by the repeated assurance that nature had made nearly all persons judges to a certain extent, and that if any were disqualified to give an opinion of nature's copyists, they were to be found among a certain set of pretending connoisseurs, whose vanity had led them to appropriate the sense and opinions of others so long, that they had lost the free use of their own. On that day my friend discovered how much he knew about paintings, and the precise points in which he was deficient; namely, that he wanted a more intimate and extensive acquaintance with nature, a knowledge of the limits of art, and correct standard of excellence in each kind of painting, as also the leading principles of perspective and composition. These are the chief points in which most common observers are deficient: therefore,

Secondly. Accustom yourself to observe landscapes, figures, &c., in nature, and compare them with paintings of similar subjects. To appreciate, for instance, the famous sea-pieces by the Vanderveldts, you must observe the degree of buoyancy in ships upon the water, of distinctness in the outlines and picturesque swelling of the sails; and so also, with reference to other pictures, observe the clouds, the tints of evening, and the foliage at different seasons, and, indeed, all other things, which works, below mentioned, will suggest.

Thirdly. Compare the paintings of those who have treated the same subject with different degrees of excellence. Do not join in decrying modern pictures, unless you can discern the exact points of their inferiority. Universal censure and universal praise are equally unphilosophical and far from truth; both must be qualified. More knowledge is required to point out beauties than defects. Things are good and bad by comparison; we must therefore study the best specimens of each kind of pictures, till they are firmly impressed upon our memory, so as to serve as a common measure or standard of excellence by which to value all others of the same class.

Fourthly. We must take every opportunity of conversing and comparing our own opinions with the opinions of others. After seeing several pictures by Claude or Titian, for example, we may read some account of their characters and a criticism on their style. Critical discussions on the styles of the ancient masters abound; every picture of celebrity has been the subject of an essay. And as to the practicability of conversing with those thoroughly conversant with art, it must be observed, that men are generally communicative on the subject of their favourite studies. It is natural with man to take an interest in those of similar taste. Doubtless the Creator ordained this sympathy between those capable of instructing each other, as a provision for the improvement of society. Such an instinct evidently prevails, and a really teachable spirit can generally find a master. The admirers of paintings of genius say, that every time they examine them they discover new beauties, and that ordinary observers frequently point out a touch of nature which the professed artist has overlooked. It is not absolutely necessary that you should meet an artist in a picture gallery. Whenever you meet a man of taste in company, the drawing-room table may furnish some book of prints taken from the works of ancient masters, which will readily furnish the occasion and the subject of a conversation. All who have money at command, if they will only inquire for one of the many ill-paid but well-deserving artists, may arrange such *peripatetic* lectures, in the National or Dulwich Gallery, as will prove a very valuable initiation into the secrets of art. Indeed, most happy should I be, if, by this casual observation, I could open a new and honourable source of emolument to a class of men who conduce very much to the refinement and ornaments of life, and receive very little in return. How many thousands are there in London, whose fathers have earned in the East sums which they are squandering in the West (end), and to whom it would, if they only thought of it, be a pleasure to be lionised for two or three mornings by a person well qualified to inform and amuse them! How many of that order of society, who are called callous, selfish, and indifferent to all wants but their own, have quite heart enough to confess that they would feel an extra relish in their own dinner, if they had earned an appetite in a way that had provided a more generous meal to one who had quite as much sensibility, though far less comfort, than themselves!

Whether my readers adopt this or any other method of improvement, they should bear in mind that their object must not be to gain mere critical knowledge, and the terms and mechanical part of the art of painting; but they should endeavour to gain a correct taste of beauty and propriety of expression, as well as a due appreciation of that invention and grandeur of conception which distinguish the highest specimens of art. Sir W. Scott exemplified the spirit in which pictures were to be studied, when he said that those of Sir David Wilkie gave him new ideas. That there are ideas in pictures is a fact which many persons have yet to learn. But, I must trust to works which will shortly follow, to show how paintings by men of genius are to be read almost like a poem, and that the conceptions of a grand imagination and a correct delineation of nature's beauties are the subject-matter of painter and poet alike, though the one conveys his impressions with the pencil and the other with the pen.

I will now enumerate the books best suited to give a general knowledge of art.

Sir Joshua Reynolds's "Discourses to the Students of the Royal Academy" have been lately published, illustrated by explanatory notes and plates by J. Burnet, F. R. S. Those who cannot procure this work may purchase, for one shilling and nine-pence, No. XXVII. of the "Student's Cabinet Library of Useful Tracts," containing a very excellent selection of those discourses. Sir Joshua, it must be observed, was a very accomplished scholar. Before Edmund Burke published his "Letters on the French Revolution," he submitted them to Sir Joshua's consideration. All of these discourses show a very superior mind, and are valuable to students of every kind of art and literature. I have scarcely known any questions arise concerning the limits and province of the imaginative arts, which these writings do not tend to elucidate.

At the same time that we read Sir Joshua's

Discourses, and all other lectures or essays on art, Pilkington's "Lives of the Painters" will be a useful handbook. Of this there is a good abstract in one small volume, by Dr. Shepherd, who selected and abridged 100 out of 1400 of the lives written by Pilkington. This is quite comprehensive enough for general purposes. I would recommend the student to procure an interleaved copy, as a convenient catalogue and critique, when he visits collections of paintings. If he sees paintings by a Claude or a Titian, by turning to their respective biographies he will have his attention directed to the peculiar characteristics of the respective styles; he will feel an interest in noting that such a landscape in such a gallery, or that such a picture exemplifies certain critical remarks.

It may be useful here to enumerate the several schools of painting. These are, —

1. The Roman school, comprehending Raphael, Cherubino Alberti, Giovanni Alberti, Caravaggio, Gauli, Michael Angelo Campidoglio, Carlo Maratti, Andrea Sacchi:

2. The Venetian school, in which are, Titian, Annibal Caracci, Tintoretto, Paolo Veronese, Ludovico Caracci, Giacomo Bassano, Francesco Bassano, Francisco Bolognese:

3. The Florentine school, with Michael Angelo

Buonarotti, Andrea del Sarto, Leonardi da Vinci:

4. The Bologna school, with Guido, Albano, Domenichino, Guercino, Lanfranc, Correggio:

5. The Flemish and Dutch, of which are Rubens, Vandyck, Rembrant, Teniers, Godfrey Kneller, Wouvermans, Vanderveldt, Albert Durer, Hans Holbein, Sir Peter Lely:

6. The French school, with Poussin, Le Brun, Perrier, Fresnoy, Claude:

7. The Spanish school, of which are Murillo, Ximenes, Velasquez, Gallego: and others in each school too many to mention.

8. Of the English school, the most remarkable are the following, noticed in Allan Cunningham's "British Painters:"— Jameson, the Scotch Vandyck; Verrio, La Guerre, and Thornhill, architectural painters; Hogarth, Wilson, Reynolds, Gainsborough, Ramsay (Scotch), Romney, Runciman (Scotch), Copley, Mortimer, Raeburn (Scotch), Hoppner, Owen, Harlow, Bonington, Cosway, Allan, Northcote, Sir T. Lawrence, Sir H. Beaumont, who aided in forming the National Gallery, Liverseege, Burnet, Fuseli, West, Bird, Barry, Blake, Opie, Morland.

Of the painters of later days, Mr. Bulwer, in his "England and the English," enumerates, in historical painting, Haydon, Hilton, Westall,

Etty, Martin; in portrait painting, Owen, Jackson, Pickersgill, Philips; in fancy painting, Wilkie, Maclise, Parris, Howard, Clint, Webster, Newton; in landscape painting, Turner, Stanfield, Fielding, Callcott, J. Wilson, Harding, Stanley, besides Landseer, Roberts, Prout, Mackensie, Lance, Derby, Cooper, Hancock, Davis.

Dr. Shepherd gives the following list of books, which he considered necessary to be consulted, in order to become a judge of painting: —

Vasari's "Lives;" Sandrart's "Lives of Painters;" Du Piles' ditto; Lord Orford's, 4 vols.; "Vertue's Life;" "Gilpin on Prints;" Dallaway's "Anecdotes;" Cochin's "Travels through Italy," 3 vols. *French;* "Richardson on Painting;" Raphael Mengs' "Works," 2 vols.; Winckelman's "Works." Forty years ago these were probably the best works; but all that is valuable in them has doubtless been adopted by later authors. The three following works, in the same list, are still popular: — Sir J. Reynolds' "Lectures," above mentioned; Cumberland's "Lives of Spanish Painters," and Fuseli's "Three Lectures;" a copy of the last is published in the "Life of Fuseli."

I have before said that a continual comparison of pictures with nature and with each other is the chief source of knowledge; still some books will quicken our observation both of nature and of art; of these the best, next to the Discourses of Sir Joshua, are "Criticisms on Art," and "Sketches of the Picture Galleries of England," by Wm. Hazlitt, containing catalogues of the principal galleries; Mrs. Jameson's "Handbook to Public Galleries of Art;" in or near London, and "Sacred and Legendary Art;" "Painting and Fine Arts," by R. B. Haydon and W. Hazlitt; Rev. R. Cattermole's "Book of the Cartoons;" "Modern Paintings," by a Graduate of Oxford, a work of much talent, and admired by the first judges of English writing. See also "Handbook of Taste," by Fabius Pictor. The works of Hogarth, with explanations of each plate, have been published in the "Penny Magazine;" but more completely in fifty-two numbers by John Nicholls, F.S.A. "Of all the paintings in the National Gallery those of Hogarth," said one of the attendants, "are examined by the greatest number of persons." Allan Cunningham's "British Painters," in the "Family Library," is a book of much general information. The same author has written a "Life of Sir David Wilkie." Much may also be derived from the "Life of Titian;" "Life of Sir Thomas Lawrence;" "Life of Fuseli."

The Art of Sculpture. Of this comparatively little remains to be said. By cultivating a taste for the highest order of painting, which is characterised, not by meretricious ornament, but by grandeur of conception and by simplicity of execution, we shall not be at a loss to judge of sculpture.

The history of sculpture is very fully given in the "Penny Cyclopædia." You will there find an enumeration of all traces of the arts found in Scripture. The extent to which it flourished among the Hebrews, Babylonians, and Phœnicians being little known, is the subject of only a few pages; but the style of sculpture, at different periods, among the Persians, Egyptians, Etrurians, Greeks, and Romans, admits of being illustrated with reference to existing remains. Of each of these schools, therefore, we have a succinct account. The history of Greek sculpture is written with peculiar care, and in the space of a few double-columned pages the reader may have a clear general view, sufficient, indeed, to give an increased interest in the collection of the British Museum, as well as in drawings of these and many other admired works not so easily accessible. The revival of the art in Italy is usually ascribed to the tenth or eleventh century, though Flaxman traces it from the age of Constantine. Fuseli remarks that the arts had never been wholly lost in Italy, because there many barbarians had been long used to behold works of art while serving in the Roman armies, and were thus animated with a nobler spirit than the less disciplined invaders of other lands. Be this as it may, the history of the revival is given in the same article, nearly down to the present time. I can recommend also the articles on Bronze, Polycletus, Phidias, Phigaleian Marbles, Elgin Marbles, Townley Marbles, Praxiteles, Benvenuto Cellini.

Allan Cunningham's "Lives of the British Sculptors" in the "Family Library" contains a good account of British art. The "Encyclopædia Britannica" has also an article on sculpture, with more criticism than that in the "Penny Cyclopædia." It is illustrated by plates, which, indeed, are almost indispensable for any essay on art which is not purely historical. Many works above mentioned, especially those on painting, throw light upon the art of sculpture: this will appear even from their titles. Mrs. Gray's "Etruria," Sir G. Wilkinson's "Egyptians," and Dr. Wordsworth's "Illustrated Greece," of course supply the best possible information on Etrurian, Egyptian, and Grecian art respectively. "Description of the Ancient Marbles in the British Museum, with Engravings," will teach the principles of criticism. "The Monumental Remains of Noble and Eminent Persons" comprises the sepulchral antiquities of Great Britain. Flaxman's "Lectures and Illustrations of Hesiod, Homer, Æschylus, and Dante," are beyond all praise. "The Life of Flaxman" and of every other sculptor will convey much general information. The British Museum, Westminster Abbey (of which a history has been written by Smith, Flaxman, and others), and almost every cathedral, must improve a visitor who carefully examines every piece of sculpture, and takes the earliest opportunity of comparing his own observations with those of men of taste.

Architecture. The same remarks as to method, prints, illustrated works, general observation, conversing with men of taste, will of course apply.

Take the article on Architecture, in Chambers' "Information for the People," price only three-halfpence — an outline, and simple woodcuts to distinguish the several Orders and Styles. Study this paper till you have a clear knowledge of its contents; and from that moment you will be much more competent to speak of architecture than most of your neighbours; so rare is it to find persons conversant with the shortest treatise, even of an easy and interesting subject. Next take Barr's "Anglican Church Architecture," an interesting detail of ecclesiastical furniture. Bloxam's "Gothic Architecture" is also very clearly written: these works have numerous engravings. As a companion or dictionary for constant reference, "The Glossary of Architecture" is admirable, containing explanations of the terms used in Grecian, Roman, Italian, and Gothic architecture, with 700 woodcuts: 400 additional examples to the same work have lately been published separately. For further information read Ruskin's "Stones of Venice," and "Lamps of Architecture," both valuable works to the man of taste; the paper on "Gally Knight's Architectural Tour," No. CXXXIX. of the "Edinburgh Review;" other papers which may be found both in the "Edinburgh" and "Quarterly," as also, in the Cyclopædias, under the terms Architecture, Arch, Architrave, Ionian, Corinthian, Pæstum, and under the name of any famous building.

Gwilt's "Encyclopædia of Architecture" is valuable for reference.

Read also, in No. XIX. of the "Family Library," the lives of William of Wykeham, Inigo Jones, Sir Christopher Wren, Sir J. Vanbrugh, James Gibbs, William Kent, and Sir W. Chambers. As an encouragement to young men of fortune to avail themselves of all the opportunities which wealth commands, I am happy to observe that Sir W. Chambers was employed by George III. when heir apparent, as a tutor in architecture.

When the student of the Fine Arts has fully availed himself of all these hints, he may be safely trusted to run alone, and choose works by the names of their authors and their titles from the classified catalogue.

CHAP. VII.

THE WAY TO STUDY THE SCRIPTURES.

LET us consider the best method of studying,

First, The text of Scripture—the Word.

Secondly, Commentaries; to which belong,

Thirdly, Biblical antiquities—Jewish history—versions of Scripture, and

Fourthly, Doctrines — Articles — the Prayer-Book.

Fifthly, The principal writers on Divinity in order.

Sixthly, Books for the closet.

1. THE TEXT OF SCRIPTURE. Select a copy of the Bible not larger than an octavo with a good margin. The one I use has uncut edges and flexible back, a minion 8vo from the Clarendon Press, without marginal references. A large

Bible is best for reading aloud, but a smaller copy for the study. Marginal references, every student blessed with an active mind should make for himself. When you make a study of the Scriptures, read with pen in hand; and decide on a few simple marks to affix to verses which are most important, as supporting doctrines, proving the genuineness or authenticity of any part of Scripture, or requiring further thought or illustration. These marks will enable you to refresh your recollection of any book of the Bible in a very short space of time. For instance, in my Bible the letters *T* mark passages most suitable for the text of a sermon, or for a rule of daily conduct. *Q* marks a difficulty, for further consideration or inquiry. When any new commentary falls in my way, I can at once test its value by passages of real difficulty. Again, *Art.* 1, 2, or 3, denotes that a verse contains a very plain proof of one of the Thirty-nine Articles. *Ch.* denotes a verse relating to the Church; besides others, as occasion suggests.

It is advisable, every time you read a book of Scripture, to propose one subject for particular attention. Read the Gospels, once, to see wherein they agree and wherein they differ, and mark M. Mk. L. J., according as St. Matthew, Mark, Luke, or John have also mentioned any parable, miracle, or other memorable part of our Lord's history occurring in the Gospel before you. Read the Gospels a second time for internal evidence of their truth. A third time with a Diatessaron to mark the order of events or any other matter of instruction. To those fond of literature, the Scriptures will have also another and a wholly different value for literary and secular purposes; for the Bible is allowed to be the most curious book in the world. It contains more knowledge of life and of the human heart than all the writings of Shakspeare, Horace, Clarendon, Thucydides, put together. The Bible comprises all that was discovered, and much more that was overlooked, by the philosophers of ancient and modern times. And the proof is this;—Butler may be said to have been the corrector of the ancient ethical writers. Mackintosh, Robert Hall, and Dr. Chalmers, no inconsiderable writers of modern times, acknowledge that they were taught by Butler, and Butler pretends only to have been taught by Scripture. Well then might the Rev. H. Melville say, "It is a truth made known to us by God, and at the same time demonstrable by reason, that in going through the courses of Bible instruction, there is a better mental discipline, whether for the child or for the adult, than in any of the cleverly devised methods for opening and strengthening the faculties."

It is advisable, however, to distinguish when we take up the Scriptures to gather the precious seed and when to examine the husk — when to read the Word and when the letter; and since the mind, no less than the heart, is a talent to improve, and since ignorance of the Scriptures is a disgrace no less to the scholar than the man; it is convenient for literary purposes to keep a separate copy, in which to enter observations, as we read of Oriental customs, Jewish antiquities, discoveries in Nineveh, or any thing illustrative of Scripture. To show the interest and satisfaction which results from being thus so methodical in the pursuit of knowledge, I will select from one of my own Bibles a few notes, which, without the method recommended, might pass unheeded through the mind.

At Gen. vi. 15., "The length, depth, and width of the 'Great Britain' steam-ship is in feet exactly what the Ark was in cubits!"

Acts, xxviii. 1. That *Melita* is Malta (though Coleridge says not) is ingeniously proved by the observation that the same wind which drifted a vessel from the Fair Havens under Clauda would in *fourteen days* carry it to Malta, and nowhere else.

Acts, xxviii. 13. "*Fetched a compass.*" A friend, in making the same voyage from Syracuse to Rhegium recently, observed that a considerable *sailing round,* as the Greek means literally, was, from the Gulf stream, unavoidable.

Deut. xxviii. 65—7. The text of the conscience-stricken Dr. Dodd, the Sunday before he was apprehended for forgery, "The Lord shall give thee there a trembling heart," &c.

Gen. viii. 9. The *dove.* Dr. Meuse says that the N. American Indians have a tradition of a *big canoe,* in which came *eight persons* across the water, *caused by the Great Spirit.* They hold the willow sacred, because *a dove flew with it from the canoe.* Many similar curiosities are found in Cardinal Wiseman's Lectures.

The 46th Psalm was Luther's favourite; the 15th, Feltham's; the 103rd and 145th, Miss Hannah More's: the 139th, she said, "surpassed any of Pindar's." The best translation of the 139th, "By the rivers of Babylon," was by Camoens while in exile. This also is about the best of all Buchanan's translations.

Isaiah, xiv. 102. was the text of the Presbyterians at Perth, before Charles Stuart, 19th September, 1745.

John, i. 1. At Otaheitc, the names of the superior deities are the Father, the Son, and the Friend Bird, which inspires the priests.—*Serle's Horæ Solitariæ.*

Job, xxix. This chapter moved Sir J. Mackintosh to tears on his death-bed.

These instances will exemplify my meaning.

Again, the poetry of the Bible and the beauties of natural and simple diction deserve attention. To commit them to memory is the best exercise for the improvement of taste. Wordsworth once remarked that he knew no poetry finer than that of Jeremiah. Mrs. Hemans justly preferred St. John to the other Evangelists. Coleridge considered the "Epistle to the Romans" the finest of St. Paul's compositions. The "Epistle to the Ephesians" exhibits a train of thought as far superior to ordinary minds and motives as anything ever written. These are hints for the exercise of criticism. Whenever you read, compare scripture with scripture. Commentaries at best are only like advisers, who may assist for the moment, but never yet made any man wise. While you trust to commentators, you will never gain the full use of your own faculties, nor enjoy anything better than an insipid spiritless dilution of scriptural truth. With respect to the difficulties of Holy Writ, either they can be solved in an obvious and satisfactory way or they cannot. If they can, a person of ordinary understanding, by examining the context and seeking similar expressions may solve the difficulties as well as any commentator; if they cannot, the opinions of commentators, though sometimes instructive, are frequently of little use, differing widely from each other, being enveloped in a cloud of words, and more fanciful than reasonable. One hour's study with marginal references is worth ten with notes. "Every reader his own commentator."

Learn by heart one verse of the Bible every day. One of my friends takes the first verse which meets his eye as the Bible happens to open. A better plan is to mark the verses you prefer in several books, and learn them in order. If one verse is too little, choose a second or a third from a different part; but do not try too much at first. The great thing is never to omit one verse each day. Do not despise the importance of this method; still less the self-command which constancy, in its performance, requires. I warn you that it is not very easy to learn 365 verses in the year without being one day in arrears. If you miss a day, do not allow yourself to make it up; but let the inequality between the number of the verses and the days remain as a punishment. Perseverance and regularity will insure a surprising knowledge of the more familiar texts of Scripture. Remember, all depends on the regularity and uninterrupted habit. Mark the 30 or 31 verses on the first day of each month, and consider you have failed, unless the number of the day and of the verse coincide. The Hebrew or Greek version is to be preferred by scholars; still none should omit the English.

One of my friends, a young lady, takes much interest in writing out the verses to which the marginal references of the Bible allude. Her paper is ruled by the stationer with one vertical column about two inches wide for the text; the rest of the page is ruled. One line also preserves a fair margin that the work may in future years admit of being bound. This is a much more profitable employment than knitting and crochet, though there is a time for both. Who would not be more proud of a mother who bequeathed him a Commentary than a Quilt?

The Society for the Diffusion of Christian Knowledge has published a prayer-book with marginal references. In the last age young ladies used to be taught at school to present their mammas with a sampler; if every young lady and young gentleman too were required to produce a neat copy of all the scripture proofs of our liturgy, or certain parts of it, what a wonderful extension of scriptural knowledge would result!

Another exercise, really invaluable to clergymen especially, is to make a scriptural common-place book. This will require the use of two books—one as a day-book, another as a ledger. The day-book must be always at hand as you read the Bible from end to end. In this you will write down promiscuously any illustration of the divine attributes, as also of faith, justification, types, prophecies, and many other topics, as you please. Then, in your ledger, you will enter each of these under its proper head, which you will also notice with the number of the page in the index. A small work of this kind was published by Dr. Chalmers.

Lastly, attend particularly to the style, dates, and proofs of the genuineness and authenticity of the several books of Scripture; and read the history of the different translations. For this purpose Gray's or Percy's "Key," Tomline, or Horne's "Introduction," will be serviceable, and especially Dr. Wordsworth's "Canons of Scripture."

2. Works of Commentary and Notes.—We will now specify some of the valuable works explanatory of the several parts of Scripture.

1. *On the whole of the Bible,* Horne's "Introduction" contains information so varied, that few persons can require more. It contains also useful instructions on theological reading. The "Epitome of Horne's Introduction," and "Key to the Bible," by the Society, will be useful for

those who have less time for study. The "Commentaries to the Bible" by Mant, Henry, Clarke, and others, and especially Scott's "Commentary" are well known; but Dr. Copleston truly said, that nothing equalled that by Whitgift and others. Simeon's Discourses or Commentary is the most useful work a country clergyman can possess for writing sermons—very sober, sensible, and practical.

2. *On the Old Testament*, Gray's "Key" is very valuable. A similar work by Bishop Tomline is also useful. Bishop Horsley's "Biblical Criticism" is highly esteemed. A new edition is now advertised in a convenient form.

3. *On separate portions and subjects of Scripture.* On the Pentateuch, Grave's "Lectures" display much useful learning. The "Horæ Mosaicæ," by G. S. Faber, 1818, is much admired for scriptural learning and truth. Warburton's "Divine Legation" is one of the standdard pieces of English literature. On the Prophecies generally, read Sir I. Newton and Davison's "Discourses upon Prophecy," also Keith. On the minor Prophets, Bishop New come and George Hutcheson (1675) have written. The first is termed "critical and useful," the second "pithy, full, and spiritual." On the historical parts, read "History of the Bible," and "History of the Jews." Also a most useful

analysis given at the end of Mant's Bible. On the whole of the New Testament, Percy's "Key to the New Testament" is very popular. Hammond, on the New Testament, has written the most learned Commentary and the most satisfactory for the scholar. Burkitt, excellent in drawing out every text into its full and legitimate signification, is better for the general reader. Campbell's "Four Gospels translated," Elsley's Annotations on the Gospels *and Acts*, are good for scholars, who should also read the "Diatessaron," to mark the order of events. On the Parables and Miracles, read two able works by Rev. Chevenix French. On the Epistles of St. Paul, Paley's "Horæ Paulinæ" will never be superseded. Shuttleworth's "Paraphrase of the Epistles" is the most concise and generally useful commentary; but the scholar may consult the new works by Dr. Peile and Mr. Alford on particular difficulties. Conybeare and Howson's "Life, &c. of St. Paul," should be in the library of every biblical student. On the Epistles of St. Peter, Dr. Leighton's book is one of the first of scripture classics.

4. *On Biblical Antiquities.* Many works combine entertainment with instruction; such as Jennings' "Jewish Antiquities;" Lightfoot's works; Shuckford's "Sacred and Profane His-

tory Connected;" Prideaux's "Connection of the Old and New Testament;" Harris's "Natural History of the Bible;" Burder's "Oriental Customs and Literature;" Calcott's "Scripture Herbal;" Townley's "Illustrations of Biblical Literature;" Carpenter's "Scripture Natural History, or an Account of the Zoology, Botany, and Geology of the Bible."

All of these works are highly valued. Those of Lightfoot, Shuckford, and Prideaux, are standard classics. The last six, though not less improving, may be termed light reading, and give agreeable relief to severer studies.

3. On Doctrine. — *Of the Person and offices of Christ.* Horne recommends Stuart's "Letters to Dr. Channing" as admirably depicting the subtle criticisms of an accomplished Unitarian, in a fine spirit of Christian philosophy. Gurney's "Biblical Notes to confirm the Deity of Christ," is considered a very able illustration of texts of Scripture. *On the offices of the Holy Spirit.* Serle's "Horæ Solitariæ" exhausts the subject. In his chapter on the Trinity, he has availed himself of his extensive classical learning. Heber's "Bampton Lectures" are on the Holy Ghost as the Comforter. Of Dr. Burton's Sermons, two treat of the sin of blasphemy against the Holy Ghost, in a very sound and consistent

manner. On the Trinity, Serle's Essay, above mentioned, and Horne's "Scripture Doctrine of the Trinity;" also sermons and works too obvious to mention. On Election and Predestination there are some very fair and reasonable remarks in "Christ our Example." Bishop Tomline's "Refutation of Calvinism" gives all that can be said on one side, and Thomas Scott's "Remarks on Bishop Tomline's 'Refutation,'" on the other. Read the 17th Article in Burnet. Copleston on "Necessity and Predestination," alludes to Scott, and terms him the most pious and temperate of modern Calvinists, though his doctrine of predestination, he says, "appears to me mistaken and dangerous." Archbishop Sumner's Sermons on this subject are the best of all his writings. The Rev. J. Scott, in the life of his father, shows that he was very cautious of bringing this doctrine before a mixed congregation, and once observed of Wilberforce's book, that it was "not Calvinistic, and so much the better, being more suited to the class of persons to whom it was addressed." In studying this doctrine, we should consider whether authors do not dispute about a word, while they agree about the thing.

On Faith and Justification, read Bishop Barlow's "Two Letters on Justification." Of this it was said by Archdeacon Browne, "The subject is treated with a degree of closeness of reasoning and logical accuracy, which defies confutation." Also Burnet's 11th Article. The sentiments of the writers of the first four centuries are given in Wall's "History of Infant Baptism." This, with Bethel's much-admired work, exhausts the subject of baptism. Read especially Burnet on the 27th Article. On the Lord's Supper, Burnet on the Articles 25, 26, 28, 29, 30, and Beveridge's Articles are equally valuable.

4. Reading for Controversialists. — 1. Against Infidelity. Paley's "Evidences of Christianity," I have already mentioned. Almost the whole is easily intelligible, and many chapters so interesting as to require but little effort. It is universally allowed to be one of the first argumentative works in the English language. Paley's "Horæ Paulinæ," is also very convincing. With this we may class Keith on the Prophecies, and the works of Bishops Hurd and Newton; as also Campbell on the Miracles. All of these combine explanation with argument. Shuttleworth's "Consistency of Revelation with Human Reason," is especially valuable, because it meets the difficulties most likely to occur to men of fair minds, honestly open to conviction. And Cardinal Wiseman's "Lectures on Science and Revealed Religion"

is a work valuable to the scholar, the general reader, and the theologian, and happily unqualified by the errors of his Church. Graves on the Pentateuch is a very learned work, yet easy to understand. Of "Watson's Apology for the Bible," George III. observed, he "did not know that the Bible needed any apology," not considering that Justin Martyr and others of the early Christians used to set forth defences of the Gospel under the name of Apologia, which, in Greek, means a defence. Watson and Graves wrote in answer to the cavils of Paine and other infidels of the French Revolution. M'Ilvaine's "Lectures on Evidences," gives an account of the death of Paine, which, if well known, would be the best antidote to the poison of his life; it is an intelligible selection from Paley and others, and containing some little original matter.

Of Butler's "Analogy," I knew one who said that he always doubted till he read it, and never doubted after. The reasoning is too deep for many readers, yet I would have all give it a trial. I have known cases in which it has been comprehended by those who had the greatest diffidence in attempting it. Gregory's "Letters" are much recommended, as giving a plain and easy exposition of difficulties. Sumner's "Evidences," Lardner's "Credibility," Gibson's "Pastoral

Letters," Jenkin's "Reasonableness," and Stillingfleet's "Origines Sacræ," are all works of authority. Paley and Butler, if well read and digested, nearly exhaust the subject. Butler shows that there is no reason why we should not believe, and Paley that there is much reason why we should. Shuttleworth is the best substitute for Butler. The value of the "Analogy" cannot be fully appreciated without considering the urgency of the times in which it was written. Butler observes, "It comes, I know not how, to be taken for granted, that Christianity is now at length discovered to be fictitious." Horace Walpole said that Queen Caroline particularly recommended his father to read it; indeed, it was wanted in high life; for Lady Mary Wortley Montagu, even while she expresses her alarm at so many young ladies being infidels, speaks in a way which shows she regarded religion as rather useful than true.

Robert Hall's sermon, on "Modern Infidelity," is very celebrated. This is a masterly composition, showing enlarged and comprehensive views.

2. In controversy with Jews, Bishop Kidder's "Demonstration of the Messiah," and Thomas Scott's "Discussion on the principal Question between the Jews and Christians," in reply to the Rabbi Crool. Of course all other works on

evidences will be of much service; but Scott's reply to the Rabbi's "Restoration of Israel," teaches us to avail ourselves of every advantage which the faith of a Jewish adversary affords, and "discuss every important question concerning the Messiah of the Old Testament, on the ground of the Old Testament only."

3. Against Popery, Finch's "Sketch of the Roman Controversy" contains a valuable collection of documents from many sources; Bishop Marsh's "Comparative View of the Churches of England and Rome;" M'Ghee's "Truth and Error contrasted," and especially Dr. Phillpott's (the Bishop of Exeter's) "Letters to Dr. Butler," occasioned by the Committee evidence given by Dr. Butler at the time of the Roman Catholic question. Pascal's "Provincial Letters" affords the most witty and keen exposure of the Jesuits. Both for the brilliancy of composition and the influence they exerted, these letters hold the highest place in the history of literature. A bookseller's catalogue will point out many other works.

The "Eclipse of Faith" will be found to be a full armoury against the assaults that have been more recently directed against the orthodox doctrines of Christianity.

4. *Against Arianism,* read Whittaker's "His-

tory of Arianism;" Burnet's "Articles," and the works which are recommended on the Trinity. This course of reading will apply also,

5. Against Socinianism; read also J. Edwards's "Preservative against Socinianism;" Wardlaw's "Discourses on the principal Points of the Socinian Controversy;" and Fuller's "Calvinistic and Socinian Systems compared."

6. Against Dissenters from the Established Church. The great champion of the Established Church is Hooker. His "Ecclesiastical Polity," like the writings of most men of true genius, is calculated to enrich and expand the reader's views on a variety of subjects. But Hooker is too grave a writer for the youthful student. Thelwall's "Letters on the Church," one volume duodecimo, explains, in a clear and familiar way, the nature of the Establishment, the excellence of our liturgy, and the importance of a national church. Boyd, on "Episcopacy," enters more deeply into the origin and authority of our Church. To those who have not time to read Mr. Boyd's larger work, I would strongly recommend his "Lecture on Episcopacy," delivered at Cheltenham. Mr. Thelwall recommends M'Neile's "Letters on the Church;" also the Rev. A. M'Caul's three sermons on "The Divine Commission of the Christian Ministry," and the

"Principles of a Church Establishment." To the general reader, a truly valuable work is "Essays on the Church," by a layman. This author modestly pretends to be only a compiler, one who, having read all the pamphlets for or against the dissenters which appeared about the year 1833, endeavours to bring the whole argument within the compass of one small volume. Add Chalmers on "Church Establishments;" also an article in the Edinburgh Review, vol. xxvi. From Dr. Dwight's "Travels in New England and New York," we learn how little the "case of America" proves against an establishment; an extract is given in "Essays on the Church." Let me not be understood to say, or even to wish, that dissenters may be reasoned down. The worst dissenting teaching, where there is no church, is better than heathen ignorance. Let churchmen maintain the true standard of pure doctrine, and this will insensibly restrain the wildness of the dissenters' tenets; and gradually, by church building and endowments, let us supply their place. Still, I doubt that the three classes, the gentry, the tradesmen, and the labourers, will ever be successfully treated by a ministry composed of the gentry alone. Then, would I institute another class, say of deacons, from a rank below?—No; a Roman Catholic hierarchy might control such an order of men, but not so the free spirit of a Protestant church. Without that self-knowledge and that discipline resulting from our public schools and universities, which characterises the present order of the clergy, any new order taken from a lower rank would be only nominally churchmen, but really as independent as dissenters are now. Besides, dissent is (partly by exclusive dealing) self-supporting; but whence shall we find a maintenance for the same men in the Church? And, would they work better? If we had greater order, should we have equal energy? Think of these things.

5. THE PRINCIPAL WRITERS ON DIVINITY.— A mere list of authors will seem of little use; but my object is to induce the student to follow some method in his selection; to read writers of the same period at the same time, in order to learn the peculiar character of each school of Theology. The different styles of composition and changes in theological writing may also be noticed; and, more particularly, the recent change from the weighty to the wordy style, with smooth sounds instead of hard sense. The number of volumes of a serious character read by some persons in the course of a year is so great that if, instead of mere casual recommendation, they would be guided by the following lists of writers, they

might soon gain a very extensive knowledge of Theological literature.

The classification is that of the Rev. E. Bickersteth, in his "Christian Student," first published in 1829. This is a valuable guide in Divinity studies. Since its publication many good works have appeared; and not a few have been rendered available by translations, selections, and reprinting.

First. The FATHERS. Dr. Chalmers fairly says, "We ought not to cast the Book of Antiquity away from us, but give it our most assiduous perusal, while at the same time we sit in the exercise of our free and independent judgment over its contents."—The Fathers are now accessible by means of English translations; and it is time that the remembrance of all the tales of pale students, dusty folios, and the midnight lamp in monastic cells, which used to be associated with the very names of the Fathers had passed away; and, as to those prejudiced persons who do not hesitate to avow an utter indifference to the writings of the Fathers, I have only to say, that to feel no curiosity about the compositions of the first and foremost of Christian champions in times the most critical to the faith, men who bequeathed to us the readiest weapons against the sceptics of modern times—to care nothing about

Justin Martyr, Tertullian, Cyprian, Chrysostom, Athanasius, Augustine — to feel no curiosity about the works of those who, like Jerome and Origen, have done much to restore and preserve the pure text of Scripture, — of Ignatius, the disciple of St. John—of Clement, "whose name is in the book of life,"— this certainly betrays a feeling hard indeed to reconcile with a due sense of our Gospel privileges. "It is difficult indeed to be insensible," says Mr. Conybeare, in his Lectures, "to the beauty, the piety, the devotion, and the spiritual feeling which are found in almost every page of the Commentary of Augustine." Whoever doubts that the works of the Fathers have a real appreciable value, founded not in the mere curiosities of ancient literature, but on good and useful service done, should read the "Evidences" of Paley, and then consider whether his leading arguments could be maintained without the testimony of the Fathers; and whether these arguments are not indispensable to the defence of Christianity upon external evidence. The reason I instance Paley's work in preference to any other evidences is, that its style and way of reasoning is of a most popular kind; and while many other works may confirm those who believe, Paley is convincing to those who doubt. It is related of the Duke of Wellington that, on hearing one of his officers speak lightly of Revelation, he asked him, "Did you ever read Paley?"— "Then you are not qualified to give an "No."— opinion."

The translations to which I alluded form the "Library of the Fathers of the Holy Catholic Church." Also in "The Christian's Family Library" there is one volume, entitled "The Christian Fathers of the First and Second Century; their Principal Remains at large; with Selections from their other Writings." Milner and Mosheim may both be consulted for the general character of the Fathers; also, Horne's "Introduction." Conybeare's "Bampton Lectures," contain an analytical examination into the character, value, and just application of the writings of the Christian Fathers during the Ante-Nicene period. Dr. Burton also published "Testimonies of the Ante-Nicene Fathers to the Divinity of Christ." In the works of N. Lardner (a Socinian writer) we have a careful examination of the testimony which the fathers have afforded to the Scriptures. Dr. Clarke's "Succession of Sacred Literature," with his "Bibliographical Miscellany," and more particularly Cave's "Lives of the Fathers of the First Four Ages of the Church," are books of high authority.

Secondly. The SCHOOLMEN. At the beginning of the Reformation a monk declared that Greek was "the mother of all heresy," and that as to Hebrew, "it is certain that all who learn it become instantly Jews." For this abhorrence of learning we must blame its abuse by the Schoolmen, of whom Luther said "they did nothing but propose paradoxes, and that their whole art was built on a contempt of Scripture." Bonaventura, Aquinas, Bradwardine, Wickliffe, Huss, and Jerome, are the names of the principal Schoolmen; the life and opinions of Wickliffe have been written by Mr. Vaughan. Estius's Sum is considered to contain the best account of the Scholastic Divinity. The best advice I can offer the general reader is conveyed in the words of Leighton; for, truly did Leighton say, "To understand and be master of those trifling disputes that prevail in the schools, is an evidence of a very mean understanding."

Thirdly. The REFORMERS. Tindal, Latimer, Cranmer, Ridley, and Philpot, Bradford, Jewell, Fox, Knox, are the writers whose lives and opinions are most worthy of attention. A work in twelve volumes by the Religious Tract Society gives selections from their works, as well as from those of Bale, Barnes, Becon, Bilney, Borthwick, Clement, Frith, Gilby, Lady J. Grey, Hamilton,

Hooper, Joye, Lambert, Queen Parr, Ponet, Rogers, Sampson, Saunders, Taylor, Wickliffe, and Wishart. More matter of the same kind will be found in Legh Richmond's "Fathers of the English Church," and in Bickersteth's "Testimony of the Reformers." Mr. Le Bas has written the lives of Cranmer, Wickliffe, Jewell, and Laud. The "English Martyrology," abridged from Foxe, by Charlotte Elizabeth, a most able writer, forms two small volumes in "The Christian's Family Library." Of the Foreign Reformers, Luther, Melancthon, Erasmus, Calvin, Zuinglius, Œcolampadius, Martyr, Bucer, Beza, Bullinger, are men with whom, either by biography (especially D'Aubigné's), or extracts, we have many opportunities of becoming acquainted. Ranke's "German Reformation" and "Lives of the Popes" are much admired, as also are Dr. Wordsworth's "Biographies" and "Christian Institutes."

Fourthly. The SUCCESSORS OF THE REFORMERS. Hooker's "Ecclesiastical Polity" is universally allowed to be the strongest bulwark of the Established Church. In this work there is a wonderful weight of words, a most appropriate selection of topics and cogent reasoning. This author is usually quoted as "the Judicious Hooker." His life, by Isaac Walton, is one of the most valuable pieces of biography in our language. He died A. D. 1600. Richard Sibbes died about thirty-five years after Hooker. The "Bruised Reed" and "Soul's Conflict" are the titles of two of Sibbes' best works. Archbishop Usher died A. D. 1656. He was called by Dr. Johnson "the great luminary of the Irish church." He is famed for having read all the Fathers. Mr. Bickersteth mentions Usher's "Answer to the Jesuit," as one of the best pieces against Romanism. Usher's works complete, fill eighteen volumes, now publishing in a handsome form, at 12*s.* each. A collection of Usher's Letters with his Life were published by his chaplain, Dr. Richard Parr. Dr. Hammond, the chaplain of Charles I. in Carisbrook Castle, wrote a Paraphrase of the New Testament, with the most learned and valuable notes. Sanderson also, attached to Charles and, to compensate for persecution, elevated to the bishopric of Lincoln at the Restoration, wrote "Nine Cases of Conscience," and "Discourse on the Church." Dr. Mede is accounted the ablest interpreter of obscure prophecy. Jeremy Taylor is a writer of great fertility and depth of thought. His defence of episcopacy and the Liturgy were much admired by Bishop Heber, who thought Taylor, in imagination and real genius, superior either to

Hooker or Barrow. Few writers have been more gleaned by modern divines. Jeremy Taylor's life has been written by Bonney and Wilmott. Bishops Babington, Cowper, Greenham, and Andrews, lived in this period.

Fifthly. The NONCONFORMISTS. These comprise all who separated from the Liturgy and ceremonies of the Church, from the Reformation till modern times. On this period, "The Christian Student" is strongly to be recommended. However great our sorrow for dissent, we must not think lightly of the writings of dissenters, or we shall forego some of the most valuable works on practical piety. When certain persons once complained to Lord Burleigh of the Liturgy, and said they only wished its amendment, he told them to make a better. Accordingly, one class of the complainants formed a new one, like that of Geneva; another class altered the new one in 600 particulars; a third, quarrelling about the alteration, proposed an entirely different model, and a fourth dissented from all! Dr. Owen was famed for sound learning and judgment. His writings are numerous, and are of a high Calvinistic character. Read the article on Baxter's life and writings in the Edinburgh Magazine, 1843. He was chaplain to Whalley's regiment after the battle of Naseby. He tried to reconcile Calvinism with

Arminianism. Baxter wrote 145 treatises, of which four were folios, seventy-three quartos, and forty-nine octavos. He wrote much in gaol, under the unjust sentence of Jeffries. Charnock was famed for masculine style and originality of thought; his "Discourses on Providence" are considered the best. Dr. Goodwin was a favourite of Cromwell, whom he attended on his death-bed; he wrote sermons, expositions, and controversial treatises. Howe is nervous and majestic. Robert Hall said Burke was the best author for earth, and Howe for heaven. Howe's "Living Temple" is very celebrated. I would particularly recommend the work by Howe among the "Sacred Classics." Dr. Bates was fluent, with beautiful similitudes. Flavel was fervent, touching the conscience, and moving the feelings. Caryl officiated with Dr. Owen as a minister to Cromwell. He wrote a "Commentary on Job" in 12 vols. 4to.

Matthew Pool: the "Synopsis Criticorum," in five folios, was his chief work. Read Neal's "Puritans."

Sixthly. The Divines of the Restoration and Revolution. This era was marked, says Bishop Heber, by a school of literature and composition, of all others which this country has seen, the least favourable to genius, and the most unlike that style of thinking and expression which had distinguished Jeremy Taylor and his contemporaries. What Augustine said of Cicero has been remarked of more than one of the following writers, "that we cease to be captivated with him, because the name of Christ does not occur in him." We may mention Bishop Burnet. Read his "Articles," "Reformation," and "Own Times."—Bishop Reynolds, very terse and full; devotional and controversial, a strong Calvinist.—Archbishop Leighton: his Commentary on St. Peter has been already mentioned.—Bishop Beveridge, very learned in Oriental literature. He wrote on the Thirty-nine Articles. His "Private Thoughts" are most known, and published among the "Sacred Classics;" and his "Sermons" are most judiciously recommended by the present Bishop of Exeter as guides in composition to candidates for ordination.—Archbishop Tillotson: Locke considered Tillotson and Chillingworth very remarkable for perspicuity. Heber speaks of "the dull good sense of Tillotson." Tillotson attended with Dr. Burnet at the execution of Lord William Russell. He was accused of Socinianism, Dr. Jortin says, because, in making some concessions to the Socinians, he had broken through one ancient rule of controversy, "allow not an adversary either common sense or common honesty." In answer to this charge he republished four of his sermons "On the Incarnation and Divinity." His sermons are best known. As to the style in which he wrote, read "Fitzosborne's Letters" by Melmoth, who qualifies the excessive praise it had long received.—Isaac Barrow was so deep and copious, that Charles II. used to call him an *unfair* preacher, because he left nothing to be said after him! Barrow's sermons are a mine of brilliant thoughts and sterling arguments. He was a great mathematician, deemed second only to Sir Isaac Newton. His sermon on "vain and idle talking" is quoted by Addison, as a specimen of singular felicity of expression.—Stillingfleet: his writings against Popery are very valuable. His "Origines Britannicæ" give antiquities of the churches of Britain. The elegance and learning of the "Origines Sacræ" has made it yet more popular. Stillingfleet had a controversy with Locke, arising from remarks made in his "Defence of the Doctrine of the Trinity."—Dr. Thomas Jackson, Southey said, was an author with whom, more than any other, one might be contented in a prison, as the most valuable of all the old Divines, though the least known — also recommended by Bishop Horne. — John Locke wrote "On the Reasonableness of Christianity," and Paraphrases and Notes to several of St. Paul's Epistles.—Robert South held a controversy with Sherlock on the Trinity. His sermons are well known. His style is nervous, with much point and even wit. His writings are in great repute.—William Sherlock wrote against the dissenters.—Thomas Sherlock, his son, wrote a tract well worth reading, called "The Trial of the Witnesses of the Resurrection."—Wilson, Bishop of the Isle of Man, published "Ecclesiastical Constitutions," of which Lord Chancellor King said that "if the ancient discipline of the Church were lost, it might be found in the Isle of Man." He wrote also sermons and tracts.—William Law: his "Serious Call to a Religious Life" was considered by Dr. Johnson one of the most powerful works of the kind. His "Practical Treatise on Christianity" is also very good.—Bishop Warburton's "Julian," "Alliance of Church and State," and "Divine Legation," are much admired. Read Dr. Johnson's character of Warburton in his "Life of Pope." It was said that Bishop Bull was his master, and Jeremy Taylor his favourite divine.— Bishop Watson answered Paine and Gibbon. His "Apology" has been already mentioned.—Archbishop Secker wrote "Sermons and Lectures on the Church Catechism."—Bishop Berkeley fell dead while hearing a sermon, written by Dr. Sherlock. He is more known as a philosopher than as a divine.

—Bishop Butler, the author of the Sermons and Analogy already mentioned.

Seventhly. MODERN WRITERS. Dr. Horne, author of the "Introduction." Jonathan Edwards, who wrote on "Justification." Romaine, author of the most popular book on Faith. Milner, author of the "Church History." Jones, of Nayland, deemed one of the most satisfactory writers on the Trinity. Newton, the history of whose life is universally recommended, as also are his letters. Scott, the author of the "Commentary." Robert Hall, one of the finest writers in the English language; clear, candid, and very powerful. Bishop Horsley, the author of "Biblical Criticism."

ON THE PRAYER-BOOK. — Read, first, the "History of the Prayer-Book," by the C. K. Society (this is a small volume, containing a useful addition to Church History); Shepherd, "On the Common Prayer;" Wheatley's "Illustration of Common Prayer;" Nelson's "Companion for the Fasts and Festivals;" and Mant "On the Liturgy," are all standard works. On "The Rubrics and Canons of the Church," a work much recommended, was written in 1753, by Thomas Sharp. "Lectures and Sermons on the Liturgy" have been published by Bishop Jebb, 2 vols. 8vo., 1830; Thomas Rogers, 2 vols.

8vo.; Bishop J. Bird Sumner, 8vo. (more particularly on the Fasts and Festivals): Matthew Hole, 4 vols. 8vo., 1838 (a new edition); and others. Bishop Taylor's "Apology for the Liturgy" Heber considered among the best of Taylor's "Polemical Discourses." Cardwell's "Liturgies," Faber's "Origines Liturgicæ," and Maskell's "Ancient Liturgy," are all able works. The Liturgies of Edward VI., published by Parker in one volume, may be compared in a single morning with much advantage.

The Rev. J. E. Riddle's "Ecclesiastical Chronology, or Annals of the Church," containing History, the relations of the Church to the State; controversies, sects, rites, discipline, writers, is a most compendious and useful book.

On the Church of England, besides the above,—

Bishop Jewell's famous "Apology for the Church of England," written in Latin, and translated by the mother of Sir Francis Bacon, is considered to have promoted the Reformation more than any other book. This, with Hooker's "Polity," Burnet's "Articles," and Nicholson "On the Book of Common Prayer," will constitute unexceptionable expositions of the doctrines of the Church of England.

Mr. Martineau's "Church History in England" contains an admirable and a very fair account of any thing relating to the Church previous to the Reformation.

CHAP. VIII.

ON THE STUDY OF POETRY — CRITICISM — TASTE.

"THEY who have known what it is," says Hallam, "in solitude, or in the intervals of worldly care, to feed on poetical recollections — to murmur over the beautiful lines whose cadence has long delighted their ear — to recall the sentiments and images with all the charm of early associations,— they will feel the inestimable value of committing to memory, in the prime of power, what it will easily and indelibly retain." Therefore, time is well spent in committing fine poetry to memory.

Lord Jeffrey says that, on an average, 10,000 lines of good poetry were published annually, and asked, "How shall posterity keep pace with the growing literature of the times?" In reply, we offer the following hints for a judicious selection:—

Johnson's "Lives of the Poets," with Campbell's "Essay," and Moir's "Sketches of the Poetical Literature of the last Half-Century," are indispensable as handbooks to direct attention to the choicest pieces.

The lives of most literary men supply notices of admired pieces, which should be read as the notices of them occur.

Of *Chaucer* few read more than one or two Tales as a specimen. Thomas Moore said he looked in vain for the qualities for which Chaucer was admired by other men of high literary character.

Spenser: one of the most poetical, and certainly the most perspicuous of all Poets; an author whom men of deep poetic feeling fondly read, and others distantly admire.

Pope said, that to hear a canto of Spenser was like seeing a gallery of pictures. When Horace Walpole was planning a bower at Strawberry Hill, he said, "I am almost afraid I must go and read Spenser, and wade through his allegories, to get at a picture." Lord Chatham's sister used to accuse him of knowing nothing but the "Fairy Queen;" "and no matter," said Burke, "for he who reads and relishes Spenser will have a strong hold of the English language."

Shakespeare. As every man of education is supposed to be familiar with Shakespeare, the following hints may be of very general service:—part are the kind suggestions, and nearly all meet the approval, of John Payne Collier, whose one volume edition, be it remembered, incorporates about 1000 corrections from the margin of his lately discovered folio, dated 1632—corrections (as a little inquiry will convince every reader) nearly as satisfactory as if made by Shakespeare's own hand.

Shakespeare's Plays are commonly divided into Comedies, Histories and Tragedies. "Pericles" was the first written, and "The Tempest" the last—a play which proves that Shakespeare's poetic spirit did not fail at fifty years of age. Chaucer and Young were never more truly poets than at sixty; Dryden was best at seventy; and Sophocles wrote his "Œdip. Coloneus" at eighty!

1. *Comedies of Shakespeare.* "The Winter's Tale" is more than marvellous; almost a miraculous composition, and the best comedy in any language. "Twelfth Night" and "As you like it" are next in merit. The least agreeable is "All's well that ends well." "The Tempest" is a play wholly unlike any other dramatic effort, and wonderful from the first line to the last.

As to "Midsummer's Night's Dream" it is a happy composition in every sense, and shows, says Thomas Campbell, that Shakespeare did once at least compose in a state of joyous ecstasy and delight. He adds, in "Measure for Measure." "Much ado about Nothing," and "Comedy of Errors," with every allowance for tales of fiction, our credulity is taxed to a fault. To eulogise "Romeo and Juliet" is gilding refined gold; and "Cymbeline," involves a refutation of old Johnson's "dictum" that we had no right to be pleased with poetry beyond our ability to say why and wherefore. This dictum certainly may be carried too far; but generally, in Poetry, as in Religion, a man should be able to render a reason for the faith that is in him.

2. *The Historical Plays.* The three parts of "Henry VI." were written first. Campbell was happy to believe that "Henry VI." pt. i. with the burning of Joan of Arc, as also "Titus Andronicus," were not by Shakespeare. Mr. Collier is convinced that Shakespeare did write "Titus Andronicus;" he also thinks that if he did not write, he certainly added to the first part of "Henry VI."

In "Henry VI.," pt. ii., the death-scene of Cardinal Beaufort is very finely drawn. "Richard III." is the best of all the plays for the stage. Its historical truth was questioned in Walpole's "Doubts." The hunchbacked Richard III. is described by a contemporary as a handsome man; still, Sir James Mackintosh lived to alter an opinion he once maintained of Richard's innocence of the crimes imputed to him.

Charles James Fox justly compared Clarence's dream to the death-scene of Alcestis in Euripides. The whole of "Richard III." evinces a power of terrific delineation; but the two parts of "Henry IV." are better plays.

"Henry IV." pt. i. is original, and rich in characters beyond all other plays. In "Henry V.," the description of the night before the Battle of Agincourt is very celebrated. "Henry VIII." is full of fine speeches and characters. In reading this play, remember that it was written in the reign of a Queen most dangerous to offend, daughter of two of the principal characters. In "King John" the scenes of "Arthur and Hubert" and "Hubert and John" are admirably adapted for private recitation. The character of the bereaved Constance ranks with Queen Margaret, Desdemona, Cleopatra, Juliet, and Lady Macbeth, the best female characters in Shakespeare.

3. *The Tragedies of Shakespeare.* In "Troilus and Cressida" Campbell thinks the Poet was not eminently successful, though the Germans (whose Shakespearian enthusiasm has made us appear comparatively cold) are as much enraptured with Troilus as with Hamlet; a play apparently more congenial to the German spirit. However, "Julius Cæsar," and "Antony and Cleopatra,"—a play more true to nature, to history and to dramatic rules,—as also "Coriolanus," fully vindicate Shakespeare's power to cope with Roman subjects. The quarrel of Brutus and Cassius has been more applauded, says Collier, than any other piece on the stage, for the last 250 years. But the scene of Coriolanus with his mother, wife and child, may be deemed the finest dramatic scene ever written.

"Hamlet" is one of the best plays to read, "Macbeth" the best to see—great in its plot, its characters and its sentiments; but "Othello" would be equally good,—so true to nature, and its plot so well developed, — were it not so painfully revolting in some parts. "King Lear" well acted would be too painful, were it not so well relieved. The madness of King Lear the physician of an asylum pronounced as true to the very life.

"Hamlet," "Macbeth," "Lear," and "Othello" are as much read as any of the plays. "Macbeth" has often been compared to the "Agamemnon" of Æschylus, from the spirit of awe and mystery that broods over the whole play, and also from the resemblance of Lady Macbeth to the daring Clytemnestra. Strong and stirring as are the thoughts of the "Agamemnon," there are twice the number in "Macbeth;" and, as to delineation of character and studies of nature, that which was first and foremost in Shakespeare was of quite a secondary consideration with the Greek Dramatists. Milton's "Samson" bears some resemblance to the Prometheus of Æschylus. In each play there is one grand figure thrown out in strong relief.

On this subject Macaulay's "Essay on Milton" has some good remarks. It was in structure and artistic finish, and not in variety of character, or fertility of thought, that the Greeks excelled. Shakespeare had not the same inducement for exact composition, otherwise no man ever could have surpassed him. Many of his speeches exhibit a matchless proportion of words to sense; they show so true a balance, and so nice a rhythm, that they seem rather tesselated than constructed. Not a syllable can you displace without loss. No play exemplifies this excellence more than the "Merchant of Venice."

The reader of Poetry must judge of beauties for himself, so widely do "doctors disagree." Byron had little appreciation either for Shakespeare or for Spenser; and Horace Walpole, as Southey quotes, said, that "The Midsummer Night's Dream" is far more nonsensical than the worst translation of an Italian opera book!

Cowley (Milton's favourite poet), Waller, Philips, Parnell, Rowe, Prior, Gay, Green, Tickell, Somerville, Swift, Collins (his lyrics very celebrated), Dyer, Churchill, Akenside, Lyttelton, Armstrong, Warton, Mason, Beattie, are authors of whom we may read such parts only as Johnson or other critics point out.

Of *Milton*, to read "Paradise Lost" is the duty of all, the pleasure of a few. Read Macaulay's admirable criticism of Milton. All the minor works are better known than "Paradise

Regained." Fuseli thought the second book of "Paradise Lost" the grandest effort of the human mind.

Of *Dryden,* "Alexander's Feast" is one of the most popular lyric odes. His "Fables," "Annus Mirabilis," and "Translation of Virgil," are the most celebrated. Dryden is considered to evince more strength and real poetry, with less smoothness, than Pope. Bolingbroke admired Pope's prose writing. Mackintosh thought "The Cock and the Fox" the best poem of Dryden.

Of *Addison,* read the "Cato," and Psalm xxiii.

Of *Pope,* the "Rape of the Lock" is the best of all heroi-comical poems; "Eloisa to Abelard" is, though very clever, a most immoral and impious poem, most unworthy of the author of "The Messiah," which should be learned by heart, and compared with Isaiah and Virgil. The "Essay on Criticism," and the "Dunciad," show that Pope could write as strong lines as any author. Of the "Essay on Man," the argument was written by Bolingbroke, and versified by Pope.

Of *Thomson,* all admire the sensibility and natural beauty of "The Seasons." He had not the art of giving effect with a few touches. His "Castle of Indolence" shows more genius, though less known than "The Seasons."

Of *Shenstone* Gray said, "He goes hopping

along his own gravel walk, and never deviates from the beaten track, for fear of being lost." "The Schoolmistress," as an imitation of Spenser, is very good, but far inferior to the "Castle of Indolence."

Of *Young*, "The Night Thoughts" hold a high place among devotional poetry. Most of the literary world read part, few read all: which, indeed, may almost be said of Milton, for reasons given in Johnson's "Life of Milton."

Of *Gray*, the "Elegy," and "Ode to Eton College," are best known. Of the rest of his odes, Sir J. Mackintosh truly said, "They are most pleasing to the artist who looks to structure." And again, "To those who are capable of that intense application, which the higher order of poetry requires, and which poetical sympathy always produces, there is no obscurity."

Of *Goldsmith*, "The Deserted Village," next to Gray's "Elegy," is the most popular piece of English poetry. The other poems are much read.

Of *Johnson*, "London," and "The Vanity of Human Wishes," much admired by Byron, every scholar should compare with the third and tenth satires of Juvenal. His "Prologue," spoken by Garrick in 1747, is very good.

Of *Cowper*, "The Task" is considered the master-piece. All his poems are much read, especially "Alexander Selkirk," "John Gilpin," and all the smaller pieces. Cowper, like Euripides, was remarkable for reconciling poetical sentiment with the language of common life. He may be considered the first of the school of Wordsworth. His letters are equal to any. Few poets have had more readers than Cowper. The public say of poetry as cottagers of religious tracts, "We like something with a tale in it."

Of later writers, *Wordsworth* is admired by all his brother poets. See Coleridge's "Biographia Literaria." Read "The Excursion." His observations of nature's beauties are too minute, and his sensibilities too acute for the sympathies of most readers. *Crabbe's* "Phœbe Dawson" was read to Fox on his death-bed! Of the "Borough" Mackintosh said what Pitt observed of Sir W. Scott's "Minstrel," "I acknowledge his unparalleled power of painting."

Byron avoid as intellectual poison—his genius serves only to wing his rankling arrow for a deeper wound. "He was inspired by the genius of pain," said Goethe. The good, wholesome, moral Southey aptly called Byron and Shelley of the "Satanic School of Poetry." Byron fills the mind with distempered views of life without contentment, humility, resignation, or repose. He not only scoffs at Religion, but diffuses a general odour of Godlessness. The true Poet is "the High Priest of Nature," eliciting our praise for beauties yet unseen, and our gratitude for mercies unfelt before; and, revealing "a soul of goodness in things evil," fits man for his mortal sphere—but Byron unfits us. He would stir up a mutiny in the voyage of life, and make believe "a soul of *badness* in thing *good*." How truly did a female friend of Southey say that there was 2lbs. of devil to every 1lb. of man in Byron's composition!

Of *Coleridge*, Scott said, translation was his *forte*. He translated "Wallenstein" from manuscript, and Schiller adopted and printed some of Coleridge's deviations. The "Ancient Mariner," composed during an evening walk with Wordsworth, as well as his "Christabel," are very celebrated. Mackintosh said Coleridge's "talents were below his understanding; he had never matured his ideas, so as to express them with clearness and order." In other words, Coleridge, like Shelley and others of the same school, often failed in the single step which would have attained to "the sublime," and therefore their writings seem in some parts to remain in the regions of "the ridiculous." Burns, Moore, Southey, Sir W. Scott, Rogers, L. E. L. (Letitia Elizabeth Landon), Heber, Milman, Keats, Shelley, James Montgomery, are names which I need only mention.

The reader may easily ascertain what are the best pieces of each; and when he thinks he knows their several styles, then he may read with interest the "Rejected Addresses," and try how many of the supposed authors he can identify. Alfred Tennyson was for some time considered the Poet of the present day who had most *admirers,* but Longfellow has far more real *lovers.* Longfellow, Lowell, Whittier, Sigourney, Bryant, and Willis are five names of which our American friends have much reason to be proud.

Thomas Hood's "Plea for the Midsummer Fairies" is of the very highest order of poetical composition. Many of his pieces are very beautiful.

On Taste.—Read Burke "On the Sublime and Beautiful," Alison "On Taste," the principles of which were espoused by Stewart and Jeffrey; but see "Burns's Letters" (lett. cc.). Read the critical articles in the "Edinburgh" and "Quarterly," and especially Lord Jeffrey's "Essays." Some admirable remarks on the poetry of a civilised, as compared with that of a ruder age, are found in T. B. Macaulay's "Essay on Milton:" and read also an able dissertation of the poetry of the present age in his "Essay on Moore's Life of Byron." Hallam recommends the papers in "Blackwood" on Spenser, by Professor Wilson. Read Coleridge's criticism of Wordsworth in his "Biographia Literaria," and the "Reviews of Wordsworth." Johnson's criticism of Gray, in his "Lives of the Poets," is termed by Mackintosh "a monstrous example of critical injustice." Gray adds, "he was unjust to Prior, because he had no feeling of the lively and the graceful." Sir James justly maintained that "there is a poetical sensibility which, in the progress of the mind, becomes as distinct a power as a musical ear or a picturesque eye," which sensibility Johnson had not. The author of "Rasselas" certainly had a talent for poetry, and so Sir James himself was "not wanting in imagery," said Robert Hall, "but it was acquired and imported, not native to his mind." The Essay in "Blackwood" on Burns's poetry, by Carlyle, was strongly recommended by Mrs. Hemans. Read and reflect on the criticisms of "Paradise Lost." Compare the papers on Milton in the "Spectator" and Johnson's "Life of Milton" with the criticisms in Coleridge's "Remains," p. 176; Hallam's "History of Literature," vol. iv. p. 419; the "Quarterly Review," June 1825; and Macaulay's "Essay on Milton." Lastly, study attentively poems of different degrees of merit; compare odes, blank verse, the different measures of Pope and Spenser, Scott, and others, and consider which best suit the English language, and what poet excels in each; then confirm or correct your own opinions by those of reputed critics. I have also known much improvement conveyed by a few hours' reading with a tutor of good taste. Coleridge, high as were his natural endowments, ascribed much of his proficiency to school lessons in criticism from Dr. Bowyer at Christ's Hospital.

CHAP. IX.

ON NATURAL PHILOSOPHY.

"In a recent catalogue by a Frenchman," says I. D'Israeli, "among works on natural history we find the 'Essay on *Irish Bulls!*'" We should rather recommend Rymer Jones's "Natural History," Humboldt's "Kosmos," and his "Aspects of Nature," Ellis's "Chemistry of Creation," "Physical Geography" by Mrs. Somerville, Kirby's "Bridgewater Treatise," and a very choice little book called the "Life of a Tree," by the C. K. Society. After these others will readily occur.

On Astronomy, Herschel's "Preliminary Discourse" all may read. Mrs. Somerville's "Connection of the Physical Sciences" was designed to teach her countrywomen science; but (1) Mitchell's "Orbs of Heaven," (2) Nichol's "Solar and Planetary Systems," and (3) Tomlinson's "Student's Manual" should smooth the way. Tomlinson clearly explains the principle of the Thermometer, Compass, Telescope, Dial, and Acoustics.

On Botany, Loudon's works will afford a clue to others.

On Chemistry, "Liebig's Letters on Chemistry" are indispensable, especially for agriculturists. "Chemistry no Mystery," by Scoffern, with one of Palmer's Chemical Chests, will furnish all implements required for common experiments; and, in every town there is a chemist who would gladly earn a guinea for a few lessons.

Lardner's "Cyclopædia" supplies Treatises on all the Sciences; he has lately published a separate course of a familiar kind. Read his work on the "Steam-Engine." Dr. Brewer's "Guide to Science" explains, in question and answer, every common phenomenon from the theory of dew to the boiling of the kettle.

On Geology, Mantell's "Wonders of Geology," Dr. Buckland, and Lyell will afford introductions. The Museums and the Crystal Palace will afford a fine school for lectures, which needy men of science are ever ready to deliver on every branch of Natural Philosophy. Science, by the many elementary treatises of the present day, has been brought within the comprehension of every intelligent person.

CHAP. X.

READING FOR A MILITARY OFFICER.

THE following is the advice of a military officer, whose name and office as lecturer in a military academy, were I allowed to mention it, would prove the value of the authority.

The following list will enable the student to become his own guide: —

I. On the ART OF WAR IN GENERAL; read,

1. Jackson on the "Formation and Discipline of Armies."

2. Jomini on "Military Combinations;" by Gilbert.

3. "King of Prussia's Military Instructions;" by Forster.

4. Duke of Wellington's "General Orders and Despatches," by Gurwood; or, "Selections from the Despatches," in one volume.

5. "Memoir of the Military Sciences," by Col. Lewis; a "Military Cyclopædia" of great merit, just completed.

II. On ARTILLERY; read,

1. Griffith's "Artillerist's Manual."

2. Sir H. Douglas's "Naval Gunnery."

N. B. I know of no reputable treatise on Artillery in the English language.

III. On FORTIFICATION; read,

1. Straith's "Fortification."

2. Macaulay's "Field Fortifications."

3. Jebb on "Attack and Defence of Ports."

4. Pasley's "Rules for conducting the practical Operations of a Siege."

IV. On MILITARY BRIDGES AND PONTOONS; read,

"Sir H. Douglas's Treatise on Military Bridges."

V. On CAVALRY; read,

1. "Remarks on the Tactics of Cavalry," by Beamish.

2. Bismark's "Field Service of Cavalry," by Beamish.

VI. On LIGHT INFANTRY; read,

1. Jarry's "Duties of Light Infantry."

2. Fitz-Clarence on the "Duty of Piquets."

VII. On TACTICS AND MILITARY ORGANISATION; read,

Mitchell.

VIII. On MILITARY LAW; read,

Simmons on "Court Martials."

IX. On SURVEYING; read,

Jackson's "Surveying and Military Sketching."

X. On MILITARY HISTORY AND BIOGRAPHY; read,

1. Coxe's "Life of Marlborough."

2. Stedman's "History of the American War."

3. Lloyd's "German War."
4. "Conquest of Canada," by Author of Hochelaga.
5. Alison's "French Revolution."
6. Napier's "Peninsular War."
7. "Napoleon's Invasion of Russia," by Segur.
8. Jones's "Sieges in Spain."
9. Drinkwater's "Siege of Gibraltar."
10. Mahon's "War of Succession in Spain."
11. Siborne's "Waterloo Campaign."
12. The Work by Frederick II. of Prussia.

The Memoirs of Napoleon, by Generals Gourgaud and Montholon, contain, what must be a matter of the greatest curiosity to the soldier, an account of the authors and the studies which formed the mind of that master of the art of war.

All the works of Jomini are instructive; his later works are the best.

The general reading of an officer should be that of any private gentleman. Though I may specify Modern History, Geographical Descriptions, Military Narratives, and accounts of the policy and interests of England and other great nations.

By translations of Arrian, Cæsar, Polybius, Tacitus, Xenophon, Herodotus, and Thucydides, the student may glean the tactics of the Greeks and Romans.

The valuable dissertation by Polybius (b. xvii.)

on the Macedonian phalanx, as compared with the Roman legion, is given in Jones's Xenophon, translated, pp. 255.

CHAP. XI.

HOW TO KEEP A COMMON-PLACE BOOK.

PROCURE "The Improved Common-place Book on the Plan of Locke." The preface contains instructions. This Common-place Book I would advise students to use as a day-book, and to keep a common ruled book of 300 or 400 pages as a ledger. The day-book should contain an analysis of every book that is read, to aid the natural defects of memory, not to supersede it; that is, we should enter time, place, and persons, and little facts, when, and only when, we can trust our memory with the chief part of the narrative. The entry should resemble the summary we find in books. We may also enter original thoughts in order as they arise. Then the ledger should be a book of topics in which every subject of interest may have a page or two assigned it, for the purpose of classifying the contents of the Common-place or Day Book. To show the advantage of this, I will copy from my own book one of the pages in which I have long stored up any casual notice and recommendation of authors to determine my choice of reading.

" *Authors recommended and characterised.*

" Read ' Collingwood's letter on Trafalgar,' cp. 2. (i. e. Common-place Book, page 2.), and Hutchinson ' On Alexandria,' cp. 8. Burke's opinion of Montesquieu, cp. 14., and of Voltaire, of Murphy's Translation and ' Ossian,' cp. 14. The prose of Dryden, Shaftesbury, and Hooker characterised, cp. 27. What Niebuhr and what Pitt considered the desiderata of literature, cp. 175. Gent. Mag. for 1747, about Hogæus. Miss Austin's ' Pride and Prejudice,' Scott thought unequalled, cp. 31. Adolphus's Letter to Heber. ' New Monthly' for 1822, about National Gallery. ' On India and Hindoos,' read Ward's Book. Swift's letters better than Pope's, cp. 150. Read Cowper's Letters, Mackintosh's opinion of Hume's ' History,' cp. 38. ' Edinb. No. XLI.' 2nd article by Sir J. Mackintosh. Canning's Eulogy of Chalmers's ' Astronomical Sermons,' cp. 257. Gray's Opinion of ' Froissart;' which was admired by Hemans, as also ' Paul and Virginia,' cp. 54."

CHAP. XII.

HOW TO REMEMBER WHAT WE READ.

Most readers, I presume, will open this chapter with no little curiosity, and a feeling which would be expressed by these words: "My memory is bad enough — would it were as good as that of a certain friend of mine. Let me see if there can be any rules to suit so bad a case as my own." Now, before you decide that you have a worse memory than your friend, let me ask, Is there no one subject on which you can equal him? You have no doubt observed, that a large class of men, who are devoted exclusively and literally to *animal* pursuits, sportsmen to wit, have the greatest difficulty in remembering matters of history or general literature, but yet are so ready with the names of all the winners of the Derby, Oaks, or St. Leger, and the progeny and pedigree of each, that a scholar would be as much surprised at their memory of horses and mares, as they could be at the scholar's memory of kings and queens. Probably you will now say, "All this we grant; it is true we have memory for some things, but not for literature." Your meaning is, that you have memory where you have attention. The sportsman cannot attend to books, nor the scholar to horses. The art of memory is the art of attention. A memory for literature will increase with that interest in literature by which attention is increased. The sportsman could remember pages of history relating to forest laws or encouragement of the breed of horses, but not the adjoining pages on the law of succession, and only because he felt an interest, and consequently paid attention, in reading the one but not the other.

Again, memory depends on association, or, on the tendency of some things to suggest and make us think of others. The geologist remembers fossils, but not flowers; and the botanist flowers, but not fossils. Each has in his mind "a cell" for the one specimen, but not for the other; and the observations which fall in with the ideas of the geologist, and link to many a subtle chain of thought, remain alone and unassociated in the mind of the botanist. Association certainly is, in some respects, an aid to attention; they are usually considered as distinct, and the basis of Memory; therefore every rule I can give for promoting either attention or association will be virtually rules for Memory.

Memory is assisted by *whatever tends to a full view and clear apprehension of a subject.* Therefore, in reading history, occasionally lay the book aside, and try if you can give a connected narrative of events. "What thou dost not know, thou canst not tell;" but clear ideas never want plain words. Do not be satisfied with feeling that the subject is too familiar for this repetition to be necessary. The better a story is known, the less time it will take to repeat. Put your "thoughts in express words." This is an invaluable exercise; for, first of all, you will greatly improve your power of expression, and gain that command of language on which one of my friends heard Fox compliment Pitt, as having not only *a* word, but *the* word, *the very* word to express his meaning. Secondly, the practice of putting your thoughts into words will improve your power of Conception. When you see a speaker, in a long argument, contract and fix his eye as if on some aëreal form, he is trying to body forth his ideas, and hold them up as a picture from which he may select, read off, and lay before his hearers such portions as he thinks will convey the desired impression. Conception is the quality for which we call a man "clear-headed;" for this enables him to grasp at one view the beginning, middle, and end of what he means to say, and have the order of his ideas at the direction of a cool judgment, instead of depending upon chance.

"Ut jam nunc dicat jam nunc debentia dici,
Pleraque differrat præsensque in tempus omittat."

HOR.

To repeat a narrative to another is better still than repeating it to yourself: you are more excited to accuracy, and your memory is assisted by the degree of attention and association which casual remarks and questions may promote. After walking round Christ Church Meadow with a late fellow of Exeter College, relating the fortunes of the Athenians in Sicily, the very trees seemed vocal, and one weather-beaten elm at the left-hand corner of the avenue next the Cherwell so regularly reminded us of Nicias, that we used to say it afforded an unanswerable argument for the transmigration of souls.

With a view to distinct conception, Writing is usually recommended to aid memory. As to mere transcribing, though much has been advanced in its favour, I believe it is by no means to be adopted. Much experience has shown me that it not only wastes time, but deceives us as to the extent of our knowledge. We are flattered at the sight of the paper we fill, while in reality we are exercising, not our wits, but our fingers. Every University student knows how common it is to find men of misguided industry with desks full, and heads empty. Writing never aids memory but when it tends to clear Conception. Most persons find it more pleasant to draw a sketch of a subject on a sheet of paper than on the tablets of the mind; but let them not suppose it is more improving.

When you want relief or variety, you may try to write, instead of repeating the subject of your morning's reading; but you will soon admit that the *vivâ voce* exercise is the better of the two. In speaking of Conception, Abercrombie relates the case of a distinguished actor, who created great surprise by learning a long part with very short notice. "When questioned respecting the mental process which he employed, he said that he lost sight entirely of the audience, and seemed to have nothing before him but the pages of the book from which he had learnt, and that, if any thing had occurred to interrupt that illusion, he should have stopped instantly."

Secondly. *Memory is assisted by whatever adds to our interest or entertainment.* Therefore all the remarks I have made relative to being guided by curiosity and inclination are hints for memory. A man rarely forgets a fact which he hears in answer to a question he has himself originated; and the art of reading is, to gain facts in such order that each shall be, as Abercrombie says, a nucleus or basis of more; in other words, that every fact may be an answer to some question already in our minds, and may suggest in its turn new questions for new answers in an endless series.

Thirdly. *Memory depends much on a thorough determination to remember.* Most persons have memory enough for the purposes of their own business. Ask the guard of the mail how he remembers the places at which he has to drop his many parcels, and he will tell you, "because he must." And if you put the same question to any number of different persons whose fortune depends on the constant exercise of memory, you will invariably receive similar answers, which is a proof from experience that our memory depends very much on our own will and determination. If, by the force of resolution, a person can wake at any hour in the morning, it is easy to believe that, by the same means, he may also have a powerful command over his memory. While at the University, I had a very remarkable proof of this. I was assisting in his studies, previous to examination, a friend who assured me he could not remember what he read; that such had been the case during fourteen University terms. But I said, "Now you must remember, —I know you can,—and I will have no more to do with you if you do not answer me correctly to-morrow on what we read to-day."

Having rallied him in this way, I heard no more of the complaint. After his examination he assured me that he was perfectly surprised at the extent to which his memory had served him, and fairly acknowledged that for years he had given way to a state of mental inactivity, never stopping to try his memory, but drinking of the Castalian stream rather after the manner of Baron Munchausen's horse, when he had lost his hinder quarters with the portcullis. A man can remember to a great extent, just as Johnson said a man might at any time compose, mastering his humour, if he will only set to work with a dogged determination: "*Possunt quia posse videntur*," "for they can conquer who believe they can," is very generally true where the mind is concerned. A very common reason that men do not remember is, that they do not try; a hearty and ever-present desire to prevail is the chief element of all success. Nothing but the fairy's wand can realise the capricious desire of the moment; but as to the objects of laudable wishes, deeply breathed and for many a night and day ever present to the mind, these are placed by Providence more within our reach than is commonly believed. When a person says, If I could only have my wish, I would excel in such an art or science, we may generally answer, The truth is, you have no such wish; all you covet is the empty applause, not the substantial accomplishment. Before we complain of want of power and mental weapons, let us be sure that we make full use of what we have. When we see one man write without hands, and another qualify himself (as in an instance within my own remembrance) for high University honours without eyes, a complaint of our memory, or other faculties, justifies the same conclusion as when workmen complain of their tools.

These, or at least other instances equally surprising, are founded on good authority. Still Abercrombie justly says, though the power of remembering unconnected facts and lists of words makes a great show, and is the kind of memory most generally admired, yet it is often combined with very little judgment, and is not so important a feature, in a cultivated mind, as that memory founded on the relations, analogies, and natural connections of different subjects, which is more in our own power. Indeed, mere parrot memory is of less use than is generally supposed. It enables a superficial person to pass off the opinions of others as his own; but educated men can generally remember enough for their own purposes, and command data sufficient for the operations of their judgment. The power and the science is the chief point, not the tools. A mathematician is always a mathematician, even without his formulæ and diagrams. The oldest judge remembers the rules of law, though he forgets the case in point, and the ablest counsel are allowed refreshers. It is enough that our minds, like our guns, carry true to the mark without being always loaded.

Fourthly. *Memory is assisted by whatever tends to connection or association of ideas.* When I asked the friend above mentioned the particular means he took to remember his lectures previous to examination, he said, that besides looking everything "more fully in the face" than he had ever done before, he tried "to match, sort, and put along-side of something similar," each event in its turn, and also to say to himself, "Here are four or five causes, circumstances, or characters relating to the same thing; by such a peculiarity in the first I shall remember the second, while something else in the second will remind me of the third and fourth." During this process, he said, he became so familiar with many facts, that he could remember without any association at all. Again, in all the works and phenomena of nature, moral or physical, men of comprehensive minds discern a marked family likeness; certain facts indicate the existence of others; so that memory is assisted by a certain key which classification suggests; and thus one effort of memory serves for all. Association and Attention are both the basis of several inventions called *Memoria Technica,* of which I will proceed to speak, more particularly for the benefit of students preparing for examinations, and those who would follow out my plan of attaining accuracy of outlines of history and other subjects. Dr. Doddridge learnt the Scripture history from his mother's lectures on the Dutch tiles in the fireplace. A series of historical pictures would form the best *Memoria Technica;* so readily do we remember the position of pictures, and associate facts with their subjects.

Of Memoria Technica, the practice of almost all men of distinction coincides with the avowed opinions of Bacon and of Abercrombie, who held that the memory of such events as these systems teach is scarcely worth the process; and, that the same degree of resolution which their use implies would supersede the necessity of them, except to that extent only to which every man of sense can, and commonly does, frame the best possible Memoria Technica, namely, one suited to his peculiar cast of mind. Of such kinds are the following: —

First. Looking at names in the index of a history, and following each separately through all the events with which it is connected. This plan with Herodotus and Thucydides I found invaluable. It aids Memory most powerfully, and leads to comparison and valuable reflection.

Secondly. Marking the names, words, or paragraphs, in your book, or numbering the separate arguments by figures, 1, 2, and 3, in the margin. This I found useful, not only with history, but especially with Aristotle, and other works of science. It tends to distinct conception; to many casual associations; you sometimes fancy you see the page itself marked with your own figures, and then one event reminds you of another; it also enables you easily to refresh your memory of a book while you leisurely turn over the pages; above all, it keeps ever present to your mind, what many students do not think of once a month, namely, that reading and remembering are two different things.

Thirdly. Making a very brief summary of the contents of each book, and thinning it by degrees, as your memory can serve, with few catchwords as well as many. This plan answers many of the same purposes as the preceding; it is valuable to one who is preparing himself to write off-hand the history of any century required. Take one sheet of paper, and write words enough on it to remind you of the whole Outline History, and after a month, try if a much more portable *skeleton-key* will not serve, and this may be reduced, in its turn, till the whole is transferred from the paper to your memory. Thus Niebuhr advised his nephew to keep a list of difficulties or new words, and blot out each as soon as he could.

Lastly, associating things with places or objects around: thus the Roman orators used to associate the parts of their speeches with the statues or pillars in the building in which they spoke. Let my readers prepare a "skeleton-key" of each of the three Outline Histories of England, Rome, and Greece, and take a walk in three different directions with each; then will they find, though I cannot say in the noble sense in which Shakespeare intended,—

"Tongues in trees — books in the running brooks,
Sermons in stones — and good in everything."

Gray's "Memoria Technica" is very useful for dates. But it must be used for kings and queens principally, the dates of other events being remembered by association.

Example is better than precept. What man has done, man may do; so we will consider a few anecdotes of men famed for powers of memory.

Xenophon, in his "Symposium," speaks of Athenians who could repeat both the "Iliad" and the "Odyssey." This statement has been recommended to the consideration of those who assert the impossibility of the Homeric poems being orally transmitted. What was practicable for one man, however extraordinary a character he might be, would be comparatively easy for a society of Rhapsodists, if each member were intrusted with the memory of a part.

The nation that exerts memory in a more surprising manner than any other at the present day is the Chinese. Medhurst, in describing their education, enumerates nine books under the names of the "Five Classics" and the "Four Books." The Classics consist of a Book of Diagrams; a Collection of Odes; The Public Ceremonies; The Life of Confucius; and the History of the Three Dynasties. The Four Books are, The Happy Medium; the Great Doctrine; Book of Discourses; and Mencius. The bulk of these nine is equal to that of the New Testament; and yet, says Medhurst, "if the whole were lost, one million persons (out of a population reckoned at 361,000,000) could restore every volume to-morrow." Public offices in China depend on examination in these books. Two per cent. of the population compete.

At Winchester and the Charter House many a boy has committed to memory 10,000 lines, so as to repeat from any part at which he was told to begin.

Mathews, the comedian, as we are told by his

widow, had so surprising a memory, that he would go through an Entertainment which he had not seen for many months. He has even been known to step aside as the curtain drew up, to ascertain by a play-bill the name of the piece advertised for the evening; and this, strange to say, at a time when he was suffering so much from cracks on the tongue, that he had not spoken a word during the whole day, and felt the greatest pain in uttering what the audience heard with raptures of delight.

Addison's daughter, said Lady Mary Wortley Montagu, was nearly imbecile, yet so powerful was her memory, that she could repeat a sermon which she had heard once, and could learn pages of a dictionary by heart.

It is related of Lord Bolingbroke that he learned Spanish enough in three weeks to correspond with the Spanish minister. I would say *credat Judæus;* but, in Sir J. Stephen's Essay on "Ignatius Loyola and the Jesuits," it is mentioned as indisputable that Xavier learnt one of the Indian languages, so as to prepare himself for his missionary duties, in the same space of time. This is an instance of the power that enthusiastic determination exerts over memory. To the same principle must we also attribute the fact that the Bishop of New Zealand preached to the natives in their own language as soon as he arrived, having studied it only during his voyage. This, however, though highly meritorious, is by no means so surprising a case as that of Xavier.

Eusebius says that to the memory of Esdras we are indebted for the Hebrew Scriptures which were destroyed by the Chaldæans. St Anthony, the Egyptian hermit, though he could not read, knew the whole Scripture by heart; while, a certain Florentine, at the age of sixteen, could repeat all the Papal bulls. Seneca tells us that the Emperor Hadrian could repeat 2000 words in the order he heard them. Petrarch says that Pope Clement V. had his memory impaired by a fall on the head (an accident which has been known to give a good memory to one who had little before), and by great application gained so much more power than he had lost, that he never forgot anything he read. Cicero says, "Lucullus had a miraculous memory for events, but Hortensius had a better memory for words." Quintilian alludes to the well-known fact that we can repeat a task more perfectly on the following morning than on the night we learn it, and observes that things digest and settle in the mind during sleep.

Many instances are recorded of men losing the memory of a language, and speaking it many years after, during a brain fever or some exciting illness. The truth of this is beyond all doubt, though it seems very much like the tunes being thawed out of the frozen trumpet.

Dr. Abercrombie knew a lady seized with apoplexy while playing at cards one Thursday evening, and on regaining consciousness three days after, her first words were, "What are trumps?"

CHAP. XIII.

ENGLISH COMPOSITION. — HOW ACQUIRED.

"WITH full command of your subject," says Horace, "you will never be at a loss, either for words, or arrangement." Composition is an art well worth studying: much as men differ in natural powers of composition, no man ever did full justice to these powers without much consideration and practice.

1. The first thing in writing is to have something to say. Strong and stirring thoughts will rarely find vent in any but a vigorous and forcible style. The next thing is to be contented to write in the style which is natural to you. At the moment of writing, express yourself as nature dictates: in the hours of study, improve that nature to the full extent of its capacity. Never

attempt to write a letter and study letter-writing at the same time. Write in your own language and in your own character without effort and without affectation. Think of nothing but your subject; and your style, however imperfect, will have far more force and fluency than any slow and laboured composition could produce.

Southey's advice on the art of composition was similar to Johnson's; namely, to think of what you have to say, and to use the first words which present themselves, — the first words will be the most natural—you may afterwards correct with a view to brevity and rhythm. From Southey's Life it appears that his advice on composition was asked very frequently; and naturally so; for Southey's prose is equal to any English writing; and the "Life of Nelson," in particular, is written in a style so lucid and natural as never was surpassed. This is the opinion of the best judges—of Byron among others—and Byron is himself pronounced by Mr. Macaulay, when speaking of that poet's correspondence, to be a perfect master of English prose.

Writing poetry is the best of all practice for prose. Poets have generally been good prose writers. Witness Cowley, Dryden, and Milton, whose prose has all the power without the affectation of Carlyle; witness Swift, Pope, Goldsmith, Cowper, Scott, Thomas Moore, and Mr. Macaulay.

Poetical exercises are recommended, on the same principle as translations from foreign languages, because they forbid the writer to shape his ideas to fit his words, and compel him to search for words adequate to his ideas.

"One thing I do know," says Southey, "to write poetry is the best preparation for writing prose. The verse-maker gets the habit of weighing the meanings and qualities of words, until he comes to know, as if by intuition, what particular word will best fit into the sentence. People talk of my style! I have only endeavoured to write plain English, and to put my thoughts into language which every one can understand." And yet how many writers appear to think that heavy latinised words, and far-fetched metaphors, and unnatural, flowery language, are all essential to fine writing!

"I am glad," writes Southey on another occasion, "that you sometimes write verses, because, if ever you become a prose writer, you will find the great advantage of having written poetry. No poet ever becomes a mannerist in prose, nor falls into those tricks of style which show that the writer is always labouring to produce effect." The great rule of composition therefore is,—NEVER TO TAKE PEN IN HAND TILL YOU HAVE SOMETHING TO SAY, AND THEN WRITE IN THE FIRST WORDS THAT COME TO MIND. This was Southey's advice, though he would afterwards correct for brevity and rhythm. That plain and forcible writer William Cobbett, said, that the order of his sentences was the natural order in which one thought suggested another, and when this suggestion failed, it was time to stop. Much of the weak diluted writing of the present day William Wilberforce ascribed to a vain attempt to write without ideas—without ideas *enough*, he should have said, to gush forth as under high-pressure, but only enough to trickle out few and far between. The voluminous Richard Baxter confessed he had too much to do in giving utterance to all the weighty truths he would impart, to afford time for selection of words or modulation of sentences; so, he fixed his thoughts on his subject, and wrote as well as he could. On this Sir George Stephen observed, that no writer ever proposed to himself a surer method for doing justice to his own powers of composition. It is the only method by which a writer will ever give full scope and freedom to his abilities, be they great or little. John Bunyan, whose "Pilgrim's Progress" Mr. Macaulay deems "an invaluable study for any man who wishes to obtain a wide command over the English language," tells the secret of his success in words that truly describe the birth of every offspring of genius,—

> "It came from mine own heart, so to my head,
> And thence into my fingers trickled;
> Then to my pen, from whence immediately
> On paper I did dribble it daintily."

2. As to the course of reading conducive to a good English style, we may learn something from Lord Brougham's remarks on the studies of Robertson:—

"That Robertson had carefully studied the best writers, with a view to acquire genuine Anglicism, cannot be doubted. He was intimately acquainted with Swift's writings; indeed, he regarded Swift as eminently skilled in the narrative art. Robertson had equal familiarity with Defoe, and had formed the same high estimation of his historical powers.

When a certain Professor consulted Robertson on the best discipline for acquiring a good narrative style, the remarkable advice he received was to read Robinson Crusoe carefully; and, when the Professor was astonished and supposed it was a jest, the historian said he was quite serious; but, if Robinson Crusoe would not help him, or if he was above studying Defoe, then he would recommend "Gulliver's Travels!"

Southey specified Cobbett as one of our best writers, having a Saxon basis, derived from his education in the heart of an English county. Cobbett writes like a man very much in earnest, and never stops to pick out pretty words or to round off polished sentences.

Gibbon studied the style of Blackstone, and Pope that of Dryden, but without any trace of imitation.

Henry Taylor says that Mr. Crabbe Robinson, being one day with Schiller in his library, and observing on the shelves a collection of German translations of Shakespeare, he inquired how it was that Schiller, who understood English, could require these translations. Schiller's answer was that he was in the habit of reading as little as possible in foreign languages, because it was his business to write German, and he thought, by reading in other languages, he should lose his nicer perceptions of what belonged to his own.

Pope, Congreve, and Chatterton were all self-educated, being left to seek in the pure "well of English undefiled," according to their own intellectual wants and tastes, those treasures of which they were so early possessed. Byron at school and college attended far more to the living languages than to the dead. Pope thought himself the better for having no regular education, but allowed to gather "sweets from every opening flower" in the rich fields of English literature. Moore acquiesces in these opinions, as he quotes them; he adds, that the perfect purity with which the Greeks wrote their own language was justly attributed to their entire abstinence from every other.

3. The above rule specifies, *till you have something to say;* something clear and familiar to your own mind, and only awaiting words for expression. With this view, some persons make a brief sketch before writing an Essay, or set down a list of topics before beginning a letter; and some writers will walk about and arrange their ideas, or converse and reason upon them with a friend. Many of our great writers have mused for years upon their favourite theory, the constant subject of their solitary and their social hours. Then, when once resolved to write, a free and natural stream of thoughts, having long since clothed themselves with words, flows forth with rapidity and effect. Great results are never attained by little labour; though the labour may not be apparent to the uninitiated, who are apt to compute by the time of actual expression, forgetting the many patient hours of antecedent thought. Thirty times over did Pascal write some of his immortal letters. Most writers would do better at a second,

or even at a third attempt, could they spare the time; and that, principally for a reason which confirms our rule, because each repetition would give them a more comprehensive view and a more full command of all their materials.

4. As to Brevity, the secret of its beauty is, that when perfectly natural, it is the result of a mind full of its subject — a symptom which every reader welcomes, that the writer had ideas ready for his words, instead of having his words and ideas to seek at the same time. Brevity is valuable rather as an omen of excellence than as an excellence in itself. Bad writers are diffuse and prosy, for the same reasons that bad speakers stammer and hesitate, because they are making a cast for ideas, and have nothing to say. Brevity, when made a point of—that is, affected brevity, is far, indeed, from being a beauty in composition.

Horace ridicules this error in *Brevis esse laboro, obscurus fio*, — "I make a great effort to be brief, and the consequence is that I am obscure."

William Wilberforce was of the same opinion. In writing his "Practical Christianity" he purposely avoided that pruning and condensation which literary taste usually prescribes. He wisely judged, that a style rather more diffuse is more easily read. The readers, like the hearers of religious discourses, are well pleased to have their attention roused by a little repetition. Brief and terse maxims are of their own nature unconnected with the context. They go by you in a single flash, whereas you have time to think and recover yourself in a longer sentence; and Wilberforce once observed to a friend—"Do not curtail too much: portable soup must be diluted before it can be used."

But as to brevity, conciseness, and that exact proportion of words to things which distinguished our great writers, this is by no means to be accomplished without careful study. Horace tells us we should observe a delicate discrimination in the choice of our words, and great nicety in their arrangement;—*In verbis etiam tenuis cautusque serendis.* Here, *serere verba* is not the same thing as *spargere verba.* We must dibble our words in exactest order, and not sow them broad cast, if we would attain to excellence. The perfection of composition is well exemplified in Sir James Mackintosh's "Laws of Nature and of Nations." For, in these truly classical compositions, every sentence reads with the utmost ease and perspicuity; yet, if you analyse the structure, you will find the words are like Mosaic work; the sentences are rather tesselated than constructed, each word fitting admirably in its own place, but defying all transposition. Such excellence no mortal man can attain without patient study.

Ariosto furnishes another instance of careful selection and patient labour. His MSS. show that many a lofty and figurative expression was written and erased, before he attained to that chaste simplicity, to the imitation of which Galileo ascribed his own success, in making science attractive to the general reader.

The mention of Lord Brougham reminds us that it is well known that no man has gone beyond Lord Brougham in the patient finish of particular passages of his speeches; he has himself recorded that the peroration on Queen Caroline's case was written ten times over before he thought it worthy of the occasion.

5. Again, our rule states, *write in the first words that come to mind:* hence, any attempt to write in the style of Addison, or in any other style than your own, is strictly prohibited. Elegant writers must be studied in the hours of preparation, and the secret of their peculiar charms considered; thus Gibbon transcribed many chapters of Blackstone; but Gibbon's History shows not the faintest trace of his copy. By throwing off your own style to attain that of another, you will fall into a style worse than either. Many a man has written in a stiff and affected style for life, by

being taught to balance sentences and count syllables at school. When general education has formed the taste, and varied and extensive reading has enriched the vocabulary, then constant practice will give facility of expression, and the result will be a style worthy of a scholar.

That choice language which we admire in the poems of Pope and in the prose of Addison is hardly the language of our mother tongue, or, at all events, it must be admitted that such smooth and chaste and varied diction is a form and dialect of that mother tongue, far superior to what we learn by nature, and only to be acquired by art.

Let us explain ourselves a little more at length. We once heard a sensible country Rector inform a new Curate that the lower classes could not understand above one fourth part of that English which the higher classes speak; and, consequently, that as often as a preacher deviated from this very limited vocabulary he was virtually speaking in an unknown tongue.

Now, if one word out of every four in the dictionary is as large a proportion of the language as the ploughman can understand, one word out of four — though, unhappily, not by any means the same — is about as many as the Squire or the Parson are able commonly to use. Words, the instruments of thought, are like other instruments, or other tools. A first-rate workman carries a great variety of tools in his flag-basket, and attains an additional finish and accuracy by the skilful application of each. But the rougher and ruder kind of labourer can handle only one or two of a sort. So is it with the ordinary vocabulary of common conversation. One word acts many parts. Nearly all persons, without special study, may be detected in ringing the changes on one set of words, and of moving round and round in one narrow circle of trite phraseology. It is one thing to understand every word in the language, but another thing to have every word ready and available for its proper use and application. Even Goldsmith, so choice and so chaste in his writings, was singularly careless and inaccurate when he conversed. It was remarked of him by one of his friends — "Goldsmith, for instance, would say, 'This is as good a guinea as was ever *born*;' *coined*, he ought to say; but such a word as *coined* would never occur to Goldsmith."

Let it be granted, therefore, that one column of the dictionary out of four is as large a proportion of our language as any one person will use by nature. It is by art — by variety of reading, and minute observation of every word in every sentence of the most effective writers —

that all the great masters of composition have studied to enrich their style, endeavouring to incorporate and make habitual as much of the other three columns as they could.

In this study of language, Pope has succeeded so far as to lay the whole language under contribution, to supply words in unison with every tone of feeling and expressive of every shade of thought. So, Johnson, struck with admiration at these varied beauties, immediately raised the question, How such command of language ever was attained?

It is a law of the human mind, that it insensibly takes the tone and colouring of those with whom it communicates. If we catch the dialect and the phrases of the land in which we live, hours and days passed amidst the pure sentiments and chaste language of Addison or Southey will tend to propriety of words and simplicity of arrangement. Still, at the moment we take pen in hand, we must avoid all imitation, and think of nothing but our subject; and, for this obvious reason, — all such terms and beauties of style as we have made thoroughly our own will present themselves in a natural way, while all others that require the least effort to recal will appear stiff and inharmonious.

6. The same rule—*to use the first words that*

come to mind—would suggest, that by attentive reading and exercises, we should endeavour to make our foremost words the most appropriate. Of the many persons who understand all the words in the language, few indeed have a tenth part ready and available for the pen. It is a great thing to have, like Sir R. Peel, a copious vocabulary; but it is a still higher excellence, says Mr. D'Israeli, that it should be "rich and rare," and, like that of the eloquent George Canning, full of the most forcible and glowing, of the most effective and spirit-stirring expressions: to this end,

Alternately read and write on the subject of your reading. This will add both to your fluency and stock of words. The ever-recurring difficulties of writing will make us observing when we read, and expressions which are new to us to-day will be uttered as our own to-morrow. Read any well-written tale, then lay aside the book, and tell it in your own words; and, many of the author's words will be embodied as your own. Every new subject will contribute new terms. The sailor abounds in nautical phrases, the lawyer uses words of jurisprudence, the physician words of exact science,—but the experienced writer should command the stores of all. So, the more varied your reading, the more copious will be your vocabulary. Shakespeare, Milton, and

John Bunyan, comprise an excellent variety of words; but Coleridge truly said, that the study of Scripture would prevent any man's style from being common or undignified.

7. Read select passages aloud, or commit them to memory and recite them, to accustom the ear to the rhythm. Cobbett's "English Grammar" has excellent observations on composition: no English scholar will regret having devoted a few hours to its perusal.

8. Translate from foreign languages, ancient and modern. Most writers sacrifice occasionally what they would say to what they can say: their ideas are at the mercy of their words, and are often clipped and mutilated for the sake of euphony. This compromise between sound and sense translation defies; it enforces a thorough searching of the language, and an accurate distinction of terms. Of translation, considered as a preparation for prose writing, Southey says, "I believe I derived great advantage from the practice sometimes of translating and sometimes of abridging the historical books read at Westminster School. And I think that a habit of speaking upon business might be acquired by giving orally the substance of what one has just read."

Sir Walter Scott also advises his son to the same effect: — "You should exercise yourself frequently in trying to make translations of the passages that most strike you, trying to invest the sense of Tacitus in as good English as you can. This will give you a command of your own language, which no person will ever have who does not study English composition in early life."

The following is Lord Brougham's account of the way Robertson, the historian, studied composition: —

"Translations from the Classics, and especially from the Greek, formed a considerable part of his labour. He considered this exercise as well calculated to give an accurate knowledge of our own language, by obliging us to weigh the shades of difference between words or phrases, and either by the selection of the terms or the turning of the idiom, to find the expression which is required for a given meaning; whereas, when composing originally, the idea may be varied in order to suit the diction which most readily presents itself."

In this advice we are but too happy to be supported by the authority of Lord Brougham. We have long maintained that writers are often at the mercy of their words, and that many persons are prevented from doing justice to their ideas, because there remains a large part of the language which they never have pressed into their service.

But, the very nature of translation compels us to extend our vocabulary as widely as our author, and so it tends to bring an entirely new order of words into requisition.

Sir Samuel Romilly follows as a witness on the same side:—"I translated, composed, and endeavoured to form for myself a correct and elegant style; I translated the whole of Sallust, and a great part of Livy, Tacitus, and Cicero." Translation insures the ideas, and enables the mind to attend chiefly to the words. This is highly necessary. Seeking for words and ideas at the same time is the worst of practice; still, this absurdity is involved in the pernicious custom of setting schoolboys to write themes on Moral Virtue or on any other subjects on which they cannot possibly have anything to say. How much better to lecture them on a given portion of history, and, having thus insured ideas, to require them to expand and illustrate these ideas with such remarks as may naturally occur!

9. A few touches from the hand of a master may give wonderful effect even to a dull composition—especially from such a master as always bears the reader in his eye. Even such aids as points and punctuation are not to be despised; though Paley said that that was the best style which was the most independent of punctuation. Southey prided

himself on his knowledge of typography; and would refer to his title-pages in proof of his skill. A printer once remarked of him, that Mr. Southey was the only man he ever knew who could tell how a page would look before it was in type.

The paper and type, with a judicious arrangement of paragraphs, and suitable spaces and capitals, tend very much to enliven a page, and to sustain the attention of the reader. "A plain tale may be marred by the telling" — so, the weariness of the eyes, as well as of the ears, may put the mind out of humour with the story. Every author has to learn that there are secrets worth knowing in the art of bookmaking, apart from the excellence of the composition. No doubt the leading publishers and printers in London will render considerable assistance; still, every author should be able to judge for himself.

Distinct Punctuation is an art which will repay attentive study. It is excellently taught, as also are some other points most essential in composition, by William Cobbett's English Grammar, a work amusing, as well as instructive, in parts; especially where he criticises a King's Speech, and shows almost as many grammatical errors as there are clauses in it.

Milton made a great point of correct punctuation. Addison was equally particular. Lord

Jeffrey was famed for his skill in giving effect by little points and the touches of a master's hand; by which many an essay which he received as Editor of the "Edinburgh Review" was set forth with a boldness of relief and lucid arrangement, almost to the surprise of its author.

Lord Cockburn says of Lord Jeffrey, his "value as *Editor* was incalculable. He had not only to revise and arrange each Number after its parts were brought together, but he had much difficult and delicate work to perform. He had to train authors—to discern the public taste—to suggest subjects. Inferior to these excellences, but still important, was his dexterity in revising the writings of others. Without altering the general tone or character of the composition, he had great skill in leaving out defective ideas or words, and in so aiding the original by lively or graceful touches, that reasonable authors were surprised and charmed in seeing how much better they looked than they thought they would."

10. Sydney Smith said, "It would be an extremely profitable thing to draw up a short and well-authenticated account of the habits of study of the most celebrated writers with whose style of literary industry we happen to be most acquainted. It would go very far to destroy the absurd and pernicious association of genius and idleness, by

showing men that the greatest poets, orators, statesmen, and historians—men of the most brilliant and imposing talents—have actually laboured as hard as the makers of dictionaries and the arrangers of indices; and, that the most obvious reason why they have been superior to other men is, that they have taken more pains than other men. Gibbon was in his study every morning, winter and summer, at six o'clock; Burke was the most laborious and indefatigable of human beings; Leibnitz was never out of his library; Pascal killed himself by study; Cicero narrowly escaped death by the same cause; Milton was at his books with as much regularity as a merchant or an attorney—he had mastered all the knowledge of his time; so had Homer; Rafaelle lived only thirty-seven years; and in that short space of time carried the art so far beyond what it had before reached, that he appears to stand alone as a model to his successors. The multitude cry out, 'A miracle of genius!' Yes, a man proves a Miracle of Genius, because he has been a miracle of labour; because he makes use of the accumulated wisdom of ages, and takes as his point of departure the very last line and boundary to which science has advanced; because it has ever been the object of his life to assist every intellectual gift of nature with every resource that art could suggest, and with every attention that diligence could bestow."

Genius is comparatively helpless and dormant without patient labour and many of the industrial virtues of common men. Even imagination and invention, says Johnson, are useless without knowledge: nature in vain gives the power of combination, unless study and observation supply materials to be combined. Sir Isaac Newton remarked, that if he excelled other men in anything, he thought it was in patient observation of facts and persevering analysis. That great philosopher attributed only to the intensity of his inspection what all the world has imputed to the superiority of his vision. Buffon also thought that "Genius is Patience;" or, as another French writer explained, "*La Patience cherche, et la Génie trouve.*" And, it is only when these two powers, Genius and Application, are found in union, that great discoveries have been made. Herschel's telescope wants Herschel's patient observation. Butler, the author of the "Analogy," forcibly remarked—"Though a man have the best eyes in the world, he can only see the way he turns them." Genius is like a great general—or like the master-mind of striking and original combinations—but without some such an aide-de-camp as Diligence or Observation to ascertain exact positions and to supply the data of his calculations, no result can be expected but confusion and dismay.

We are happy to be able to quote the following testimony from a man of real genius, Thomas Moore.

"There are some exceptions, it is true, to this rule. But the records of immortality furnish very few such exceptions; all we know of the works that she has hitherto marked with her seal sufficiently authorise the general position—that nothing great and durable has ever been produced with ease; and that labour is the parent of all the lasting wonders of this world, whether in verse or stone, Poetry or Pyramids."

THE END.

London:
A. and G. A. Spottiswoode,
New-street-Square.

A CATALOGUE

OF

NEW WORKS

IN GENERAL LITERATURE,

PUBLISHED BY

LONGMAN, BROWN, GREEN, AND LONGMANS,

39, PATERNOSTER ROW, LONDON.

CLASSIFIED INDEX.

Agriculture and Rural Affairs.

Arts, Manufactures, and Architecture.

Biography.

Books of General Utility.

Botany and Gardening.

London: Printed by M. Mason, Ivy Lane, Paternoster Row.

Chronology.

Commerce and Mercantile Affairs.

Criticism, History, and Memoirs.

Geography and Atlases.

Juvenile Books.

Medicine and Surgery.

Miscellaneous and General Literature.

Natural History in General.

1-Volume Encyclopædias and Dictionaries.

Religious and Moral Works.

Poetry and the Drama.

Political Economy & Statistics.

The Sciences in General and Mathematics.

Rural Sports.

Veterinary Medicine, etc.

Voyages and Travels.

Works of Fiction.

ALPHABETICAL CATALOGUE

OF

NEW WORKS AND NEW EDITIONS

PUBLISHED BY

MESSRS. LONGMAN, BROWN, GREEN, AND LONGMANS,

PATERNOSTER ROW, LONDON.

Miss Acton's Modern Cookery- Book.—Modern Cookery in all its Branches, reduced to a System of Easy Practice. For the use of Private Families. In a Series of Receipts, all of which have been strictly tested, and are given with the most minute exactness. By ELIZA ACTON. New Edition; with Directions for Carving, and other Additions, Plates and Woodcuts. Fcp. 8vo. price 7*s*. 6*d*.

Adams.—A Spring in the Can-terbury Settlement. By C. WARREN ADAMS, Esq. With Five Illustrations. Post 8vo. price 5*s*. 6*d*.

Aikin. — Select Works of the British Poets, from Ben Jonson to Beattie. With Biographical and Critical Prefaces by Dr. AIKIN. New Edition, with Supplement by LUCY AIKIN; consisting of additional Selections, from more recent Poets. 8vo. price 18*s*.

Arnold.—Poems. By Matthew Arnold, Author of *Poems by A.* A New Edition, greatly altered; With a Preface. Fcp. 8vo. price 5*s*. 6*d*.

**** More than one-third of the contents of this volume consists of Poems now first published.*

Austin.—Germany from 1760 to 1814; Or, Sketches of German Life from the Decay of the Empire to the Expulsion of the French. Reprinted from the *Edinburgh Review*; with large Additions. By Mrs. AUSTIN. Post 8vo. [*Nearly ready*.

Joanna Baillie's Dramatic and Poetical Works, complete in One Volume: Comprising the Plays of the Passions, Miscellaneous Dramas, Metrical Legends, Fugitive Pieces, (several now first published), and Ahalya Baee. Second Edition, including a new Life of Joanna Baillie; with a Portrait, and a View of Bothwell Manse. Square crown 8vo. 21*s*. cloth or 42*s*. bound in morocco.

Baker.—The Rifle and the Hound in Ceylon. By S. W. BAKER, Esq. With several Illustrations printed in Colours, and Engravings on Wood. 8vo. price 14*s*.

Balfour.—Sketches of English Literature from the Fourteenth to the Present Century. By CLARA LUCAS BALFOUR. Fcp. 8vo. 7*s*.

Bayldon's Art of Valuing Rents and Tillages, and Tenant's Right of Entering and Quitting Farms, explained by several Specimens of Valuations; with Remarks on the Cultivation pursued on Soils in different Situations. Adapted to the Use of Landlords, Land Agents, Appraisers, Farmers, and Tenants. New Edition; corrected and revised by JOHN DONALDSON. 8vo. 10*s*. 6*d*.

Banfield.—The Statistical Com-panion for 1854: Exhibiting the most Interesting Facts in Moral and Intellectual, Vital, Economical, and Political Statistics, at Home and Abroad. Corrected to the Present Time: and including the Census of the British Population taken in 1851. Compiled from Official and other Authentic Sources, by T. C. BANFIELD, Esq., Statistical Clerk to the Council of Education. Fcp. 8vo. price 5*s*.

Lord Belfast.—Lectures on the English Poets and Poetry of the Nineteenth Century. By the Right Hon. the EARL OF BELFAST. 8vo. price 6*s*. 6*d*.

Berkeley.—Reminiscences of a Huntsman. By the Honourable GRANTLEY F. BERKELEY. With four Etchings by John Leech (one coloured). 8vo. price 14*s*.

Bewley. — Decimal Interest Tables, calculated at 5 per Cent. from 1 Day to 365 Days, and from 1 Month to 12 Months, on from £1 to £40,000: To which are added, Tables of Commission, from $\frac{1}{8}$ per Cent. to 5 per Cent. advancing by Eighths. By JOHN BEWLEY. 8vo. price 21*s*.

Black's Practical Treatise on Brewing, Based on Chemical and Economical Principles: With Formulæ for Public Brewers, and Instructions for Private Families. New Edition, with Additions. 8vo. price 10s. 6d.

Blaine's Encyclopædia of Rural Sports; or, a complete Account, Historical, Practical, and Descriptive, of Hunting, Shooting, Fishing, Racing, and other Field Sports and Athletic Amusements of the present day. A New and thoroughly revised Edition; with numerous additional Illustrations. The Hunting, Racing, and all relative to Horses and Horsemanship, revised by HARRY HIEOVER; Shooting and Fishing by EPHEMERA; and Coursing by Mr. A. GRAHAM. With upwards of 600 Woodcuts. 8vo. price 50s.

Blair's Chronological and His-torical Tables, from the Creation to the present Time: with Additions and Corrections from the most authentic Writers; including the Computation of St. Paul, as connecting the Period from the Exode to the Temple. Under the revision of SIR HENRY ELLIS, K.H. New Edition with corrections. Imperial 8vo. price 31s. 6d.

Bloomfield.—The Greek Testa-ment: With copious English Notes, Critical, Philological, and Explanatory. Especially formed for the use of advanced Students and Candidates for Holy Orders. By the Rev. S. T. BLOOMFIELD, D.D. F.S.A. New Edition. 2 vols. 8vo. with Map, price £2.

Dr. Bloomfield's Additional Annotations on the above. 8vo. price 15s.

Bloomfield.—College and School Greek Testament: with shorter English Notes, Critical, Philological, and Explanatory, formed for use in Colleges and the Public Schools. By the Rev. S. T. BLOOMFIELD, D.D., F.S.A. New Edition, greatly enlarged and improved. Fcp. 8vo. 10s. 6d.

Dr. Bloomfield's College and School Lexicon to the Greek Testament. Fcp. 8vo. price 10s. 6d.

Bode.—Ballads from Herodotus: With an Introductory Poem. By the Rev. J. E. BODE, M.A., late Student of Christ Church. 16mo. price 5s.

A Treatise on the Steam Engine, in its Application to Mines, Mills, Steam Navigation, and Railways. By the Artisan Club. Edited by JOHN BOURNE, C.E. New Edition. With 30 Steel Plates, and 349 Wood Engravings. 4to. price 27s.

Bourne. — A Treatise on the Screw Propeller: With various Suggestions of Improvement. By JOHN BOURNE, C.E. With 20 large Plates and numerous Woodcuts. 4to. price 38s.

Bourne.—A Catechism of the Steam Engine, illustrative of the Scientific Principles upon which its Operation depends, and the Practical Details of its Structure, in its Applications to Mines, Mills, Steam Navigation, and Railways; with various Suggestions of Improvement. By JOHN BOURNE, C. E. New Edition. Fcp. 8vo. price 6s.

Brande.—A Dictionary of Sci-ence, Literature, and Art; comprising the History, Description and Scientific Principles of every Branch of Human Knowledge; with the Derivation and Definition of all the Terms in general use. Edited by W. T. BRANDE, F.R.S.L. and E.; assisted by Dr. J. CAUVIN. The Second Edition, revised and corrected; including a Supplement, and numerous Wood Engravings. 8vo. price 60s.

The SUPPLEMENT separately, price 3s. 6d.

Bull.—The Maternal Manage-ment of Children in Health and Disease. By T. BULL, M.D., Member of the Royal College of Physicians; formerly Physician Accoucheur to the Finsbury Midwifery Institution. New Edition, Fcap. 8vo. 5s.

Bull.—Hints to Mothers, for the Management of their Health during the Period of Pregnancy and in the Lying-in Room: with an Exposure of Popular Errors in connexion with those subjects, etc.; and Hints on Nursing. By T. BULL, M.D. New Edition. Fcp. price 5s.

Bunsen.—Hippolytus and his Age; Or, Doctrine and Practice of the Church of Rome under Commodus and Alexander Severus: and Ancient and Modern Christianity and Divinity compared. By C. C. J. BUNSEN, D.D., D.C.L. A New Edition, corrected, remodeled, and extended. 7 vols. 8vo. [*Nearly ready.*

1. Hippolytus and his Age; or, the Beginnings and Prospects of Christianity New Edition, 2 vols. 8vo.

Separate Works connected with *Hippolytus and his Age*, as forming its Philosophical and Philological Key:—

2. Sketch of the Philosophy of Language and Religion; or, the Beginnings and Prospects of Mankind. 2 vols. 8vo.

3. Analecta Ante-Nicæna.. 3 vols. 8vo.
I. Reliquiæ Literariæ;
II. Reliquiæ Canonicæ;
III. Reliquiæ Liturgicæ.

Bunsen.—Egypt's Place in Universal History: An Historical Investigation, in Five Books. By C. C. J. BUNSEN, D.D., D.C.L. Translated from the German, by C. H. COTTRELL, Esq. M.A.—Vol. I. containing the First Book, or Sources and Primeval Facts of Egyptian History: With an Egyptian Grammar and Dictionary, and a complete List of Hieroglyphical Signs; an Appendix of Authorities, embracing the complete Text of Manetho and Eratosthenes, Ægyptiaca from Pliny, Strabo, etc., and Plates representing the Egyptian Divinities. With many Illustrations. 8vo. price 28*s*.

*** The second Volume is preparing for publication.

Burton.—The History of Scotland, from the Revolution to the Extinction of the last Jacobite Insurrection (1689—1748.) By JOHN HILL BURTON, Author of *The Life of David Hume*, etc. 2 vols. 8vo. price 26*s*.

Bishop Butler's General Atlas of Modern and Ancient Geography; comprising Fifty-two full-coloured Maps; with complete Indexes. New Edition, nearly all re-engraved, enlarged, and greatly improved; with Corrections from the most authentic Sources in both the Ancient and Modern Maps, many of which are entirely new. Edited by the Author's Son, the Rev. T. BUTLER. Royal 8vo. price 24*s*. half-bound.

Separately { The Modern Atlas, of 28 full-coloured Maps. Rl. 8vo. 12*s*. The Ancient Atlas of 24 full-coloured Maps. Rl. 8vo. 12*s*.

Bishop Butler's Sketch of Modern and Ancient Geography. New Edition, carefully revised, with such Alterations introduced as continually progressive Discoveries and the latest Information have rendered necessary. Edited by the Author's Son, the Rev. T. BUTLER. 8vo. price 9*s*.

The Cabinet Gazetteer: A Popular Exposition of all the Countries of the World; their Government, Population, Revenues, Commerce and Industries; Agricultural, Manufactured, and Mineral Products; Religion, Laws, Manners, and Social State: *with brief Notices of their* History and Antiquities. From the latest Authorities. By the Author of *The Cabinet Lawyer*. Fcap. 8vo. price 10*s*. 6*d*. cloth; or 13*s*. calf lettered.

The Cabinet Lawyer: A Popular Digest of the Laws of England, Civil and Criminal; with a Dictionary of Law Terms, Maxims, Statutes, and Judicial Antiquities; Correct Tables of Assessed Taxes, Stamp Duties, Excise Licences, and Post-Horse Duties; Post-Office Regulations, and Prison Discipline. 16th Edition, comprising the Public Acts of the Session 1858. Fcap. 8vo. price 10*s*. 6*d*.—SUPPLEMENT, price 1*s*.

Caird.—English Agriculture in 1850 and 1851; Its Condition and Prospects. By JAMES CAIRD, Esq., of Baldoon, Agricultural Commissioner of *The Times*. The Second Edition. 8vo. price 14*s*.

Calvert.—The Wife's Manual; or, Prayers and Thoughts on Several Occasions of a Matron's Life. By the Rev. WILLIAM CALVERT, Rector of St. Antholin, and one of the Minor Canons of St. Paul's. Post 8vo. [*In the Press.*

The Calling & Responsibilities of a Governess. By AMICA. Fcp. 8vo. price 4*s*. 6*d*.

Catlow.—Popular Conchology; or, the Shell Cabinet arranged: being an Introduction to the modern System of Conchology; with a Sketch of the Natural History of the Animals, an Account of the Formation of the Shells, and a complete Descriptive List of the Families and Genera. By AGNES CATLOW. New Edition, with numerous additional Woodcuts. Post 8vo. [*In the Press.*

Cecil.—The Stud Farm; or, Hints on Breeding Horses for the Turf, the Chase, and the Road. Addressed to Breeders of Race Horses and Hunters, Landed Proprietors, and especially to Tenant Farmers. By CECIL. Fcp. 8vo. with Frontispiece, 5*s*.

Cecil.—Records of the Chase, and Memoirs of Celebrated Sportsmen, illustrating some of the Usages of Olden Times and comparing them with prevailing Customs: Together with an Introduction to most of the Fashionable Hunting Countries; and Comments. By CECIL. With two Plates by B. Herring. Fcp. 8vo. price 7*s*. 6*d*.

Cecil.—Stable Practice; or Hints on Training for the Turf, the Chase, and the Road, with Observations on Racing and Hunting, Wasting, Race Riding, and Handicapping. Addressed to Owners of Racers, *Hunters, and other Horses, and to all who* are concerned in Racing, Steeple-Chasing, and Fox Hunting. By CECIL. Fcap. 8vo. with Plate, price 5*s*. half-bound.

Chalybaeus's Historical Survey of Modern Speculative Philosophy, from Kant to Hegel. Translated from the German by ALFRED TULK. Post 8vo. [*Just ready.*

Conversations on Botany. New Edition, improved; with 22 Plates. Fcp. 8vo. price 7*s*. 6*d*.; or with the Plates coloured, 12*s*.

Captain Chesterton's Autobiography. — Peace, War, and Adventure: Being an Autobiographical Memoir of George Laval Chesterton, formerly of the Field-Train Department of the Royal Artillery, subsequently a Captain in the Army of Columbia, and at present Governor of the House of Correction at Cold Bath Fields. 2 vols. post 8vo. price 16*s*.

Chevreul on Colour.—The Principles of Harmony and Contrast of Colours, and their Applications to the Arts: Including Painting, Interior Decoration, Tapestries, Carpets, Mosaics, Coloured Glazing, Paper-Staining, Calico Printing, Letterpress Printing, Map Colouring, Dress, Landscape and Flower Gardening, etc. By M. E. CHEVREUL, Membre de l'Institut de France, etc. Translated from the French by CHARLES MARTEL. Illustrated with Diagrams, etc. Crown 8vo. [*In the press.*

Conybeare and Howson.—The Life and Epistles of Saint Paul: Comprising a complete Biography of the Apostle, and a Translation of his Epistles inserted in Chronological order. By the Rev. W. J. CONYBEARE, M.A., late Fellow of Trinity College, Cambridge; and the Rev. J. S. HOWSON, M.A. Principal of the Collegiate Institution, Liverpool. With 40 Engravings on Steel and 100 Woodcuts, 2 vols. 4to. price £2. 8*s*.

Copland.—A Dictionary of Practical Medicine: Comprising General Pathology, the Nature and Treatment of Diseases, Morbid Structures, and the Disorders especially incidental to Climates, to Sex, and to the different Epochs of Life, with numerous approved Formulæ of the Medicines recommended. By JAMES COPLAND, M.D., Consulting Physician to Queen Charlotte's Lying-in Hospital, etc. Vols. I. and II. 8vo. price £3; and Parts X. to XVI. 4*s*. 6*d*. each.

The Children's Own Sunday-Book. By Miss JULIA CORNER, Author of *Questions on the History of Europe.* With Two Illustrations. Square fcp. 8vo. price 5*s*.

Cresy.— An Encyclopædia of Civil Engineering, Historical, Theoretical, and Practical. By EDW. CRESY, F.S.A., C.E. Illustrated by upwards of 3000 Woodcuts, explanatory of the Principles, Machinery, and Constructions which come under the Direction of the Civil Engineer. 8vo. price £3. 13*s*. 6*d*.

The Cricket-Field; or, the Sci-ence and History of the Game. Illustrated with Diagrams, and enlivened with Anecdotes. By the Author of *Principles of Scientific Batting*. Fcp. 8vo. with 2 Plates price 5*s*. half-bound.

Lady Cust's Invalid's Book.— The Invalid's Own Book: A Collection of Recipes from various Books and various Countries. By the Honourable LADY CUST. Fcp. 8vo. price 3*s*. 6*d*.

Dale.—The Domestic Liturgy and Family Chaplain, in Two Parts: The First Part being Church Services adapted for Domestic Use, with Prayers for every Day of the Week, selected exclusively from the Book of Common Prayer. Part II. Comprising an appropriate Sermon for every Sunday in the Year. By the Rev. THOMAS DALE, M.A., Canon-Residentiary of St. Paul's Cathedral. 2d Edition. Post 4to. 21*s*. cloth; 31*s*. 6*d*. calf; or £2. 10*s*. morocco.

Separately { THE FAMILY CHAPLAIN, 12*s*.
THE DOMESTIC LITURGY, 10*s*. 6*d*.

Davis.—China during the War and since the Peace. By Sir J. F. DAVIS, Bart., F.R.S., late H.M. Plenipotentiary in China; Governor and Commander-in-Chief of the Colony of Hongkong. 2 vols. post 8vo. price 21*s*.

De Felice.—History of the Pro-testants of France, from the Commencement of the Reformation to the Present Time. Translated from the French of G. DE FELICE, D.D., Professor of Theology at Montauban, by E. WEST: With a Supplemental Chapter, written expressly for this translation by Dr. DE FELICE. 2 vols. post 8vo. price 12*s*.

"We can speak with confidence of the idiomatic accuracy of Mr. West's translation, whose critical acquaintance with the French language has enabled him to produce a rendering of the French Professor's work in the highest degree creditable to his scholarly ability and taste. He has turned good French into good English, without taking unclassical liberties with either one language or the other. As the work is from the pen of a writer of singular perspicuity, enlarged research, and fervent devotion to the cause of evangelical Protestantism, it will be justly regarded by all competent judges as a valuable addition to the literature of our country."—*Evangelical Magazine.*

Delabeche.—The Geological Ob-server. By Sir HENRY T. DELABECHE, F.R.S. Director-General of the Geological Survey of the United Kingdom. New Edition; with numerous Woodcuts. 8vo. price 18*s*.

Delabeche.—Report on the Geo-logy of Cornwall, Devon, and West Somerset. By Sir HENRY T. DELABECHE, F.R.S., Director-General of the Geological Survey. With Maps, Woodcuts, and 12 Plates. 8vo. price 14*s*.

De la Rive.—A Treatise on Elec-tricity, in Theory and Practice. By A. DE LA RIVE, Professor in the Academy of Geneva. In Two Volumes, with numerous Wood Engravings. Vol. I. 8vo. price 18*s*.

Discipline. By the Author of "Letters to My Unknown Friends," etc. Second Edition, enlarged. 18mo. price 2*s.* 6*d.*

Eastlake.—Materials for a History of Oil Painting. By Sir Charles Lock Eastlake, F.R.S., F.S.A., President of the Royal Academy. 8vo. price 16*s.*

The Eclipse of Faith; or, a Visit to a Religious Sceptic. New Edition. Post 8vo. price 9*s.* 6*d.*

A Defence of The Eclipse of Faith, by its Author: Being a Rejoinder to Professor Newman's *Reply.* Post 8vo. price 5*s.* 6*d.*

The Englishman's Greek Concordance of the New Testament: Being an attempt at a Verbal Connexion between the Greek and the English Texts; including a Concordance to the Proper Names, with Indexes Greek-English and English-Greek. New Edition, with a new Index. Royal 8vo. price 42*s.*

The Englishman's Hebrew and Chaldee Concordance of the Old Testament: Being an attempt at a Verbal Connexion between the Original and the English Translations: with Indexes, a List of the Proper Names and their Occurrences, etc. 2 vols. royal 8vo. price £3. 13*s.* 6*d.*; large paper, £4. 14*s.* 6*d.*

Ephemera.—A Handbook of Angling; Teaching Fly Fishing, Trolling, Bottom Fishing, and Salmon Fishing; with the Natural History of River Fish, and the best Modes of Catching them. By Ephemera. Third and cheaper Edition, corrected and improved; with Woodcuts. Fcp. 8vo. 5*s.*

Ephemera.—The Book of the Salmon; Comprising the Theory, Principles, and Practice of Fly-Fishing for Salmon; Lists of good Salmon Flies for every good River in the Empire; the Natural History of the Salmon, all its known Habits described, and the best way of artificially Breeding it explained. With numerous coloured Engravings of Salmon Flies and Salmon Fry. By Ephemera; assisted by Andrew Young. Fcp. 8vo. with coloured Plates, price 14*s.*

W. Erskine, Esq.—History of India under the House of Taimur (1526 to 1707). By Wm. Erskine, Esq., Editor of *Memoirs of the Emperor Baber.* The First Volume—History of Baber; His Early Life, 1483-1526; his Reign in India, 1526-1530. The Second Volume,—History of Humayun, 1530-1556. Vols. I. and II. 8vo. [*Just ready.*

Faraday (Professor).—The Subject-Matter of Six Lectures on the Non-Metallic Elements, delivered before the Members of the Royal Institution in 1852, by Professor Faraday, D.C.L., F.R.S., etc. Arranged by permission from the Lecturer's Notes by J. Scoffern, M.B., late Professor of Chemistry in the Aldersgate College of Medicine. To which are appended Remarks on the Quality and Tendencies of Chemical Philosophy, on Allotropism, and on Ozone; together with Manipulative Details relating to the Performances of Experiments indicated by Professor Faraday. Fcp. 8vo. price 5*s.* 6*d.*

Forester and Biddulph's Norway.—Norway in 1848 and 1849: Containing Rambles among the Fjelds and Fjords of the Central and Western Districts; and including Remarks on its Political, Military, Ecclesiastical, and Social Organisation. By Thomas Forester, Esq.; and Lieutenant M. S. Biddulph, Royal Artillery. With Map, Woodcuts, and Plates. 8vo. price 18s.

Francis.—Annals, Anecdotes, and Legends: A Chronicle of Life Assurance. By John Francis, Author of *The History of the Bank of England,* "Chronicles and Characters of the Stock Exchange," and *A History of the English Railway.* Post 8vo. price 8*s.* 6*d.*

The Poetical Works of Oliver Goldsmith. Edited by Bolton Corney, Esq. Illustrated by Wood Engravings, from Designs by Members of the Etching Club. Square crown 8vo. cloth, 21*s.*; morocco £1. 16*s.*

Mr. W. R. Greg's Contributions to the Edinburgh Review.—Essays on Political and Social Science. Contributed chiefly to the *Edinburgh Review.* By William R. Greg, 2 vols. 8vo. price 24*s.*

Gurney.—Historical Sketches; Illustrating some Memorable Events and Epochs, from A.D. 1400 to A.D. 1546. By the Rev. John Hampden Gurney, M.A., Rector of St. Mary's, Mary-le-bone. Fcp. 8vo. 7*s.* 6*d.*

Gosse.—A Naturalist's Sojourn in Jamaica. By P. H. Gosse, Esq. With Plates. Post 8vo. price 14*s.*

Gwilt.—An Encyclopædia of Architecture, Historical, Theoretical, and Practical. By Joseph Gwilt. Illustrated with more than One Thousand Engravings on Wood, from Designs by J. S. Gwilt. Second Edition, with a Supplemental View of the Symmetry and Stability of Gothic Architecture: Comprising upwards of Eighty additional Woodcuts. 8vo. price 52*s.* 6*d.*

The SUPPLEMENT separately, price 6*s.*

Sidney Hall's General Large Library Atlas of Fifty-three Maps (size 20 in. by 16 in.), with the Divisions and Boundaries carefully coloured; and an Alphabetical Index of all the Names contained in the Maps. New Edition, corrected from the best and most recent Authorities; with the Railways laid down, and many entirely new Maps. Colombier 4to. price £5. 5s. half-russia.

Hamilton.—Discussions in Philosophy and Literature, Education and University Reform. Chiefly from the *Edinburgh Review*; corrected, vindicated, enlarged, in Notes and Appendices. By Sir William Hamilton, Bart. Second Edition, with Additions. 8vo. price 21s.

Hare (Archdeacon).—The Life of Luther, in Forty-eight Historical Engravings. By Gustav König. With Explanations by Archdeacon Hare. Square crown 8vo. [*In the press.*

Harrison.—The Light of the Forge; or, Counsels drawn from the Sick-Bed of E. M. By the Rev. William Harrison, M.A., Rector of Birch, Essex, and Domestic Chaplain to H. R. H. the Duchess of Cambridge. With 2 Woodcuts. Fcp. 8vo. price 5s.

Harry Hieover.—The Hunting-Field. By Harry Hieover. With Two Plates, one representing *The Right Sort*; the other, *The Wrong Sort.* Fcp. 8vo. 5s.

Harry Hieover.—Practical Horsemanship. By Harry Hieover. With 2 Plates, one representing *Going like Workmen*; the other, *Going like Muffs.* Fcp. 8vo. 5s. half-bound.

Harry Hieover.—The Stud, for Practical Purposes and Practical Men: being a Guide to the Choice of a Horse for use more than for show. By Harry Hieover. With 2 Plates, one representing *A pretty good sort for most purposes*; the other, *Rayther a bad sort for any purpose.* Fcp. 8vo. price 5s. half-bound.

Harry Hieover.—The Pocket and the Stud; or, Practical Hints on the Management of the Stable. By Harry Hieover. Second Edition; with Portrait of the Author on his favourite Horse *Harlequin.* Fcp. 8vo. price 5s. half-bound.

Harry Hieover.—Stable Talk and Table Talk; or Spectacles for Young Sportsmen. By Harry Hieover. New Edition, 2 vols. 8vo. with Portrait, 24s.

Haydn's Book of Dignities: con-taining Rolls of the Official Personages of the British Empire, Civil, Ecclesiastical, Judicial, Military, Naval, and Municipal, from the Earliest Periods to the Present Time: compiled chiefly from the Records of the Public Offices. Together with the Sovereigns of Europe, from the Foundation of their respective States; the Peerage and Nobility of Great Britain; and numerous other Lists. Being a New Edition, improved and continued, of Beatson's Political Index. By Joseph Haydn, Compiler of *The Dictionary of Dates*, and other Works. 8vo. price 25s. half-bound.

Haydon.—The Life of Benjamin Robert Haydon, Historical Painter, from his Autobiography and Journals. Edited and compiled by Tom Taylor, M.A., of the Inner Temple, Esq.; late Fellow of Trinity College, Cambridge; and late Professor of the English Language and Literature in University College, London. Second Edition, with Additions and an Index. 3 vols. post 8vo. price 31s. 6d.

Sir John Herschel.—Outlines of Astronomy. By Sir John F. W. Herschel, Bart. etc. New Edition; with Plates and Wood Engravings. 8vo. price 18s.

Hill.—Travels in Siberia and Russia. By S. S. Hill, Esq. 2 vols. post 8vo. with Map.

Hints on Etiquette and the Usages of Society: With a Glance at Bad Habits. By Αγωγός. "Manners make the Man." New Edition, revised (with Additions) by a Lady of Rank. Fcp. 8vo. price Half-a-Crown.

Hole.—Prize Essay on the His-tory and Management of Literary, Scientific, and Mechanics' Institutions, and especially how far they may be developed and combined so as to promote the Moral Well-being and Industry of the Country. By James Hole, Hon. Secretary of the Yorkshire Union of Mechanics' Institutes. 8vo. price 5s.

Lord Holland's Memoirs.— Memoirs of the Whig Party during My Time. By Henry Richard Lord Holland. Edited by his Son, Henry Edward Lord Holland. Vols. I. and II. post 8vo. price 9s. 6d. each.

Lord Holland's Foreign Remi-niscences. Edited by his Son, Henry Edward Lord Holland. Second Edition; with Facsimile. Post 8vo. price 10s. 6d.

Holland.—Chapters on Mental Physiology. By Sir HENRY HOLLAND, Bart., F. R. S., Physician-Extraordinary to the Queen; and Physician in Ordinary to His Royal Highness Prince Albert. Founded chiefly on Chapters contained in *Medical Notes and Reflections*, by the same Author. Fcp. 8vo. price 10*s*. 6*d*.

Hook. — The Last Days of Our Lord's Ministry: A Course of Lectures on the principal Events of Passion Week. By WALTER FARQUHAR HOOK, D.D., Chaplain in Ordinary to the Queen. New Edition. Fcp. 8vo. price 6*s*.

Hooker and Arnott.—The British Flora; Comprising the Phænogamous or Flowering Plants, and the Ferns. The Sixth Edition, with Additions and Corrections, and numerous Figures, illustrative of the Umbelliferous Plants, the Composite Plants, the Grasses, and the Ferns. By Sir W. J. HOOKER, F.R.A. and L.S. etc., and G. A. WALKER ARNOTT, LL.D., F.L.S. 12mo. with 12 Plates, price 14*s*., with the Plates coloured, price 21*s*.

Hooker.—Kew Gardens; or, a Popular Guide to the Royal Botanic Gardens of Kew. By Sir WILLIAM JACKSON HOOKER, K.H., D.C.L., F.R.A. and L.S., etc. etc. Director. New Edition; with numerous Wood Engravings. 16mo. price Sixpence.

Horne.—An Introduction to the Critical Study and Knowledge of the Holy Scriptures. By THOMAS HARTWELL HORNE, B.D. of St. John's College, Cambridge. Prebendary of St. Paul's. New Edition, revised and corrected: with numerous Maps, and Facsimiles of Biblical Manuscripts, 5 vols. 8vo. price 63*s*.

Horne.—A Compendious Intro-duction to the Study of the Bible. By THOMAS HARTWELL HORNE, B.D. of St. John's College, Cambridge. Being an Analysis of his *Introduction to the Critical Study and Knowledge of the Holy Scriptures*. New Edition, corrected and enlarged; with Maps and other Engravings. 12mo. price 9*s*.

Howitt.—(A. M.) An Art Stu-dent in Munich, By ANNA MARY HOWITT, 2 vols. post 8vo. price 14*s*.

Howitt.—The Children's Year. By MARY HOWITT. With Four Illustrations, engraved by John Absolon, from Original Designs by ANNA MARY HOWITT. Square 16mo. price 5*s*.

William Howitt's Boy's Coun-try Book. Being the real Life of a Country Boy, written by Himself: Exhibiting all the Amusements, Pleasures, and Pursuits of Children in the Country. New Edition; with 40 Woodcuts. Fcp. 8vo. price 6*s*.

Howitt.—The Rural Life of En-gland. By WILLIAM HOWITT. New Edition, corrected and revised; with Woodcuts by Bewick and Williams; uniform with *Visits to Remarkable Places*. Medium 8vo. 21*s*.

Howitt.—Visits to Remarkable Places; Old Halls, Battle-Fields, and Scenes illustrative of Striking Passages in English History and Poetry. By WILLIAM HOWITT. New Edition; with 40 Woodcuts. Medium 8vo. 21*s*.

Second Series, chiefly in the Counties of Northumberland and Durham, with a Stroll along the Border. With upwards of 40 Woodcuts. Medium 8vo. 21*s*.

Hudson. — Plain Directions for Making Wills in conformity with the Law: with a clear Exposition of the Law relating to the Distribution of Personal Estate in the case of Intestacy, two Forms of Wills, and much useful Information. By J. C. HUDSON, Esq., late of the Legacy Duty Office, London. New and enlarged Edition; including the provisions of the Wills Act Amendment Act of 1852, (introduced by Lord St. Leonards). Fcp. 8vo. 2*s*. 6*d*.

Hudson.—The Executor's Guide. By J. C. HUDSON, Esq., New and enlarged Edition; with the Addition of Directions for paying Succession Duties on Real Property under Wills and Intestacies, and a Table for finding the Values of Annuities and the Amount of Legacy and Succession Duty thereon. Fcp. 8vo. price 6*s*.

Humboldt's Aspects of Nature. Translated, with the Author's authority, by Mrs. SABINE. New Edition. 16mo. price 6*s*.: or in 2 vols. 3*s*. 6*d*. each cloth; 2*s*. 6*d*. each sewed.

Humboldt's Cosmos. — Trans-lated with the Author's authority, by Mrs. SABINE. Vols. I. and II. 16mo. Half-a-Crown each, sewed; 3*s*. 6*d*. each cloth: or in post 8vo. 12*s*. 6*d*. each cloth. Vol. III. post 8vo. 12*s*. 6*d*. each cloth: or in 16mo. Part I. 2*s*. 6*d*. sewed, 3*s*. 6*d*. cloth; and Part II. 3*s*. sewed, 4*s*. cloth.

Humphreys. — Sentiments and Similes of Shakspeare: A Classified Selection of Similes, Definitions, Descriptions, and other remarkable Passages in Shakspeare's Plays and Poems. With an elaborately illuminated border in the characteristic style of the Elizabethan Period, massive carved covers, and other Embellishments, designed and executed by H. N. HUMPHREYS. Square, post 8vo. price 21*s*.

The Report of the Committee appointed by the Council of the Society of Arts to inquire into the Subject of Industrial Instruction. With the Evidences. 8vo. price 5*s*.

Jameson.—A Commonplace Book of Thoughts, Memories, and Fancies, Original and Selected. Part I. Ethics and Character; Part II. Literature and Art. By Mrs. JAMESON. With Etchings and Wood Engravings. Square crown 8vo. [*Just ready.*

Mrs. Jameson's Legends of the Saints and Martyrs. Forming the First Series of *Sacred and Legendary Art.* Second Edition; with numerous Woodcuts, and 16 Etchings by the Author. Square crown 8vo. price 28*s.*

Mrs. Jameson's Legends of the Monastic Order, as represented in the Fine Arts. Forming the Second Series of *Sacred and Legendary Art.* Second Edition, corrected and enlarged; with 11 Etchings by the Author, and 88 Woodcuts. Square crown 8vo. price 28*s.*

Mrs. Jameson's Legends of the Madonna, as represented in the Fine Arts. Forming the Third Series of *Sacred and Legendary Art.* With 55 Drawings by the Author, and 152 Wood Engravings. Square crown 8vo. price 28*s.*

Lord Jeffrey's Contributions to the Edinburgh Review. A New Edition, complete in One Volume, with a Portrait engraved by HENRY ROBINSON, and a Vignette View of Craigcrook, engraved by J. Cousen. Square crown 8vo. 21*s.* cloth; or 30*s.* calf.

*** Also a LIBRARY EDITION, in 3 ols. 8vo. price 42*s.*

Bishop Jeremy Taylor's Entire Works: with Life, by Bishop HEBER. Revised and corrected by the Rev. CHARLES PAGE EDEN, Fellow of Oriel College, Oxford. In Ten Volumes. Vols. II. to X. 8vo. price Half-a-Guinea each. Vol. I. comprising Bishop Heber's Life of Jeremy Taylor, extended by the Editor, is *nearly ready.*

Johnston.—A New Dictionary of Geography, Descriptive, Physical, Statistical, and Historical: Forming a complete General Gazetteer of the World. By ALEXANDER KEITH JOHNSTON, F.R.S.E., F.R.G.S.F.G.S.; Geographer at Edinburgh in Ordinary to Her Majesty. In One Volume of 1,440 pages, comprising nearly 50,000 Names of Places. 8vo. price 36*s.* cloth; or half-bound in russia, 41*s.*

Kemble.—The Saxons in Eng-land; A History of the English Commonwealth till the period of the Norman Conquest. By JOHN MITCHELL KEMBLE, M.A., F.C.P.S., etc. 2 vols. 8vo. price 28*s.*

Kippis's Collection of Hymns and Psalms for Public and Private Worship. New Edition; including a New Supplement by the Rev. EDMUND KELL, M.A. 18mo. price 4*s.* cloth; or 4*s.* 6*d.* roan.—The SUPPLEMENT, separately, price Eightpence.

Kirby.—The Life of the Rev. WILLIAM KIRBY, M.A., F.R.S., F.L.S., etc. Rector of Barham. Author of one of the Bridgewater Treatises, and Joint-Author of the *Introduction to Entomology.* By the Rev. JOHN FREEMAN, M.A., Rector of Ashwicken, Norfolk, and Rural Dean. With Portrait, Vignette, and Facsimile. 8vo. price 15*s.*

Kirby & Spence's Introduction to Entomology; or, Elements of the Natural History of Insects: comprising an account of noxious and useful Insects, of their Metamorphoses, Food, Stratagems, Habitations, Societies, Motions, Noises, Hybernation, Instinct, etc. New Edition, 2 vols. 8vo. with Plates, price 31*s.* 6*d.*

Laing's (S.) Observations on the Social and Political State of Denmark and the Duchies of Sleswick and Holstein in 1851: Being the Third Series of *Notes of a Traveller.* 8vo. price 12*s.*

Laing's (S.) Observations on the Social and Political State of the European People in 1848 and 1849: Being the Second Series of *Notes of a Traveller.* 8vo. price 14*s.*

L. E. L.—The Poetical Works of Letitia Elizabeth Landon; comprising the *Improvisatrice,* the *Venetian Bracelet,* the *Golden Violet,* the *Troubadour,* and Poetical Remains. New Edition; with 2 Vignettes by Richard Doyle. 2 vols. 16mo. 10*s.* cloth; morocco, 21*s.*

Dr. Latham on Diseases of the Heart. Lectures on Subjects connected with Clinical Medicine: Diseases of the Heart. By P. M. LATHAM, M.D., Physician Extraordinary to the Queen. New Edition. 2 vols. 12mo. price 16*s.*

Mrs. R. Lee's Elements of Na-tural History; or First Principles of Zoology: comprising the Principles of Classification, interspersed with amusing and instructive Accounts of the most remarkable Animals. New Edition, enlarged; with numerous additional Woodcuts. Fcp. 8vo. price 7*s.* 6*d.*

Letters on Happiness, addressed to a Friend. By the Author of *Letters to My Unknown Friends,* etc. Fcp. 8vo. price 6*s.*

LARDNER'S CABINET CYCLOPÆDIA.

Of History, Biography, Literature, the Arts and Sciences, Natural History, and Manufactures: A Series of Original Works by

SIR JOHN HERSCHEL,
SIR JAMES MACKINTOSH,
ROBERT SOUTHEY,
SIR DAVID BREWSTER,
THOMAS KEIGHTLEY,
JOHN FORSTER,
SIR WALTER SCOTT,
THOMAS MOORE,
BISHOP THIRLWALL,
THE REV G. R. GLEIG,
J. C. L. DE SISMONDI,
JOHN PHILLIPS, F.R.S., G.S.

AND OTHER EMINENT WRITERS.

Complete in 132 vols. cp. 8vo. with Vignette Titles, price, in cloth, Nineteen Guineas.
The Works *separately*, in Sets or Series, price Three Shillings and Sixpence each Volume.

A List of the WORKS *composing the* CABINET CYCLOPÆDIA:—

1. Bell's History of Russia . 3 vols. 10*s*. 6*d*.
2. Bell's Lives of British Poets, 2 vols. 7*s*.
3. Brewster's Optics, . . 1 vol. 3*s*. 6*d*.
4. Cooley's Maritime and Inland Discovery . . 3 vols. 10*s*. 6*d*.
5. Crowe's History of France, 3 vols. 10*s*. 6*d*.
6. De Morgan on Probabilities, 1 vol. 3*s*. 6*d*.
7. De Sismondi's History of the Italian Republics . 1 vol. 3*s*. 6*d*.
8. De Sismondi's Fall of the Roman Empire . . 2 vols. 7*s*.
9. Donovan's Chemistry . 1 vol. 3*s*. 6*d*.
10. Donovan's Domestic Economy . . . . 2 vols. 7*s*.
11. Dunham's Spain and Portugal . . . . 5 vols. 17*s*. 6*d*.
12. Dunham's History of Denmark, Sweden, and Norway . . . . 3 vols. 10*s*. 6*d*.
13. Dunham's History of Poland . . . . 1 vol. 3*s*. 6*d*.
14. Dunham's Germanic Empire . . . . 3 vols. 10*s*. 6*d*.
15. Dunham's Europe during the Middle Ages . . 4 vols. 14*s*.
16. Dunham's British Dramatists . . . . 2 vols. 7*s*.
17. Dunham's Lives of Early Writers of Great Britain, 1 vol. 3*s*. 6*d*.
18. Fergus's History of the United States . . 2 vols. 7*s*.
19. Fosbroke's Greek and Roman Antiquities . . 2 vols. 7*s*.
20. Forster's Lives of the Statesmen of the Commonwealth . . . 5 vols. 17*s*. 6*d*.
21. Gleig's Lives of British Military Commanders 3 vols. 10*s*. 6*d*.
22. Grattan's History of the Netherlands . . . 1 vol. 3*s*. 6*d*.
23. Henslow's Botany . . 1 vol. 3*s*. 6*d*.
24. Herschel's Astronomy . 1 vol. 3*s*. 6*d*.
25. Herschel's Discourse on Natural Philosophy . 1 vol. 3*s*. 6*d*.
26. History of Rome . 2 vols. 7*s*.
27. History of Switzerland . 1 vol. 3*s*. 6*d*.
28. Holland's Manufactures in Metal, ... 3 vols. 10*s*. 6*d*.
29. James's Lives of Foreign Statesmen . . . 5 vols. 17*s*. 6*d*.
30. Kater and Lardner's Mechanics . . . 1 vol. 3*s*. 6*d*.
31. Keightley's Outlines of History . . . . 1 vol. 3*s*. 6*d*.
32. Lardner's Arithmetic . 1 vol. 3*s*. 6*d*.
33. Lardner's Geometry . 1 vol. 3*s*. 6*d*.
34. Lardner on Heat . . 1 vol. 3*s*. 6*d*.
35. Lardner's Hydrostatics and Pneumatics . . . 1 vol. 3*s*. 6*d*.
36. Lardner and Walker's Electricity and Magnetism, 2 vols. 7*s*.
37. Mackintosh, Forster, and Courtenay's Lives of British Statesmen . . 7 vols. 24*s*. 6*d*.
38. Mackintosh, Wallace, and Bell's History of England . . . . 10 vols. 35*s*.
39. Montgomery and Shelley's Eminent Italian, Spanish, and Portuguese Authors, 3 vols. 10*s*. 6*d*.
40. Moore's History of Ireland, 4 vols. 14*s*.
41. Nicolas's Chronology of History . . . 1 vol. 3*s*. 6*d*.
42. Phillips' Treatise on Geology . . . . 2 vols. 7*s*.
43. Powell's History of Natural Philosophy . . . 1 vol. 3*s*. 6*d*.
44. Porter's Treatise on the Manufacture of Silk . 1 vol. 3*s*. 6*d*.
45. Porter's Manufacture of Porcelain and Glass . 1 vol. 3*s*. 6*d*.
46. Roscoe's British Lawyers, 1 vol. 3*s*. 6*d*.
47. Scott's History of Scotland . . . . 2 vols. 7*s*.
48. Shelley's Lives of Eminent French Authors . . 2 vols. 7*s*.
49. Shuckard and Swainson's Insects . . . . 1 vol. 3*s*. 6*d*.
50. Southey's Lives of British Admirals . . . 5 vols. 17*s*. 6*d*.
51. Stebbing's Church History, 2 vols. 7*s*.
52. Stebbing's History of the Reformation . . 2 vols. 7*s*.
53. Swainson's Discourse on Natural History . . 1 vol. 3*s*. 6*d*.
54. Swainson's Natural History and Classification of Animals . . . 1 vol. 3*s*. 6*d*.
55. Swainson's Habits and Instincts of Animals . 1 vol. 3*s*. 6*d*.
56. Swainson's Birds . . 2 vols. 7*s*.
57. Swainson's Fish, Reptiles, etc. . . . . . 2 vols. 7*s*.
58. Swainson's Quadrupeds . 1 vol. 3*s*. 6*d*.
59. Swainson's Shells and Shell-fish . . . 1 vol. 3*s*. 6*d*.
60. Swainson's Animals in Menageries . . . . 1 vol. 3*s*. 6*d*.
61. Swainson's Taxidermy and Biography of Zoologists 1 vol. 3*s*. 6*d*.
62. Thirlwall's History of Greece . . . . 8 vols. 28*s*.

Letters to my Unknown Friends By a Lady, Author of *Letters on Happiness.* Fourth *and cheaper* Edition. Fcp. 8vo. price 5*s.*

Lindley.—The Theory of Horticulture; Or, an Attempt to explain the principal Operations of Gardening upon Physiological Principles. By JOHN LINDLEY, Ph.D. F.R.S. New Edition, revised and improved; with Wood Engravings. 8vo. [*In the press.*

Dr. John Lindley's Introduction to Botany. New Edition, with Corrections and copious Additions. 2 vols. 8vo. with Six Plates and numerous Woodcuts, 24*s.*

Linwood.—Anthologia Oxoniensis, sive, Florilegium e lusibus poeticis diversorum Oxoniensium Græcis et Latinis decerptum. Curante GULIELMO LINWOOD, M.A. Ædis Christi Alummo. 8vo. price 14*s.*

Dr. Little on Deformities.—On the Nature and Treatment of Deformities of the Human Frame. By W. J. LITTLE, M.D., Physician to the London Hospital, Founder of the Royal Orthopædic Hospital, etc. With 160 Woodcuts and Diagrams. 8vo. price 15*s.*

Litton.—The Church of Christ, in its Idea, Attributes, and Ministry: With a particular Reference to the Controversy on the Subject between Romanists and Protestants. By the Rev. EDWARD ARTHUR LITTON, M.A., Vice-Principal of St. Edmund Hall, Oxford. 8vo. price 16*s.*

Lorimer's (C.) Letters to a Young Master Mariner on some Subjects connected with his Calling. New Edition. Fcp. 8vo. price 5*s.* 6*d.*

Loudon's Self-Instruction for Young Gardeners, Foresters, Bailiffs, Land Stewards, and Farmers; in Arithmetic, Book-keeping, Geometry, Mensuration, Practical Trigonometry, Mechanics, Land-Surveying, Levelling, Planning and Mapping, Architectural Drawing, and Isometrical Projection and Perspective: With Examples shewing their applications to Horticultural and Agricultural Purposes; a Memoir, Portrait, and Woodcuts. 8vo. price 7*s.* 6*d.*

Loudon's Encyclopædia of Gardening; comprising the Theory and Practice of Horticulture, Floriculture, Arboriculture, and Landscape Gardening: Including all the latest improvements, a General History of Gardening in all Countries; a Statistical View of its Present State; and Suggestions for its Future Progress in the British Isles. With many hundred Woodcuts. New Edition, corrected and improved by Mrs. LOUDON. 8vo. price 50*s.*

Loudon's Encyclopædia of Trees and Shrubs; or the *Arboretum et Fruticetum Britannicum* abridged: Containing the Hardy Trees and Shrubs of Great Britain, Native and Foreign, Scientifically and Popularly Described: with their Propagation, Culture, and Uses in the Arts; and with Engravings of nearly all the Species. Adapted for the use of Nurserymen, Gardeners, and Foresters. With about 2,000 Woodcuts, 8vo. price 50*s.*

Loudon's Encyclopædia of Agriculture: comprising the Theory and Practice of the Valuation, Transfer, Laying-out, Improvement, and Management of Landed Property, and of the Cultivation and Economy of the Animal and Vegetable Productions of Agriculture; Including all the latest improvements, a general History of Agriculture in all Countries, a Statistical View of its present State, and Suggestions for its future progress in the British Isles. New Edition; with 1,100 Woodcuts. 8vo. price 50*s.*

Loudon's Encyclopædia of Plants, including all the Plants which are now found in, or have been introduced into, Great Britain, giving their Natural History, accompanied by such descriptions, engraved Figures, and elementary details, as may enable a beginner, who is a mere English reader, to discover the name of every Plant which he may find in flower, and acquire all the information respecting it which is useful and interesting. New Edition, corrected throughout and brought down to the year 1854, by Mrs. LOUDON and GEORGE DON, Esq., F.L.S., etc. 8vo [*In the Spring.*

Loudon's Encyclopædia of Cottage, Farm, and Villa Architecture and Furniture: containing numerous Designs, from the Villa to the Cottage and the Farm, including Farm Houses, Farmeries, and other Agricultural Buildings; Country Inns, Public Houses, and Parochial Schools, with the requisite Fittings-up, Fixtures, and Furniture, and appropriate Offices, Gardens, and Garden Scenery: Each Design accompanied by Analytical and Critical Remarks. New Edition, edited by Mrs. LOUDON; with more than 2,000 Woodcuts. 8vo. price 63*s.*

Loudon's Hortus Britannicus; Or, Catalogue of all the Plants indigenous to, cultivated in, or introduced into Britain. An entirely New Edition corrected throughout: With a Supplement, including all the New Plants, and a New General Index to the whole Work. Edited by Mrs. LOUDON; assisted by W. H. BAXTER and DAVID WOOSTER. 8vo. price 31*s.* 6*d.*—The SUPPLEMENT separately, price 14*s.*

Mrs. Loudon's Amateur Gardener's Calendar; Being a Monthly Guide as to what should be avoided as well as what should be done in a Garden in each Month: with plain Rules *how to do* what is requisite; Directions for Laying Out and Planting Kitchen and Flower Gardens, Pleasure Grounds, and Shrubberies; and a short account, in each Month, of the Quadrupeds, Birds, and Insects, then most injurious to Gardens. 16mo. with Woodcuts, price 7*s*. 6*d*.

Mrs. Loudon's Lady's Country Companion; or, How to Enjoy a Country Life Rationally. Fourth Edition, with Plates and Wood Engravings. Fcp. 8vo. price 5*s*.

Low.—A Treatise on the Domesticated Animals of the British Islands: comprehending the Natural and Economical History of Species and Varieties; the Description of the Properties of external Form; and Observations on the Principles and Practice of Breeding. By D. Low, Esq., F.R.S.E. With Wood Engravings. 8vo. price 25*s*.

Low.—Elements of Practical Agriculture; comprehending the Cultivation of Plants, the Husbandry of the Domestic Animals, and the Economy of the Farm. By D. Low, Esq., F.R.S.E. New Edition; with 200 Woodcuts, 8vo. price 21*s*.

Macaulay.—Speeches of the Right Hon. T. B. Macaulay, M.P. Corrected by Himself. 8vo. price 12*s*.

Macaulay.—The History of England from the Accession of James II. By Thomas Babington Macaulay. New Edition. Vols. I. and II. 8vo. price 32*s*.

Mr. Macaulay's Critical and Historical Essays contributed to the Edinburgh Review. Four Editions, as follows:—

1. Library Edition (the *Seventh*), in 3 vols. 8vo. price 36*s*.
2. Complete in One Volume, with Portrait and Vignette. Square crown 8vo. price 21*s*. cloth; or 30*s*. calf.
3. Another Edition, in 3 vols. fcp. 8vo. price 21*s*.
4. People's Edition, in course of publication, crown 8vo. in Weekly Numbers at 1½*d*. and in 7 Monthly Parts, price One Shilling each.

Macaulay.—Lays of Ancient Rome, with Ivry and the Armada. By Thomas Babington Macaulay. New Edition. 16mo. price 4*s*. 6*d*. cloth; or 10*s*. 6*d*. bound in morocco.

Mr. Macaulay's Lays of Ancient Rome. With numerous Illustrations, Original and from the Antique, drawn on Wood by George Scarf, jun., and engraved by Samuel Williams. New Edition. Fcp. 4to. price 21*s*. boards; or 42*s*. bound in morocco.

Macdonald.—Villa Verocchio; or the Youth of Leonardo da Vinci: A Tale. By the late Diana Louisa Macdonald. Fcp. 8vo. price 6*s*.

Sir James Mackintosh's History of England from the Earliest Times to the final Establishment of the Reformation. Being that portion of the *History of England* published in Dr. Lardner's *Cabinet Cyclopædia*, which was contributed by Sir James Mackintosh. Library Edition, revised by the Author's Son. 2 vols. 8vo. price 21*s*.

Mackintosh.—Sir James Mackintosh's Miscellaneous Works: Including his Contributions to the Edinburgh Review. A New Edition, complete in One Volume; with Portrait and Vignette. Square crown 8vo. price 21*s*. cloth; or 30*s*. bound in calf.

M'Culloch.—A Dictionary, Practical, Theoretical, and Historical, of Commerce and Commercial Navigation. Illustrated with Maps and Plans. By J. R. M'Culloch, Esq. New Edition (1854), adapted to the Present Time; and embracing a large mass of new and important Information in regard to the Trade, Commercial Law, and Navigation of this and other Countries. 8vo. price 50*s*. cloth; half-russia, with flexible back, 55*s*.

M'Culloch.—A Dictionary, Geographical, Statistical, and Historical, of the various Countries, Places, and Principal Natural Objects in the World. By J. R. M'Culloch, Esq. Illustrated with Six large Maps. New Edition, with a Supplement, comprising the Population of Great Britain from the Census of 1851. 2 vols. 8vo. price 63*s*.

M'Culloch.—An Account, Descriptive and Statistical of the British Empire; Exhibiting its Extent, Physical Capacities, Population, Industry, and Civil and Religious Institutions. By J. R. M'Culloch, Esq. New Edition, corrected, enlarged, and greatly improved. 2 vols. 8vo. price 42*s*.

Maitland.—The Church in the Catacombs: A Description of the Primitive Church of Rome, illustrated by its Sepulchral Remains. By the Rev. CHARLES MAITLAND. New Edition, with many Woodcuts. 8vo. price 14s.

Mrs. Marcet's Conversations on Chemistry, in which the Elements of that Science are familiarly Explained and Illustrated by Experiments. New Edition, enlarged and improved. 2 vols. fcp. 8vo. price 14s.

Mrs. Marcet's Conversations on Natural Philosophy, in which the Elements of that Science are familiarly explained. New Edition, enlarged and corrected; with 23 Plates. Fcp. 8vo. price 10s. 6d.

Mrs. Marcet's Conversations on Political Economy, in which the Elements of that Science are familiarly explained. New Edition. Fcp. 8vo. price 7s. 6d.

Mrs. Marcet's Conversations on Vegetable Physiology; comprehending the Elements of Botany, with their Application to Agriculture. New Edition; with Four Plates. Fcp. 8vo. price 9s.

Mrs. Marcet's Conversations on Land and Water. New Edition, revised and corrected; with a coloured Map, shewing the comparative Altitude of Mountains. Fcp. 8vo. price 5s. 6d.

Martineau.—Church History in England: Being a Sketch of the History of the Church of England from the Earliest Times to the Period of the Reformation. By the Rev. ARTHUR MARTINEAU, M.A., late Fellow of Trinity College, Cambridge. 12mo. price 6s.

Maunder's Biographical Treasury; consisting of Memoirs, Sketches, and brief Notices of above 12,000 Eminent Persons of all Ages and Nations, from the Earliest Period of History; forming a new and complete Dictionary of Universal Biography. The Eighth Edition, revised throughout, and brought down to the close of the year 1853. Fcp. 8vo. 10s. cloth; bound in roan, 12s.; calf lettered, 12s. 6d.

Maunder's Historical Treasury; comprising a General Introductory Outline of Universal History, Ancient and Modern, and a Series of separate Histories of every principal Nation that exists; their Rise, Progress, and Present Condition, the Moral and Social Character of their respective Inhabitants, their Religion, Manners, and Customs, etc., etc. New Edition; revised throughout, and brought down to the Present Time. Fcp. 8vo. 10s. cloth; roan, 12s.; calf, 12s. 6d.

Maunder's Scientific and Literary Treasury: A New and Popular Encyclopædia of Science and the Belles-Lettres; including all Branches of Science, and every subject connected with Literature and Art. New Edition. Fcp. 8vo. price 10s. cloth; bound in roan, 12s.; calf lettered, 12s. 6d.

Maunder's Treasury of Natural History; Or, a Popular Dictionary of Animated Nature: In which the Zoological Characteristics that distinguish the different Classes, Genera, and Species, are combined with a variety of interesting Information illustrative of the Habits, Instincts, and General Economy of the Animal Kingdom. With 900 Woodcuts. New Edition. Fcp. 8vo. price 10s. cloth; roan, 12s.; calf, 12s. 6d.

Maunder's Treasury of Knowledge, and Library of Reference. Comprising an English Dictionary and Grammar, an Universal Gazetteer, a Classical Dictionary, a Chronology, a Law Dictionary, a Synopsis of the Peerage, numerous useful Tables, etc. The Twentieth Edition carefully revised and corrected throughout: With some Additions. Fcp 8vo. price 10s. cloth; bound in roan, 12s.; calf, 12s. 6d.

Merivale.—A History of the Romans under the Empire. By the Rev. CHARLES MERIVALE, B.D., late Fellow of St. John's College, Cambridge. Vols. I. and II. 8vo. price 28s.; and Vol. III. completing the History to the Establishment of the Monarchy by Augustus, price 14s.

Merivale.—The Fall of the Roman Republic: A Short History of the last Century of the Commonwealth. By the Rev. CHARLES MERIVALE, B.D., late Fellow of St. John's College, Cambridge. 12mo. price 7s. 6d.

Merivale.—Memoirs of Cicero: A Translation of *Cicero in his Letters*, by Bernard Rudolph Abeken. Edited by the Rev. CHARLES MERIVALE, B.D. 12mo.

Milner's History of the Church of Christ. With Additions by the late Rev. ISAAC MILNER, D.D., F.R.S. A New Edition, revised, with additional Notes by the Rev. T. GRANTHAM, B.D. 4 vols. 8vo. price 52s.

Montgomery.—Original Hymns for Public, Social, and Private Devotion. By JAMES MONTGOMERY. 18mo. 5s. 6d.

James Montgomery's Poetical Works: Collective Edition; with the Author's Autobiographical Prefaces. A New Edition, complete in One Volume; with Portrait and Vignette. Square crown 8vo. price 10*s*. 6*d*. cloth; morocco, 21*s*.—Or in 4 vols. fcp. 8vo. with Portrait, and Seven other Plates, price 20*s*. cloth; morocco, 36*s*.

Moore.—Man and his Motives. By George Moore, M.D., Member of the Royal College of Physicians. *Third* and cheaper *Edition*. Fcp. 8vo. price 6*s*.

Moore.—The Power of the Soul over the Body, considered in relation to Health and Morals. By George Moore, M.D., Member of the Royal College of Physicians, etc. *Fifth* and cheaper *Edition*. Fcp. 8vo. price 6*s*.

Moore.—The Use of the Body in relation to the Mind. By George Moore, M.D., Member of the Royal College of Physicians. *Third* and cheaper *Edition*. Fcp. 8vo. price 6*s*.

Moore. — Health, Disease, and Remedy, familiarly and practically considered in a few of their Relations to the Blood. By George Moore, M.D. Post 8vo. 7*s*. 6*d*.

Moore.—Memoirs, Journal, and Correspondence of Thomas Moore. Edited by the Right Hon. Lord John Russell, M.P. With Portraits and Vignette Illustrations. Vols. I. to IV. post 8vo. price 10*s*. 6*d*. each.

The Fifth and Sixth Volumes of MOORE'S MEMOIRS, JOURNAL, and CORRESPONDENCE, with Portraits of Lord John Russell and Mr. Corry, and Vignettes, by T. Creswick, R.A., of Moore's Residence at Paris and at Sloperton. Vols. V. and VI. post 8vo. price 21*s*.

Thomas Moore's Poetical Works. Containing the Author's recent Introduction and Notes. Complete in One Volume; with a Portrait, and a View of Sloperton Cottage. Medium 8vo. price 21*s*. cloth; morocco 42*s*.

*** Also a New and Cheaper Issue of the First collected Edition of the above, in 10 vols. fcp. 8vo. with Portrait, and 19 Plates, price 35*s*.

Moore. — Songs, Ballads, and Sacred Songs. By Thomas Moore, Author of *Lalla Rookh*, etc. First collected Edition, with Vignette by R. Doyle. 16mo. price 5*s*. cloth; 12*s*. 6*d*. bound in morocco.

Moore's Irish Melodies. New Edition, with the Autobiographical Preface from the Collective Edition of Mr. Moore's Poetical Works, and a Vignette Title by D. Maclise, R.A. 16mo. price 5*s*. cloth; 12*s*. 6*d*. bound in morocco.

Moore's Irish Melodies. Illus-trated by D. Maclise, R.A. New and cheaper Edition; with 161 Designs, and the whole of the Letter-press engraved on Steel, by F. P. Becker. Super royal 8vo. price 31*s*. 6*d*. boards; bound in morocco, £2. 12*s*. 6*d*.

The Original Edition of the above, in Imperial 8vo. price 63*s*. boards; morocco, £4. 14*s*. 6*d*.; proofs, £6. 6*s*. boards,—*may still be had.*

Moore's Lalla Rookh: An Ori-ental Romance. New Edition; with the Autobiographical Preface from the Collective Edition of Mr. Moore's Poetical Works, and a Vignette Title by D. Maclise, R.A. 16mo. price 5*s*. cloth; 12*s*. 6*d*. bound in morocco.

Moore's Lalla Rookh: An Ori-ental Romance. With 13 highly-finished Steel Plates, from Designs by Corbould, Meadows, and Stephanoff, engraved under the superintendence of the late Charles Heath. New Edition. Square crown 8vo. price 15*s*. cloth; morocco, 28*s*.

A few copies of the Original Edition, in royal 8vo. price One Guinea, *still remain.*

Morton.—A Manual of Pharmacy for the Student of Veterinary Medicine: Containing the Substances employed at the Royal Veterinary College, with an attempt at their Classification; and the Pharmacopœia of that Institution. By W. J. T. Morton, Professor of Chemistry and Materia Medica in the College. *Fifth Edition* (1854). Fcp. 8vo. price 10*s*.

Moseley.—The Mechanical Prin-ciples of Engineering and Architecture. By the Rev. H. Moseley, M.A., F.R.S., Professor of Natural Philosophy and Astronomy in King's College, London. 8vo. price 24*s*.

Mure.—A Critical History of the Language and Literature of Ancient Greece. By William Mure, M.P. of Caldwell. 3 vols. 8vo. price 36*s*.

Vol. IV. comprising His-torical Literature from the Rise of Prose Composition to the Death of Herodotus. 8vo. with Map, price 15*s*.

Murray's Encyclopædia of Geography: Comprising a complete Description of the Earth: exhibiting its Relation to the Heavenly Bodies, its Physical Structure, the Natural History of each Country, and the Industry, Commerce, Political Institutions, and Civil and Social State of All Nations. Second Edition; with 82 Maps, and upwards of 1,000 other Woodcuts. 8vo. price 60*s.*

Neale. — "Risen from the Ranks;" Or, Conduct *versus* Caste. By the Rev. ERSKINE NEALE, M.A., Rector of Kirton, Suffolk. Fcap. 8vo. price 6*s.*

Neale.—The Riches that bring no Sorrow. By the Rev. ERSKINE NEALE, M.A., Rector of Kirton, Suffolk. Fcp. 8vo. price 6*s.*

Neale. — The Earthly Resting Places of the Just. By the Rev. ERSKINE NEALE, M.A., Rector of Kirton, Suffolk. Fcp. 8vo. with Woodcuts, price 7*s.*

Neale.— The Closing Scene; or Christianity and Infidelity contrasted in the Last Hours of Remarkable Persons. By the Rev. ERSKINE NEALE, M.A., Rector of Kirton, Suffolk. New Editions of the First and Second Series. 2 vols. fcp. 8vo. price 12*s.*; or separately, 6*s.* each.

Newman.—Discourses addressed to Mixed Congregations. By JOHN HENRY NEWMAN, Priest of the Oratory of St. Philip Neri. Second Edition. 8vo. price 12*s.*

Lieutenant Osborn's Arctic Journal. Stray Leaves from an Arctic Journal; or, Eighteen Months in the Polar Regions in search of Sir John Franklin's Expedition. By Lieut. SHERARD OSBORN, R.N., Commanding H.M.S.V. *Pioneer.* With Map and Four coloured Plates. Post 8vo. price 12*s.*

Owen Jones.—Flowers and their Kindred Thoughts. A Series of Stanzas. By MARY ANNE BACON. With beautiful Illustrations of Flowers printed in Colours by Owen Jones. Imperial 8vo. price 31*s.* 6*d.* elegantly bound in calf.

Owen. — Lectures on the Comparative Anatomy and Physiology of the Invertebrate Animals, delivered at the Royal College of Surgeons in 1843. By RICHARD OWEN, F.R.S. Hunterian Professor to the College. New Edition, corrected. 8vo. with Wood Engravings. [*In the press.*

Professor Owen's Lectures on the Comparative Anatomy and Physiology of the Vertebrate Animals, delivered at the Royal College of Surgeons in 1844 and 1846. With numerous Woodcuts. Vol. I. 8vo. price 14*s.*

The Complete Works of Blaise Pascal. Translated from the French, with Memoir, Introductions to the various Works, Editorial Notes, and Appendices, by GEORGE PEARCE, Esq. 3 vols. post 8vo. with Portrait, 25*s.* 6*d.*

Vol. 1. Pascal's Provincial Letters: with M. Villemain's Essay on Pascal prefixed, and a new Memoir. Post 8vo. Portrait, 8*s.* 6*d.*

Vol. 2. Pascal's Thoughts on Religion and Evidences of Christianity, with Additions from original MSS.: from M. Faugère's Edition. Post 8vo. 8*s.* 6*d.*

Vol. 3. Pascal's Miscellaneous Writings, Correspondence, Detached Thoughts, etc. from M. Faugère's Edition. Post 8vo. 8*s.* 6*d.*

Captain Peel's Travels in Nubia. —A Ride through the Nubian Desert. By Captain W. PEEL, R.N. Post 8vo. with a Route Map, price 5*s.*

Pereira's Treatise on Food and Diet. With Observations on the Dietetical Regimen suited for Disordered States of the Digestive Organs; and an Account of the Dietaries of some of the principal Metropolitan and other Establishments for Paupers, Lunatics, Criminals, Children, the Sick, etc. 8vo. 16*s.*

Peschel's Elements of Physics. Translated from the German, with Notes, by E. WEST. With Diagrams and Woodcuts. 3 vols. fcp. 8vo. 21*s.*

Peterborough. — A Memoir of Charles Mordaunt, Earl of Peterborough and Monmouth. With Selections from his Correspondence. By the Author of *Hochelaga*, etc. 2 vols. post 8vo. price 18*s.*

Phillips.—A Guide to Geology. By JOHN PHILLIPS, M.A. F.R.S. F.G.S., Deputy Reader in Geology in the University of Oxford; Honorary Member of the Imperial Academy of Sciences of Moscow, etc. Fourth Edition, corrected to the Present Time; with 4 Plates. Fcp. 8vo. price 5*s.*

Phillips's Elementary Introduction to Mineralogy. A New Edition, with extensive Alterations and Additions, by H. J. BROOKE, F.R.S., F.G.S.; and W. H. MILLER, M.A., F.G.S., Professor of Mineralogy in the University of Cambridge. With numerous Wood Engravings. Post 8vo. price 18*s.*

Phillips.—Figures and Descriptions of the Palæozoic Fossils of Cornwall, Devon, and West Somerset; observed in the course of the Ordnance Geological Survey of that District. By JOHN PHILLIPS, F.R.S. F.G.S. etc. 8vo. with 60 Plates, price 9*s.*

Captain Portlock's Report on the Geology of the County of Londonderry, and of Parts of Tyrone and Fermanagh, examined and described under the Authority of the Master-General and Board o Ordnance. 8vo. with 48 Plates, price 24*s*.

Power's Sketches in New Zealand, with Pen and Pencil. From a Journal kept in that Country, from July 1846 to June 1848. With Plates and Woodcuts. Post 8vo. 12*s*.

Pulman's Vade-Mecum of Fly-Fishing for Trout; being a complete Practical Treatise on that Branch of the Art of Angling; with plain and copious Instructions for the Manufacture of Artificial Flies. Third Edition, with Woodcuts. Fcp. 8vo. price 6*s*.

Pycroft's Course of English Reading, adapted to every Taste and Capacity; With Literary Anecdotes. New and cheaper Edition. Fcp. 8vo. price 5*s*.

Dr. Reece's Medical Guide; for the use of the Clergy, Heads of Families, Schools, and Junior Medical Practitioners: Comprising a complete Modern Dispensatory, and a Practical Treatise on the distinguishing Symptoms, Causes, Prevention, Cure, and Palliation of the Diseases incident to the Human Frame. With the latest Discoveries in the different departments of the Healing Art, Materia Medica, etc. Seventeenth Edition, corrected and enlarged by the Author's Son, Dr. H. Reece, M.R.C.S. etc. 8vo. price 12*s*.

Rich's Illustrated Companion to the Latin Dictionary and Greek Lexicon: Forming a Glossary of all the Words representing Visible Objects connected with the Arts, Manufactures, and Every-day Life of the Ancients. With Woodcut Representations of nearly 2,000 Objects from the Antique. Post 8vo. price 21*s*.

Sir J. Richardson's Journal of a Boat Voyage through Rupert's Land and the Arctic Sea, in Search of the Discovery Ships under Command of Sir John Franklin. With an Appendix on the Physical Geography of North America; a Map, Plates, and Woodcuts. 2 vols. 8vo. price 31*s*. 6*d*.

Richardson (Captain).—Horsemanship; or, the Art of Riding and Managing a Horse, adapted to the Guidance of Ladies and Gentlemen on the Road and in the Field: With Instructions for Breaking-in Colts and Young Horses. By Captain Richardson, late of the 4th Light Dragoons. With 5 Line Engravings. Square crown 8vo. price 14*s*.

Riddle's Complete Latin-English and English-Latin Dictionary, for the use of Colleges and Schools. *New* and cheaper *Edition*, revised and corrected. 8vo. 21*s*.

Separately { The English-Latin Dictionary, 7*s*. The Latin-English Dictionary, 15*s*.

Riddle's Copious and Critical Latin-English Lexicon, founded on the German-Latin Dictionaries of Dr. William Freund. New Edition. Post 4to. price 31*s*. 6*d*.

Riddle's Diamond Latin-English Dictionary: A Guide to the Meaning, Quality, and right Accentuation of Latin Classical Words. Royal 32mo. price 4*s*.

Rivers's Rose-Amateur's Guide; containing ample Descriptions of all the fine leading varieties of Roses, regularly classed in their respective Families; their History and Mode of Culture. New Edition, Fcp. 8vo. 6*s*.

Dr. E. Robinson's Greek and English Lexicon of the Greek Testament. A New Edition, revised and in great part re-written. 8vo. price 18*s*.

Roby.—Remains, Legendary & Poetical, of John Roby, Author of *Traditions of Lancashire*. With a Sketch of his Literary Life and Character by his Widow; and a Portrait. Post 8vo. price 10*s*. 6*d*.

Rogers.—Essays selected from Contributions to the Edinburgh Review. By Henry Rogers. 2 vols. 8vo. price 24*s*.

Dr. Roget's Thesaurus of English Words and Phrases classified and arranged so as to facilitate the Expression of Ideas and assist in Literary Composition. New Edition, revised and enlarged. Medium 8vo. price 14*s*.

Rowton's Debater: A Series of complete Debates, Outlines of Debates, and Questions for Discussion; with ample references to the best Sources of Information on each particular Topic. New Edition. Fcp. 8vo. price 6*s*.

Letters of Rachael Lady Russell. A New Edition, including several unpublished Letters, together with those edited by Miss Berry. With Portraits, Vignettes, and Facsimile. 2 vols. post 8vo. price 15*s*.

The Life of William Lord Russell. By the Right Hon. Lord John Russell, M.P. The Fourth Edition, complete in One Volume; with a Portrait engraved on Steel by S. Bellin, from the original by Sir Peter Lely at Woburn Abbey. Post 8vo. price 10*s*. 6*d*.

St. John (the Hon. F.)—Rambles in Search of Sport, in Germany, France, Italy, and Russia. By the Honourable FERDINAND ST. JOHN. With Four coloured Plates. Post 8vo. price 9*s*. 6*d*.

St. John (H.)—The Indian Archipelago; Its History and Present State. By HORACE ST. JOHN, Author of *The British Conquests in India*, etc. 2 vols. post 8vo. price 21*s*.

St. John (J. A.)—There and Back Again in Search of Beauty. By JAMES AUGUSTUS ST. JOHN, Author of *Isis*, etc. 2 vols. post 8vo. price 21*s*.

St. John (J. A.)—The Nemesis of Power: Causes and Forms of Political Revolutions. By JAMES AUGUSTUS ST. JOHN, Author of *There and Back again*, etc. Fcp. 8vo. [*Just ready*.

Mr. St. John's Work on Egypt. Isis: An Egyptian Pilgrimage. By JAMES AUGUSTUS ST. JOHN. 2 vols. post 8vo. 21*s*.

The Saints our Example. By the Author of *Letters to my Unknown Friends*, etc. Fcp. 8vo. price 7*s*.

Schmitz.—History of Greece, from the Earliest Times to the Taking of Corinth by the Romans, B.C. 146, mainly based upon Bishop Thirlwall's History of Greece. By Dr. LEONHARD SCHMITZ, F.R.S.E. Rector of the High School of Edinburgh. New Edition. 12mo. price 7*s*. 6*d*.

A Schoolmaster's Difficulties at Home and Abroad:—1. In regard to his Calling; 2. In relation to Himself; 3. As concerning his Charge; 4. About Committees; 5. With Pupil-Teachers; 6. Touching Inspectors; 7. On the Matter of Society; 8. In Prospect of the Future; and 9. Affecting Personal Relations. Fcp. 8vo. 4*s*. 6*d*.

Sir Edward Seaward's Narrative of his Shipwreck, and consequent Discovery of certain Islands in the Caribbean Sea: With a detail of many extraordinary and highly interesting Events in his Life, from 1733 to 1749. Third Edition; 2 vols. post 8vo. 21*s*.

An ABRIDGMENT, in 16mo. price 2*s*. 6*d*.

The Sermon on the Mount. Printed on Silver; with Picture Subjects, numerous Landscape and Illustrative Vignettes, and Illuminated Borders in Gold and Colours, designed expressly for this work by M. LEPELLE DU BOIS-GALLAIS, formerly employed by the French Government on the great work of Count Bastard. Square 18mo. price in ornamental boards, One Guinea; or 31*s*. 6*d*. bound in morocco.

Self-Denial the Preparation for Easter. By the Author of *Letters to my Unknown Friends, Letters on Happiness*, etc. Fcp. 8vo. price 2*s*. 6*d*.

Sewell.—Amy Herbert. By a Lady. Edited by the Rev. WILLIAM SEWELL, B.D. Fellow and Tutor of Exeter College, Oxford. New Edition. Fcp. 8vo. price 6*s*.

Sewell.—The Earl's Daughter. By the Author of *Amy Herbert*. Edited by the Rev. W. SEWELL, B.D. 2 vols. fcp. 8vo. 9*s*.

Sewell.—Gertrude: A Tale. By the Author of *Amy Herbert*. Edited by the Rev. W SEWELL, B.D. New Edition. Fcp. 8vo. price 6*s*.

Sewell.—Laneton Parsonage: A Tale for Children, on the practical Use of a Portion of the Church Catechism. By the Author *Amy Herbert*. Edited by the Rev. W. SEWELL, B.D. New Edition. 3 vols. fcp. 8vo. price 16*s*.

Sewell.—Margaret Percival. By the Author of *Amy Herbert*. Edited by the Rev. W. SEWELL, B.D. New Edition. 2 vols. fcp. 8vo. price 12*s*.

By the same Author,

The Experience of Life. New Edition. Fcp. 8vo. price 7*s*. 6*d*.

Readings for a Month Preparatory to Confirmation: Compiled from the Works of Writers of the Early and of the English Church. Fcp. 8vo. price 5*s*. 6*d*.

Readings for Every Day in Lent: Compiled from the Writings of BISHOP JEREMY TAYLOR. Fcp. 8vo. 5*s*.

Sharp's New British Gazetteer, or Topographical Dictionary of the British Islands and Narrow Seas: Comprising concise Descriptions of about Sixty Thousand Places, Seats, Natural Features, and Objects of Note, founded on the best Authorities; full Particulars of the Boundaries, Registered Electors, etc. of the Parliamentary Boroughs; with a reference under every name to the Sheet of the Ordnance Survey, as far as completed; and an Appendix, containing a General View of the Resources of the United Kingdom, a Short Chronology, and an Abstract of certain Results of the Census of 1851. 2 vols. 8vo. price £2. 16*s*.

The Family Shakspeare; in which nothing is added to the Original Text; but those Words and Expressions are *omitted* which cannot with propriety be read aloud. By T. BOWDLER, Esq. F.R.S. New Edition, in volumes for the Pocket. 6 vols. fcp. 8vo. price 30*s.*

₊ Also a LIBRARY EDITION; with 36 Wood Engravings from designs by Smirke, Howard, and other Artists. 8vo. price 21*s.*

Short Whist; Its Rise, Progress, and Laws: With Observations to make any one a Whist Player. Containing also the Laws of Piquet, Cassino, Ecarté, Cribbage, Backgammon. By Major A * * * * * New Edition; to which are added, Precepts for Tyros. By Mrs. B * * * * Fcp. 8vo. 3*s.*

Sinclair.—The Journey of Life. By CATHERINE SINCLAIR, Author of *The Business of Life* (2 vols. fcp. 8vo. price 10*s.*) New Edition, corrected and enlarged. Fcp. 8vo. price 5*s.*

Sinclair.—Popish Legends or Bible Truths. By CATHERINE SINCLAIR. Dedicated to her Nieces. Fcp. 8vo. 6*s.*

Sir Roger de Coverley. From *The Spectator.* With Notes and Illustrations by W. HENRY WILLS; and Twelve fine Wood Engravings, by John Thompson from Designs by FREDERICK TAYLER. Crown 8vo. price 15*s.* boards; or 27*s.* bound in morocco.—Also a Cheap Edition, without Woodcuts, in 16mo. price One Shilling.

Smee's Elements of Electro-Metallurgy. Third Edition, revised, corrected, and considerably enlarged; with Electrotypes and numerous Woodcuts. Post 8vo. price 10*s.* 6*d.*

Smith's Sacred Annals.—Sacred Annals: Vol. III. The Gentile Nations; or, The History and Religion of the Egyptians, Assyrians, Babylonians, Medes, Persians, Greeks, and Romans, collected from ancient authors and Holy Scripture, and including the recent discoveries in Egyptian, Persian, and Assyrian Inscriptions: Forming a complete connection of Sacred and Profane History, and shewing the Fulfilment of Sacred Prophecy. By GEORGE SMITH, F.A.S., etc. In Two Parts, crown 8vo. price 12*s.*

By the same Author,

Sacred Annals: Vol. I. The Patriarchal Age; or, Researches into the History and Religion of Mankind, from the Creation of the World to the Death of Isaac. Crown 8vo. 10*s.*

Sacred Annals: Vol. II. The Hebrew People; or, The History and Religion of the Israelites, from the Origin of the Nation to the Time of Christ. In Two Parts, crown 8vo. price 12*s.*

The Works of the Rev. Sydney Smith; including his Contributions to the Edinburgh Review. New Edition, complete in One Volume; with Portrait and Vignette. Square crown 8vo. price 21*s.*; or 30*s.* bound in calf.

₊ Also a LIBRARY EDITION (the Fourth), in 3 vols. 8vo. with Portrait, price 36*s.*

The Rev. Sydney Smith's Ele-mentary Sketches of Moral Philosophy, delivered at the Royal Institution in the Years 1804, 1805, and 1806. Second Edition. 8vo. price 12*s.*

The Life and Correspondence of the late Robert Southey. Edited by his Son, the Rev. C. C. SOUTHEY, M.A. Vicar of Ardleigh. With Portraits; and Landscape Illustrations. 6 vols. post 8vo. 63*s.*

Southey's Life of Wesley; and Rise and Progress of Methodism. New Edition, with Notes and Additions, by the late Samuel Taylor Coleridge, Esq., and the late Alexander Knox, Esq. Edited by the Rev. C. C. SOUTHEY, M.A. 2 vols. 8vo. with 2 Portraits, price 28*s.*

Southey's Commonplace Books. Comprising—1. Choice Passages: with Collections for the History of Manners and Literature in England; 2. Special Collections on various Historical and Theological Subjects; 3. Analytical Readings in various branches of Literature; and 4. Original Memoranda, Literary and Miscellaneous. Edited by the Rev. J W. WARTER, B.D. 4 vols. square crown 8vo. price £3 18*s.*

Each *Commonplace Book*, complete in itself, may be had separately as follows:—

FIRST SERIES—CHOICE PASSAGES, etc. 18*s.*

SECOND SERIES — SPECIAL COLLECTIONS. 18*s.*

THIRD SERIES — ANALYTICAL READINGS. 21*s.*

FOURTH SERIES — ORIGINAL MEMORANDA, etc. 21*s.*

Robert Southey's Complete Poet-ical Works; containing all the Author's last Introductions and Notes. Complete in One Volume, with Portrait and Vignette. Medium 8vo. price 21*s.* cloth; 42*s.* bound in morocco.

₊ Also a New and Cheaper Issue of the First collected Edition of the above, in 10 vols. fcp. 8vo. with Portrait and 19 Plates, price 35*s.*

Select Works of the British Poets; from Chaucer to Lovelace, inclusive. With Biographical Sketches by the late ROBERT SOUTHEY. Medium 8vo. 30*s.*

Southey's The Doctor etc. Complete in One Volume. Edited by the Rev. J. W. WARTER, B.D. With Portrait, Vignette, Bust, and coloured Plate. New Edition. Square crown 8vo. price 21*s*.

Stephen.—Lectures on the History of France; By the Right Hon. Sir JAMES STEPHEN, K.C.B., LL.D., Professor of Modern History in the University of Cambridge. Second Edition, 2 vols. 8vo. price 24*s*.

Stephen.—Essays in Ecclesiastical Biography; from the Edinburgh Review. By the Right Hon. Sir JAMES STEPHEN, K.C.B., LL.D. Third Edition. 2 vols. 8vo. 24*s*.

Steel's Shipmaster's Assistant, for the use of Merchants, Owners and Masters of Ships, Officers of Customs, and all Persons connected with Shipping or Commerce; containing the Law and Local Regulations affecting the Ownership, Charge, and Management of Ships and their Cargoes; together with Notices of other Matters, and all necessary Information for Mariners. New Edition, rewritten, by G. WILLMORE, Esq., M.A., Barrister-at-Law; G. CLEMENTS, of the Customs, London; and W. TATE, Author of *The Modern Cambist*. 8vo. price 28*s*.

Stonehenge.—The Greyhound: Being a Treatise on the Art of Breeding, Rearing, and Training Greyhounds for Public Running; their Diseases and Treatment: Containing also, Rules for the Management of Coursing Meetings, and for the Decision of Courses. By STONEHENGE, With numerous Portraits of Greyhounds, etc., engraved on Wood, and a Frontispiece engraved on Steel. Square crown 8vo. price 21*s*.

Stow.—The Training System, the Moral Training School, and the Normal Seminary or College. By DAVID STOW, Esq., Honorary Secretary to the Glasgow Normal Free Seminary. Ninth Edition; with Plates and Woodcuts. Post 8vo. price 6*s*.

Dr. Sutherland's Journal of a Voyage in Baffin's Bay and Barrow's Straits, in the Years 1850 and 1851, performed by H. M. Ships *Lady Franklin* and *Sophia*, under the command of Mr. William Penny, in search of the Missing Crews of H. M. Ships *Erebus* and *Terror*. with Charts and Illustrations. 2 vols. post 8vo. price 27*s*.

Swain.—English Melodies. By CHARLES SWAIN. Fcp. 8vo. price 6*s*. cloth; bound in morocco, 12*s*.

Swain.—Letters of Laura D'Auverne. By CHARLES SWAIN. Fcp. 8vo. 3*s*. 6*d*.

Tate.—On the Strength of Materials; containing various original and useful Formulæ, specially applied to Tubular Bridges, Wrought Iron and Cast Iron Beams, etc. By THOMAS TATE, F.R.A.S. 8vo. price 5*s*. 6*d*.

Taylor.—Loyola: and Jesuitism in its Rudiments. By ISAAC TAYLOR. Post 8vo. with a Medallion, price 10*s*. 6*d*.

Taylor.—Wesley and Methodism. By ISAAC TAYLOR. Post 8vo. with a Portrait, price 10*s*. 6*d*.

Thirlwall.—The History of Greece. By the Right Rev the LORD BISHOP of ST. DAVID'S (the Rev. Connop Thirlwall). An improved Library Edition; with Maps. 8 vols. 8vo. price £4. 16*s*.

Also, an Edition in 8 vols. fcp. 8vo. with Vignette Titles, price 28*s*.

Thomson (The Rev. W.)—An Outline of the Laws of Thought: Being a Treatise on Pure and Applied Logic. By the Rev. W. THOMSON, M.A. Fellow and Tutor of Queen's College, Oxford. Third Edition, enlarged. Fcp. 8vo. price 7*s*. 6*d*.

Thomson's Tables of Interest, at Three, Four, Four-and-a-half, and Five per Cent., from One Pound to Ten Thousand, and from 1 to 365 Days, in a regular progression of Single Days; with Interest at all the above Rates, from One to Twelve Months, and from One to Ten Years. Also, numerous other Tables of Exchanges, Time, and Discounts. New Edition. 12mo. 8*s*.

Thomson's Seasons. Edited by BOLTON CORNEY, Esq. Illustrated with Seventy-seven fine Wood Engravings from Designs by Members of the Etching Club. Square crown 8vo. price 21*s*. cloth; or, 36*s*. bound in morocco.

Thornton.—Zohrab; or, a Midsummer Day's Dream: And other Poems. By WILLIAM THOMAS THORNTON, Author of *An Essay on Over-Population*, etc. Fcp. 8vo. price 4*s*. 6*d*.

Todd (Charles).—A Series of Tables of the Area and Circumference of Circles; the Solidity and Superficies of Spheres; the Area and Length of the Diagonal of Squares; and the Specific Gravity of Bodies, etc.: To which is added, an Explanation of the Author's Method of Calculating these Tables. Intended as a Facility to Engineers, Surveyors, Architects, Mechanics, and Artizans in General. By CHARLES TODD, Engineer. The Second Edition, improved and extended. Post 8vo. price 6*s*.

THE TRAVELLERS LIBRARY,

In course of Publication in Volumes at Half-a-Crown, and in Parts price One Shilling each. Comprising books of valuable information and acknowledged merit, in a form adapted for reading while Travelling, and also of a character that will render them worthy of preservation.

		s.	d.
Vol. I.	MACAULAY'S ESSAYS on WARREN HASTINGS and LORD CLIVE ..	2	6
II.	——— ESSAYS on PITT & CHATHAM, RANKE & GLADSTONE	2	6
III.	LAING'S RESIDENCE in NORWAY	2	6
IV.	PFEIFFER'S VOYAGE ROUND the WORLD	2	6
V.	EOTHEN, TRACES of TRAVEL from the EAST	2	6
VI.	MACAULAY'S ESSAYS on ADDISON, WALPOLE, and LORD BACON	2	6
VII.	HUC'S TRAVELS IN TARTARY, etc.	2	6
VIII.	THOMAS HOLCROFT'S MEMOIRS	2	6
IX.	WERNE'S AFRICAN WANDERINGS	2	6
X.	Mrs. JAMESON'S SKETCHES in CANADA	2	6
XI.	JERRMANN'S PICTURES from ST. PETERSBURG	2	6
XII.	The Rev. G. R. GLEIG'S LEIPSIC CAMPAIGN	2	6
XIII.	HUGHES'S AUSTRALIAN COLONIES	2	6
XIV.	SIR EDWARD SEAWARD'S NARRATIVE	2	6
XV.	ALEXANDRE DUMAS' MEMOIRS of a MAITRE-D'ARMES	2	6
XVI.	OUR COAL-FIELDS and OUR COAL-PITS	2	6
XVII.	M'CULLOCH'S LONDON and GIRONIERE'S PHILIPPINES	2	6
XVIII.	SIR ROGER DE COVERLEY and SOUTHEY'S LOVE STORY	2	6
XIX.	JEFFREY'S ESSAYS on SWIFT and RICHARDSON and LORD CARLISLE'S LECTURES AND ADDRESSES	2	6
XX.	HOPE'S BIBLE in BRITTANY and CHASE in BRITTANY	2	6
XXI.	THE ELECTRIC TELEGRAPH and NATURAL HISTORY of CREATION	2	6
XXII.	MEMOIR of DUKE of WELLINGTON and LIFE of MARSHAL TURENNE	2	6
XXIII.	TURKEY and CHRISTENDOM and RANKE'S FERDINAND and MAXIMILIAN	2	6
XXIV.	FERGUSON'S SWISS MEN and SWISS MOUNTAINS and BARROW'S CONTINENTAL TOUR	2	6
XXV.	SOUVESTRE'S WORKING MAN'S CONFESSIONS and ATTIC PHILOSOPHER in PARIS	2	6
XXVI.	MACAULAY'S ESSAYS on LORD BYRON, and the COMIC DRAMATISTS and his SPEECHES on PARLIAMENTARY REFORM (1831-32)	2	6
XXVII.	SHIRLEY BROOKS'S RUSSIANS of the SOUTH and Dr. KEMP'S INDICATIONS of INSTINCT	2	6
XXVIII.	LANMAN'S ADVENTURES in the WILDS of NORTH AMERICA......	2	6
XXIX.	De CUSTINE'S RUSSIA, Abridged	3	6

The Thumb Bible; or, Verbum Sempiternum. By J. Taylor. Being an Epitome of the Old and New Testaments in English Verse. Reprinted from the Edition, of 1693, bound and clasped. In 64mo. price Eighteenpence.

Townsend.—The Lives of Twelve Eminent Judges of the Last and of the Present Century. By W. C. Townsend, Esq., M.A., Q.C. 2 vols. 8vo. price 28*s*.

Townsend.—Modern State Trials, revised and illustrated with Essays and Notes. By W. C. Townsend, Esq., M.A. Q.C. 2 vols. 8vo. price 30*s*.

Sharon Turner's Sacred History of the World, attempted to be Philosophically considered, in a Series of Letters to a Son. New Edition, edited by the Author's Son, the Rev. S. Turner. 3 vols. post 8vo. price 31*s*. 6*d*.

Sharon Turner's History of England during the Middle Ages: Comprising the Reigns from the Norman Conquest to the Accession of Henry VIII. Fifth Edition, revised by the Rev. S. Turner. 4 vols. 8vo. price 50*s*.

Sharon Turner's History of the Anglo-Saxons, from the Earliest Period to the Norman Conquest. The Seventh Edition, revised by the Rev. S. Turner. 3 vols. 8vo. price 36*s*.

Dr. Turton's Manual of the Land and Freshwater Shells of the British Islands. New Edition, with considerable Additions. By John Edward Gray: with Woodcuts, and 12 coloured Plates. Post 8vo. price 15*s*.

Dr. Ure's Dictionary of Arts, Manufactures and Mines: Containing a clear Exposition of their Principles and Practice. The Fourth Edition, much enlarged and corrected throughout; with all the Information comprised in the *Supplement of Recent Improvements* brought down to the Present Time, and incorporated in the *Dictionary*. Most of the Articles being entirely re-written, and many New Articles now first added. With nearly 1,600 Woodcuts. 2 vols. 8vo. price 60*s*.

Waterton.—Essays on Natural History, chiefly Ornithology. By C. Waterton, Esq. With an Autobiography of the Author and Views of Walton Hall. New and cheaper Edition. 2 vols. fcp. 8vo. 10*s*.

Separately: Vol. I. (First Series), 5*s*. 6*d*. Vol. II. (Second Series), 4*s*. 6*d*.

Alaric Watts's Lyrics of the Heart, and other Poems. With 41 highly-finished Line Engravings, executed expressly for the work by the most eminent Painters and Engravers. Square crown 8vo. price 31*s*. 6*d*. boards, or 45*s*. bound in morocco; Proof Impressions, 63*s*. boards.

Webster and Parkes's Encyclopædia of Domestic Economy; Comprising such subjects as are most immediately connected with Housekeeping; As, The Construction of Domestic Edifices, with the Modes of Warming, Ventilating, and Lighting them—A Description of the various Articles of Furniture, with the Nature of their Materials—Duties of Servants, etc. New Edition; with nearly 1,000 Woodcuts, 8vo. price 50*s*.

Willich's Popular Tables for ascertaining the Value of Lifehold, Leasehold, and Church Property, Renewal Fines, etc. Third Edition, with additional Tables of Natural or Hyperbolic Logarithms, Trigonometry, Astronomy, Geography, etc. Post 8vo. price 9*s*.

Lady Willoughby's Diary (1635 to 1663). Printed, ornamented, and bound in the style of the period to which *The Diary* refers. New Edition; in Two Parts. Square fcp. 8vo. price 8*s*. each, boards; or, bound in morocco, 18*s*. each.

Wilmot's Abridgment of Blackstone's Commentaries on the Laws of England, intended for the use of Young Persons, and comprised in a series of Letters from a Father to his Daughter. A New Edition, corrected and brought down to the Present Day, by Sir John E. Eardley Wilmot, Bart., Barrister-at-Law, Recorder of Warwick. 12mo. price 6*s*. 6*d*.

Youatt.—The Horse. By William Youatt. With a Treatise of Draught. A New Edition; with numerous Wood Engravings from Designs by William Harvey. (Messrs. Longman and Co.'s Edition should be ordered). 8vo. price 10*s*.

Youatt.—The Dog. By William Youatt. A New Edition; with numerous Engravings from Designs by William Harvey. 8vo. 6*s*.

Zumpt's Larger Grammar of the Latin Language. Translated and adapted for the use of the English Students, by Dr. L. Schmitz, F.R.S.E., Rector of the High School of Edinburgh: With numerous Additions and Corrections by the Author and Translator. The Third Edition, thoroughly revised; to which is added, an Index (by the Rev. J. T. White, M.A.) of all the Passages of Latin Authors referred to and explained in the Grammar. 8vo. price 14*s*.

March, 1854.

London: Printed by M. Mason, Ivy Lane, Paternoster Row.

www.ingramcontent.com/pod-product-compliance
Lightning Source LLC
LaVergne TN
LVHW010156110826
845151LV00002B/536

* 9 7 8 1 4 2 5 5 3 6 0 0 8 *